C0-BYG-932

COLUMBIA UNIVERSITY STUDIES IN ENGLISH
AND COMPARATIVE LITERATURE

DISGUISE PLOTS IN ELIZABETHAN DRAMA

DISGUISE PLOTS IN ELIZABETHAN DRAMA

A STUDY IN STAGE TRADITION

BY

VICTOR OSCAR FREEBURG

Submitted in Partial Fulfilment of the Requirements
for the Degree of Doctor of Philosophy, in the
Faculty of Philosophy, Columbia University

WITHDRAWN OCCIDENTAL COLLEGE LIBRARY

Benjamin Blom

OCCIDENTAL COLLEGE LIBRARY

822.309 F853d 1965

202497

First published by Columbia University Press, 1915
Reissued by Benjamin Blom, Inc., 1965
Library of Congress Catalog Card No. 65-19616

Printed in U.S.A. by
NOBLE OFFSET PRINTERS, INC.
NEW YORK 3, N. Y.

This Monograph has been approved by the Department of English and Comparative Literature in Columbia University as a contribution to knowledge worthy of publication.

A. H. THORNDIKE,
Executive Officer.

PREFACE

In this book the dramatic construction and stage representation of the plays of Shakespeare and his brother playwrights have been inspected from a new angle of observation; and it is believed that the results obtained may help the reader to understand more completely the practice of Elizabethan playwrights, the nature of their medium, and the tastes of their audience.

It is hoped that the illustrative significance of the four hundred and twenty-five plots here discussed may in some measure palliate the offense of many omissions. It should perhaps be explained that certain disguise situations, even though occurring in well-known plays, have been deliberately omitted in favor of other situations which served better to illustrate the point being made. Incidentally, this comparative study of Elizabethan plays in a new alignment has revealed a number of inter-relations which are here discussed for the first time.

I take pleasure in expressing my obligation to Doctor Orie L. Hatcher of Bryn Mawr College, who suggested the subject and has offered many constructive criticisms of this work; to Doctor Winifred Smith of Vassar College, who kindly loaned me her translations of the *commedie dell' arte* in the Scala collection; and to Miss Vera Parsons for pointing out a great many disguise plots in Italian *novelle*. To Professor Brander Matthews and to Professor G. C. D. Odell, who have read the manuscript, I am greatly indebted for careful and illuminating criticisms. To my colleague Professor Francis B. Gummere I wish to express my heartfelt thanks for warm

sympathy and encouragement. To a patient and inspiring
teacher, Professor Ashley H. Thorndike, more is due than
can easily be expressed. His extensive and exact knowledge
of the drama has often been appealed to, and never in vain;
and his searching comments have frequently stolen their
way bodily into the pages of this book.

V. O. F.

HAVERFORD COLLEGE,
    January 25, 1915

CONTENTS

DISGUISE PLOTS
IN ELIZABETHAN DRAMA

CHAPTER I

INTRODUCTION

THE use of disguise is an old stratagem in literature as well as in life. Achilles lived for a time undisturbed with his love because he was disguised as a maiden. Apollo in the stress of battle appeared in the guise of a common soldier and encouraged his favorite hero. Odysseus returned from his wanderings in the shape of a beggar in order that he might not be recognized at home. Haroun al Raschid dressed himself in lowly costume and pursued adventures among his people. Up in the icebound North, Thor had to utilize a female impersonation before he could regain his stolen hammer from Thrym. Down in the pastoral valley of Beersheba Jacob disguised himself as Esau and by a brief dissimulation gained his brother's birthright.

If we narrow our view to a single type of literature, the drama, we shall find a long succession of disguise situations reaching its height in the Renaissance drama of Italy, England, and Spain. On the London stage alone disguise occurs with important dramatic functions in more than two hundred extant plays which were produced before the death of Shakespeare.

A dramatic device so frequently used must be worthy of particular attention.[1] If we analyze *Twelfth Night*, for

[1] The only previous studies that have come to my attention are Schulz's monograph on the sources of the disguises in eight of Shake-

example, we find that Viola's disguise has definite functions in the development and termination of the plot. When we learn that Ben Jonson did not dare to produce the same kind of plots as Plautus for fear his audience would not accept certain stage improbabilities, we become interested in the theatrical methods of representing disguise situations. The study of dramaturgy and stagecraft involves dramatic history; and this history reveals interesting relations which perpetuated definite traditions in disguise plots. The English dramatists, like Molière, took their treasures where they could find them. Obviously these dramatists took the treasures, not because they found them, but because they recognized their value in the theater. This recognition of dramatic values resulted in repetition and conventionalizing. Our chief interest in this book, as may be guessed from the chapter headings, is to follow out the careers, so to speak, of the various traditional disguises in Elizabethan drama.

First of all we must make sure of our terms. Dramatic disguise, in our discussion, means a change of personal appearance which leads to mistaken identity. There is a double test, change and confusion. Disguise has a large number of relatives, and we ourselves must make no mistakes in identity. We cannot refer to the twin motive in the *Comedy of Errors* as disguise, because the confusion in that play is not due to a change of costume and facial appearance. Nor can we apply the term "disguise" to the trick of substitution in a dark chamber, or to the verbal misrepresentations of a stranger who misleads us with respect to his identity. Eavesdropping is similar to spying in dis-

speare's plays, Züge's monograph on disguises in the English and Scottish ballads, Jackson's paper on disguise in Sanskrit drama, and Creizenach's half dozen pages of remarks on the use of disguise in English drama. Dr. H. W. L. Dana has an excellent unpublished article entitled "The Disguised Heroine in the Sixteenth Century."

guise; it results in the same sort of complication for the person under observation. The pretence of deafness may also have the same results as spying in disguise. Yet in the cases of twins, substitution, misrepresentation, eavesdropping, and deafness the dramatic mistakes are not due to change of appearance.

On the other hand, change of appearance may not always lead to mistaken identity. Volpone makes up to seem at death's door, which results in deception, but the victims mistake his condition and not his identity. The wearing of a mask or fantastic costume by a person would not naturally induce another to decide on his identity. On the contrary, it would suspend the decision until the mask was removed or until some individual mark or manner betrayed the person. Let us understand then that the plots we are to study contain confusion of identity resulting from the alteration of personal appearance.

As a basis for the division of our material we shall use the disguise situation as such. We shall place in one category all cases of girls disguised as boys, whether such disguises have been prompted by love, hate, the spirit of adventure, curiosity, jealousy, or infidelity, and whether the action occurs in tragedy, comedy, or farce. The most definite division of disguises is according to sex. All women disguised as boys or men we shall call female pages, even though, for example, Bess Bridges masquerades as a sea captain, and not as a mere page. Boys or men disguised as women we shall include in the chapter entitled *The Boy Bride*. To be sure, Bartholomew, in the Induction to the *Taming of The Shrew*, does not actually become a boy bride; but the complication is essentially of the same nature as that in *Epicœne*. The spy in disguise became a traditional figure, appearing in situations that also became traditional. Hence we must classify spy plays in a group by themselves.

Plays in which a single character, usually a rogue, impersonates many parts with lightning changes, are grouped in the chapter entitled *The Rogue in Multi-Disguise.* Situations in which the lover employs disguise constitute another group. Thus we have five types of disguise situation, identified by the female page, the boy bride, the rogue in multi-disguise, the disguised spy, and the disguised lover. Each type is classified according to the dramatic pattern of plot weaving, and named according to the distinctive feature in that pattern. In the situations of the female page and the boy bride the changes of sex are more distinctive than the purposes which inspired those changes. The action derives its characteristic dramatic value from the costumes rather than from what is in the minds of the persons. In the disguised spy and disguised lover plays, however, the purposes, not the costumes, are paramount. Even though the spy be a woman dressed as a man, the plot pattern does not usually resemble that of a female page play. These five types then may be considered mutually exclusive; they are sufficiently inclusive for all the important disguises in English drama.

The year 1616 has been chosen as an arbitrary terminal in tracing out disguise traditions. Disguise appears frequently after that time but lacks novelty in dramatic method. Many of the later plays will be alluded to, but no exhaustive study of them will be made. Our limitation gives opportunity for a somewhat detailed study of the plays of Shakespeare and his immediate contemporaries.

CHAPTER II

THE TECHNIC OF DRAMATIC DISGUISE

To counterfet well is a good consayte.— *Magnificence.*

I

BEFORE we can intelligently follow the course of any traditional disguise situation, we must consider the technical aspects of disguise in general. Let us examine briefly the constructive function of the motive, from the point of view of the playwright, and its physical or theatrical value from the point of view of the stage manager. Disguise is an effective dramatic contrivance because the deception which produces action and the recognition which ends it are fundamentally dramatic transactions; and because the change of costume together with the mimetic action of body and dissimulation of voice involve the essence of theatricality. For dramaturgic effectiveness there are few better mechanical devices. Yet it must be understood from the beginning that disguise is only a mechanical and external cause of action. When a dramatist builds a tragedy on the basis of mad ambition or vacillating desire for revenge, he is using an abstract or psychological cause. When comic action results from gullibility, or braggadocio, the motive is again abstract. But when pity and fear are aroused by the clashing of bloody swords, or when laughter comes at the sight of unctuous avoirdupois or ridiculous grimacings, the dramatic causes are physical and concrete. Such a physical device is the disguise motive.

The test of plot structure needs no very elaborate formula. It is perhaps better to limit ourselves to two elements of

5

plot action, the complication and ultimate resolution. A playwright, before constructing a plot, must find a factor which is capable of producing dramatic complication. He must also find a factor which will produce a sure resolution of this complication. It stands to reason then that a device which complicates and is at the same time capable of resolving, is especially desirable to him. Disguise is such a device. For as soon as disguise is successfully assumed there is probability of complication which involves the persons deceived and the one deceiving; and when the disguise is discovered there is an end to the complication. We shall consider disguise basic when it initiates and develops, as well as resolves, the action of the given plot.

As a complicating factor disguise is useful because its results seem natural. The results are also partly foreseen, an important consideration, since expectancy is one of the keenest joys of the spectator. When a girl disguises herself as a page and goes out into the world we know that there will be trouble before the day is over. She may fall in love with some man and regret that she cannot display her charms in feminine raiment. Some Olivia, mistaking her sex, may fall in love with her, and some rival may challenge her to a duel. She may meet her lover, and he may unknowingly utilize her disguise to deepen his own infidelity towards her. Other types of disguise may initiate similar dramatic actions. Suppose we have an amorous gull who is disposed to fall in love with any petticoat; he meets some boy disguised as a girl, and the farcical results are inevitable. Suppose we hear a ruler say that he is going on a vacation. We suspect that the mice intend to play. But the shrewd ruler, instead of departing, remains in disguise. Again the complications are probable and interesting. On some dark night a lover steals to his beloved in the disguise of her husband. We learn that the husband is returning and we eagerly anticipate the results. These are only a few typical examples to illustrate how easily disguise may initiate a convincing plot.

The plot once started, complications will accumulate with every circumstance until the revelation of disguise unties the knot. Many of the dramatic difficulties which beset the disguised person or his victims may be entirely unforeseen by the audience; in constructing such situations the playwright needs considerable dramaturgic skill if he would hold his audience balanced between suspense and surprise.

The most common use of disguise in constructing a plot is illustrated by *Twelfth Night*. The disguise of Viola is basic, and the results are manifold and highly dramatic; yet the use of this disguise is simple. Viola changes to male costume at the beginning of the story, and chance does the rest. She had not foreseen the complications and was simply a victim in the play. It was her disguise which constantly led her into difficulties.

A different method of producing action is illustrated by the spy in *Measure for Measure*. In such a spy situation the disguised person is decidedly active. He is, as it were, the stage manager of the plot; for he initiates, oversees, and terminates the action; but he is the chief actor too. In the simpler spying situations the spy may stand safely aloof and watch the process of events; but in *Measure for Measure*, as in many spy plays, he utilizes disguise not only to observe but to shape events as well.

In multi-disguise plays disguise is by the definition basic. But it is not basic in the sense that the disguises in *Twelfth Night* or in *Measure for Measure* are basic, where a single and simple change of appearance operates with cumulative effect. A multi-disguise play is rather a series of transitions from one situation to another. Each disguise is an episode in itself, and the unity of the whole is like the unity in a string of beads. The complexity does not usually reach a logical crisis. Whether there shall be four changes of costume or four dozen, is settled arbitrarily by the playwright. A motive similar to multi-disguise is the device of shifting out of disguise into the real character, then into the disguise, then back into the real character again. It occurs in the *Malcontent, Measure for Measure,* and elsewhere.

The types above mentioned illustrate dramatic procedure when the audience is aware of the disguise and expectant of results. But in some plays, *Epicœne* and *Philaster,* for example, the presence of disguise is not known by the audience, and consequently cannot be used as an impelling cause of action. The plot must be woven apparently by some other agency. This subject of unforeseen discovery of disguise is so important that we shall discuss it somewhat in detail a few pages below.

Sometimes disguise is apparently a subsidiary, but actually a very important, factor in a play. *Every Man in His Humour,* for example, is appreciated chiefly as a comedy of "humours." But it is interesting to note that the movement from one situation to another is largely effected through the machinations of Brainworm with his disguises.

The use of a disguise episode as a dramatic link between two situations is a simple but effective dramaturgic device. It is best illustrated by Portia's manœuvre in the *Merchant of Venice.* Her disguise enables her to terminate the tragic part of the plot, but it initiates a new set of comic complications, which end by her revelation of the stratagem only when she has sufficiently teased her husband.

A common disguise expedient was the costume exchange. For example, a prisoner escapes by exchanging costumes with a visitor who has come to see him. When the ruse is discovered the episode generally ends. This device is frequently used in the *commedia dell' arte* (Creiz. IV, 252). It can be traced back through the *Captivi* of Plautus as far as the *Frogs* of Aristophanes, where master and slave exchange costumes. In England a rapid series of costume exchanges characterizes such multi-disguise plays as *Look About You*.

Thus we see how the disguise motive may become a useful part in the machinery of a plot, and how the machinery is kept in motion as long as the disguise remains an active part. The disguise ceases to be active as soon as it is discovered.

Every writer knows that it is easier to start a plot than to stop it. But the playwright who motivated an entire plot on the disguise of some character had no difficulty; the plot could stop anywhere, and almost every complication could be satisfactorily resolved by merely exposing the disguise. As to the proper ending of a play, dramatists by their practice, and critics by their precept, are not agreed. Price says that the end must be organic, and that "to deviate from the logical result is to destroy at one blow all unity" (*Technique*, 109). Professor Brander Matthews, shrewdly observant of what is, as well as what should be, says: "But if an audience has sat for three hours, following with keen enjoyment the successive episodes of a complication between forces evenly balanced, it does not insist upon logic; it is often better pleased to have the knot cut arbitrarily than to be delayed by the process of untying" (*Study*, 195). The resolution by the disguise motive can satisfy both critics, because the revelation of the identity which we had originally seen concealed is an organic, immediate, and final dénouement. The resolution by discovery of identity is absolute, even when the original assumption of disguise was not probable or convincing.

The dénouement of a play always tests the skill of a

dramatist. We have just said that a disguise dénouement can be logical and convincing, for it is simply the removal of the cause which produced the difficulties. However, there are exceptions. Some disguise dénouements are crude and ineffective because the writer was in haste, or was not alert to dramatic opportunity. In the Induction of *The Shrew*, for example, when Sly is victimized by a boy dressed as a girl the whole episode loses point because the disguise is not revealed and Sly does not discover that he is the victim of a practical joke. Another case of ineffective action is the last act of Greene's *James IV*, where the author deliberately altered the disguise plot of his source and brought the heroine on the stage in her own character instead of in disguise, thus missing an opportunity for the stage business of undisguising and its dramatic effect upon the other characters in the play.

Letting the plot run into a blind alley is still another technical error. In Lyly's *Gallathea* we have two girls disguised as boys. Each thinks the other really is a boy and falls deeply in love with "him." Obviously the revelation of the two disguises in no way satisfies the love-sick girls. The resolution of this play cannot be organic, and must be effected by some outside agency. Venus steps in and changes one girl into a boy.

These are interesting exceptions. But we find many ingenious and effective resolutions of plot by the discovery of disguise. The simultaneous appearance of doubles at the end of a play was an unusually theatrical means of forcing the revelation of identity. We have a situation of real doubles in such a play as the *Comedy of Errors*, where the resemblance of the pair is not artificial. But in *Twelfth Night* there is an artificial resemblance between Viola as page and Sebastian. The dramatic consequence of their simultaneous appearance is the revelation of Viola's artificial likeness. The entry of the doubles upon the scene produces a dramatic pause on a full stage, and while we are amused by the puzzled mien of some of the persons, we watch the expressions of brother and sister growing into recognition.

If the doubles in a play were both disguised like some third person, fictitious or real, their simultaneous appearance served as an exposure of fraud on both sides. Such a situation occurs very effectively at the end of *Look About You*,[1] where the two men disguised as the "hermit" appear, and each one, while maintaining his own genuineness, accuses the other of being an impostor.

The most subtle doubles situation of all is in Marston's *What You Will*. A man is impersonating another who is supposedly dead. A rival of this impersonator proposes to disguise a second impersonator like the absent man, and the knowledge of this counterplot leaks out. But this second disguise is never effected, a fact which does not leak out. The consequence is that when the supposedly dead man appears, the counterplotters think he is the first impersonator and the plotters think he is the second impersonator. Presently when the genuine character and his impersonator appear simultaneously, both are considered bogus. Thus the theatrical effect of a stock situation from Plautus was enriched by a slight touch in the spring of action.

Our study of the dramaturgic effect of basic disguises leads us into more and more intricate plots. The most elaborately motivated disguise situation of all is what I term the "retro-disguise." This will be discussed more fully in connection with a number of female page plays.[2] The formula is as follows: First, a girl disguises herself as a boy. Second, somebody who thinks this female page really is a boy dis-

[1] The plot of *Look About You* is summarized in Chapter VI.
[2] See Chapter IV, pages, 80–3.

guises "him" as a girl, which constitutes a retro-disguise, or an unconscious restoring of the right appearance and identity. The results during the play are highly involved and the dénouement is double in structure. First, a number of victims have to be told that the girl is only a disguised page; then all the persons of the play have to learn that the page, as a matter of fact, is of the female sex, and had originally been in disguise. Such a plot, though intricate, is not too hard to follow when the audience is taken completely into confidence concerning all the action. But when the first disguise is not known by the spectators, but is revealed as a surprise at the end of the play, the plot seems a little too highly involved. An example of retro-disguise combined with surprise is Jonson's *New Inn*.[3]

The surprise motive, which became very popular during the Jacobean drama, is, I believe, an English contribution to the technic of disguise plots. In the conventional disguise plot the character who was to disguise himself always told the audience of his intention,[4] sometimes directly in a monolog, and sometimes in discussion with a confidant. Usually the costume too was specified. Hence the audience not only knew that there was going to be a disguise, but was able to recognize the disguised character immediately upon appearance.

But in the surprise plot the audience was completely deceived and did not know until the end of the play that there had been disguise. In such a plot therefore the action could not be impelled by the disguise motive, for

---

[3] See Chapter IV.

[4] Such practice goes back at least as far as Aristophanes. In *Acharnians* when Dicæopolis dresses as a beggar he says: "The spectators must know who I am; but the chorus, on the other hand, must stand by like fools, that I may fillip them with quibbles." Hickie, I, 18. See Arnold (56–58) for a discussion of the identification of disguised persons by the use of soliloquies.

that factor did not yet exist as far as the observer was concerned. But incidents had to have dramatic significance. Significance would come, to be sure, by the spectators' discovery of the disguise when the play ended, but during the progress of the play the incidents must not seem devoid of dramatic meaning. Therefore in surprise plots the playwright had to motivate the action by some cause which was independent of the concealed disguise motive. In *Epicœne* it is the bridegroom's hatred of noise that gives dramatic significance to the career of the boisterous bride. The startling revelation of the bride's sex is unsuspected, because the audience finds the action amusing and complete without seeking further motives. The dénouement is a complete surprise.

Whether such surprise is good dramaturgy may be a question of taste. But I think the average spectator would rather be given certain dramatic causes and conflicts with a chance to guess at the probable outcome, than watch the unfolding of a dramatic story which ends with the disconcerting revelation that he had all the way through been ignorant of the cardinal fact in the story. If there is a secret, the spectator wants to be let in, so that he may enjoy the perplexed action of the characters during complications and their amazement when the cause of the complications is revealed. But if the secret is held back, the spectator may feel that he has been victimized as much as the gulls in the play. In *Epicœne* even Truewit, one of the comic conspirators, is deceived. He has the sympathy of the spectator when he says: "Well, Dauphine, you have lurched your friends of the better half of the garland by concealing this part of the plot." Perhaps this statement really represents a serious query of Jonson himself, who may have doubted the success of his departure from traditional technic in disguise intrigue.

We must remember that the surprise motive is operative only at the first witnessing of the play; and even then some obliging initiate may assume the responsibility of disclosing the secret.[5]

A compromise between confided disguise and surprise is employed by Chapman in *May Day* (see Chapter IV, page 87). By two or three hints he arouses the suspicion of the audience that a certain boy might in reality be a girl. This type of a dimly suspected discovery of disguise would seem to be dramaturgically desirable; but for some reason it did not flourish.

If the dramatist grew tired of conventional disguise in its various functions, or if the retro-disguise and the surprise discovery lost their novelty, he could still amuse his audience with the same kind of complications as from disguise by simply pretending disguise when there was none at all.[6] In *Honest Man's Fortune* (see Chapter IV, page 97) a credulous character gets the notion that a certain page is a girl in disguise. The page, seeing an opportunity for a joke, says to himself substantially, "Very well, whoop la, I am in disguise," and acts as though he were a female page instead of a mischievous lad. We have already alluded to Marston's effective use of a supposed impersonation in *What You Will*.[7] The most laughable supposition of all is when the character imagines himself in disguise although there is no change of appearance. This is the situation in *Albumazar* (see Chapter VIII, page 186), where a farmer is made to believe that he has been magically transformed into another man, and conducts himself accordingly.

In the above paragraphs we have briefly pointed out the

[5] This type of disguise is further discussed and illustrated in Chapter IV, pages 84–9, and in Chapter V, pages 114–18.

[6] For Italian examples of supposed disguise see Chapter VIII, page 185.

[7] See above, page 11.

various structural functions of the disguise motive. It remains for us to point out two or three other qualities which recommend it as a dramatic device.

The dialog of a disguise situation is especially capable of theatrical effectiveness. A disguised character is virtually two persons. One personality is maintained for the companions, who are deceived; and the other personality for the spectators, who are not deceived. This immediately gives an opportunity for double meanings or veiled allusions. Such subtlety of dialog is a valuable element of style, especially in Lyly and Shakespeare.[8] Furthermore, these subtleties are not subtleties of speech merely; they permit pretty shadings in the physical language of pantomime, and are therefore peculiarly important in theatrical art.[9]

The dramatic economy of a playwright may be discovered by studying his use of disguise, which is always, even in simple use, an economic motive. By economy we mean getting the maximum dramatic value from every dramatic action. Disguise gives dramatic compactness by compressing two characters into one person. One is the fictitious character, who seems real enough to the people in the play; and the other is the real character, whose presence they do not suspect. The value of such duality may be illustrated by Chapman's *Widow's Tears*. Chapman found a story containing a dead husband, a widow, and a soldier lover. He made a play out of it by conceiving the husband supposedly dead but really disguised as the soldier lover. Thus he actually eliminated a character, but multiplied the dramatic results.

Dramatic irony is one of the best dramaturgic products of disguise. There is poetic irony in the conception of Viola in love with the duke, yet carrying his love messages

[8] See Chapter IV, pages 65-6; 75-8.
[9] In surprise plays veiled allusions are naturally impossible.

to Olivia, or in Julia's emotions as she carries her own
betrothal ring as a love token to a rival mistress. Comic
irony is exhibited in *Measure for Measure* when the duke,
who has been spying, pretends to have returned from
abroad, expresses confidence in his notorious deputy, and
listens to the deputy's accusations of a certain "friar "
(himself in disguise). Other examples of comic irony are
Justice Overdo's spying out loose women only to find his wife
among them, and Gremio's employing a rival lover, Lucentio,
as his love agent. Tragic irony of disguise is illustrated by
the death of the disguised lover in *I Ieronimo*, and in
Beaumont and Fletcher's *Captain*, where a daughter amorously solicits her disguised father.[10]

Absolute probability versus dramatic probability has been
a topic of discussion ever since the sage remarks of Aristotle.
The question naturally arises in analyzing the basis and
development of any dramatic plot, but is especially pertinent in testing the technic of a disguise plot. In considering the disguise motive one critic says: "Il n'y a rien de
plus invraisemblable" (Mézières, 65). Another says that
the disguise motive often is accompanied by "die krassesten
Unwahrscheinlichkeiten" (Creiz. IV, 254). And there can
be no quarrel with the criticisms. Looking for improbabilities in disguise plots, or in Elizabethan drama in general, is like fishing in a pool that has been stocked. Let
us apply to the disguise motive the words which Professor
Matthews has written concerning the twin motive. He
says: "If the play which the author builds on an arbitrary

[10] The tragic irony of the play scene in the *Spanish Tragedy* is not
due to disguise; no one mistakes the identity of Ieronimo or of the
other performers of the play within the play. The victims are mistaken
in Ieronimo's intention, not in his identity. Compare the scene
where a rogue is disguised as a player in Middleton's *Mad World, My
Masters*. See Chapter VI, page 136.

supposition of this sort catches the interest of the spectators and holds them enthralled as the story unrolls itself, then they forget all about its artificial basis and they have no leisure to cavil" (*Study*, 209). We can accept disguise as conventionally probable, but we do well to remember that an increasing improbability accelerates the transition into farce.

A play differs essentially from a story, which is merely to be imagined. Consequently we have two kinds of probability. One is the probability of the plot as we see it in the mind's eye, and the other is the probability of the action as we actually see it represented physically with mechanical aids on a fixed spot and within a limited time. It is conceivable that a real Rosalind might deceive a real Orlando in a real forest of Arden. That is at least one aspect of the question of probability. But that a hundred and sixty pound, well-molded actress should deceive a hundred and thirty-five pound, slender, fifteen year younger actor into believing that she is a sentimental shepherd boy is preposterous. Yet such a *reductio ad absurdum* has been known even on our contemporary stage.[11]

The vision of the mind's eye must not be obscured by the

[11] White discusses stage Rosalinds in his *Studies in Shakespeare*, 233–257. After condemning all the performances he has ever seen, he says that the following costuming of the part would be historically correct, would make the confusions more probable, and would bring out the real humor of the situation in Arden. Rosalind should first "with a kind of umber smirch" her face. She should wear a doublet and trunk-hose, with tawny boots "almost meeting the puffed and bombasted trunk-hose." A coarse russet cloak, and "a black felt hat with narrow brim and high and slightly conical crown" should complete the costume. She should be armed with a boar-spear and a cutlass.

This comment should be compared with Winter's description (80–82) of Viola Allen's performance of *Twelfth Night*. He criticises the actress severely for being too literal and matter-of-fact in her conception of the female page.

rough beams of the theater. All the art of the actor and
the stage manager must unite to obviate jarring improbabilities, and to make a disguise situation seem at least
poetically probable. It will be interesting in the succeeding
paragraphs to note the development of the art of representing
disguise situations on the English stage. It is a record, not
only of a development of skill in theatrical costuming and
make-up, but also of an awakening consciousness of the
rich theatricality in disguise situations.

II

The staging of disguise may be considered as advancing
in three steps. First, there was only a change of name, but
no change at all in appearance. Second, there was a partial
change of appearance, or merely a symbol to represent a
change. Third, there came a consistent attempt to make
the disguised person really look his part in detail. Thus the
acting of disguise parts developed from the mere pretending
of children at play, to the art of the well-equipped and
practiced mimic.

In Skelton's *Magnificence* the whole plot depends on the
hero's mistaking Fancy for Largess, Crafty Conveyance for
Sure Surveyance, Courtly Abusion for Lusty Pleasure,
Folly for Conceit, and Cloaked Collusion for Sober Sadness.
Yet all except one of these characters have remained un-
changed in appearance.[12] They have confessedly merely
changed their names. The disguise which these characters
pretend is a disguise of abstract character, a spiritual metamorphosis, which is after all best indicated by a change of
name. We may imagine such a disguise but cannot easily
represent it by physical garments.

[12] Cloaked Collusion wears some sort of vestment or priestly garment (11, 601–609) to represent "sober sadness."

Some progress is made in Lyndsay's *Satire of the Three Estates*. Flattery, Falsehood, and Deceit change their names to Devotion, Sapience, and Discretion, thus assuming the same sort of spiritual disguise as the characters in *Magnificence*. But the play is an advance in theatricality, for the three vices actually put on the costumes of friars. These garments appropriately symbolize devotion, wisdom, and discretion, and, what is more important, they add to the stage picture and permit new stage business.

When the characters in a play ceased being abstractions and became human individuals, the disguise, too, had to become individual and specific. The transition is represented in the interlude called the *Marriage of Wit and Wisdom* (probably considerably earlier than the manuscript, which is dated 1579). The author pretends to disguise Idleness into five different characters. In scene 2, Idleness gulls the credulous Wit by saying that his name is Honest Recreation. But he does not alter his appearance in the least. In scene 3, Idleness enters and says that now he is "nue araid like a phesitien." He evidently is not much altered, however, for two comrades address him as Idleness, and Wit recognizes him as Honest Recreation, the name by which he knows him. In scene 4, Idleness enters "halting with a stilt, and shall cary a cloth upon a stafe, like a rat-catcher." This is confessedly pseudo-disguise but, accepting the symbol, we behold a very good scene, for Idleness has a merry time with the constable who carries a warrant to arrest Idleness! Since the constable does not appear in any other scene with Idleness, the disguise may be considered sufficiently convincing. In scene 6, Idleness says he is "a bould beggar," but, since this scene is a monolog and nobody sees him, he might as safely say that he is Charlemagne. The same conditions of isolation apply to scene 9, where Idleness enters "like a priest." The superficial changes in

order to impersonate the types of rat-catcher, physician,
beggar, and priest represent a slight advance in disguise
usage, while the changing of the name Idleness to Honest
Recreation is a relic of the pure moralities.

The next step is the disguise which involves only individuals
and has nothing to do with general abstractions. There is,
by the way, no very definite chronological order in the development we are tracing.[13] Our next illustration, *Tom Tyler
and His Wife*, may be an older piece than the *Marriage of
Wit and Wisdom*. *Tom Tyler*, which may date about 1550,
contains perhaps the earliest English impersonation motive.[14]
The situation is this: Tom Tyler is strangely afraid to
beat his wife. But his friend Tom Tayler performs the
task by disguising in Tyler's coat. The wife takes her
thrashing without discovering Tayler's identity. There
was no attempt at facial make-up or change of appearance, but the mid-century audience was not hypercritical,
and a change of coat was sufficient to indicate the impersonation.

The words of Chapman in *May Day* (II, 4) could have
been written more pertinently at least a generation before
May Day, for after 1600 his criticism had surely lost point.
He refers to "the stale refuge of miserable poets, by change
of a hat or a cloak to alter the whole state of a comedy."
Then his comment is "unless your disguise be such that your

---

[13] The change of names and symbolic disguising continued till the
end of the century. For a comparison of these disguises see, besides
the plays already mentioned, *Lusty Juventus* (before 1553), *New Custom* (before 1563), *Albion Knight* (1566), *Common Conditions* (1570),
Three Lords and Three Ladies of London (1585), *Cobbler's Prophecy*
(before 1593), and the *Case is Altered* (1598), and the dumb show in
the *Whore of Babylon* (1604). The dates are from Schelling's list.

[14] An impersonation motive of a different kind appears in *Jack
Juggler* (see below, page 29). Whether that interlude precedes *Tom
Tyler* or vice versa cannot be determined.

face may bear as great a part in it as the rest, the rest is nothing."

If a playwright realized the improbability in partial disguise he might make this improbability less obvious to the spectator by letting the person in disguise act only in monolog scenes, while the actual dramatic contact with other persons took place off the stage. This method, as we have just seen, was used in the *Marriage of Wit and Wisdom.* Whetstone in *Promos and Cassandra* presents Cassandra, "apparelled like a page" (Part I, III, 7) only for a brief soliloquy, and she meets no one on the stage. So also Andrugio, disguised "in some long black cloak" (Part II, V, 1), appears only in monolog scenes.

Acting in the Shakespearian theater was probably well developed into a finished art. By studying disguise situations we may form some general conclusion concerning the attention to detail in stage presentation. Of course, we are handicapped by not having any prompter's copies of the plays, but even in the text and stage directions of printed plays we have interesting evidence of the stage manager's practice. We shall illustrate briefly the acting of the disguise motive with reference to costume, facial make-up, voice, and stage business.

Actors and actresses are fond of appearing in different costumes during a play. The practice is very common in contemporary staging, even in "straight" parts of the serious "legitimate" drama. Disguise furnished an opportunity to display an actor in various costumes.[15] All of Shakespeare's female pages appeared first as women, then,

[15] Pepys thought Kynaston especially fortunate in playing the rôle of Epicœne. He says: "Kinaston the boy had the good turn to appear in three shapes; first, as a poor gentlewoman in ordinary clothes, . . . then in fine clothes, as a gallant; . . . and lastly as a man" (January 7, 1661).

after talking of disguising, appeared in the fictitious male character. Rosalind, Portia, Nerissa, and Jessica re-appear dressed as women. But Julia, Viola, and Imogen confess their identities and remain in page costumes. Julia dresses in "such weeds as may beseem some well reputed page" (II, 7). Rosalind decides to "suit me all points like a man" (I, 3). Imogen receives from her servant "Doublet, hat, hose, all that answer to them" (III, 4). Portia's habit is not specified but she was doubtless dressed like a doctor of laws. Viola enters in "man's attire."

A woodcut published in the 1622 edition of the *Maid's Tragedy* shows Aspatia disguised in "man's apparel." There is practically no difference between her and Amintor in dress and appearance.[16] The fact that the actor of a female page part was actually a young man, made the part absolutely convincing as it cannot be when an actress assumes the rôle. "What an odd double confusion it must have made, to see a boy play a woman playing a man: one cannot disentangle the perplexity without some violence to the imagination," said Lamb in his notes on *Philaster*. But in this book we shall have occasion several times for an odder and triple confusion, for we shall see a boy play a woman playing a man disguised as a woman. The necessity of using boy actors for female rôles doubtless bore a vital relation to the popularity of the heroine-pages. The stage manager and boy actor had an easy time of it. But it was the poet's art to create the illusion of real life by letting the women of a play discuss and plan their disguises as though they might have some difficulty in looking like boys.

Sometimes various causes united to make a costume or

[16] An interesting comment on woman's dress is furnished by Middleton's *Mad World, My Masters* (III, 3) where Follywit, when disguising as a woman, uses only a skirt. He explains that the "upper bodies" (doublet) is the same for woman as for man and that he will be in "fashion to a hair."

character popular with a playwright. The friar's gown, with its ample folds and long hood, furnished a convenient means of concealment in many plays. The disguise of an old soldier often appears. Both of these costumes were especially desirable because they were easily procurable in London and did not have to be made to order for any particular performance or play. Besides, these two — the friar and the soldier — were familiar figures and were easily imitated or burlesqued. The custom of getting what was convenient is reflected in the *Alchemist* (IV, 4) when Face instructs Drugger to go to the players and borrow "Hieronimo's old cloak, ruff and hat" in order to disguise as a Spaniard.

Conventional symbolic disguises were doubtless used when a character wished to pose as Revenge, Rapine, or Murder (see *Titus Andronicus*), or as a ghost. What these conventional costumes were we can only guess.[17]

Special costumes may possibly have been manufactured to facilitate disguising. In the *Devil is an Ass* a character mentions "double clokes" (III, 2). Gifford says in a note that the garment referred to was "a cloke adapted for disguises, which might be worn on either side. It was of different colours, and fashions. This turned cloke . . . furnished a ready and effectual mode of concealment, which is now lost to the stage." Such a cloak might have been very useful in multi-disguise plays, but I can find no references to one, nor any situation where it was needed.[18]

The references given above show that playwrights gave a great deal of attention to the garments of the disguised

[17] Haigh (*Attic Theatre*, 221) implies that the Greeks had special masks to represent figures such as Justice, Persuasion, Deceit, Jealousy.

[18] Note in *Magnificence*, line 605, that when Cloaked Collusion appears disguised in a priestly vestment he is addressed as "Sir John Double Cloak" (or "Double Cope").

person. But the principle of probability demanded that the change of appearance should extend farther than the clothes. The face also had to be disguised. There were, however, two subterfuges. One was the wearing of a high bandage or muffler. Thus Wilie posing as a girl in *George a Greene* pretends to have a toothache and naturally has his face pretty well covered. Thus, also, Falstaff as witch wears a muffler. The other evasion was the wearing of a mask, or visor, concealing, not disguising, the face.[19] Folly-wit, disguised as a courtesan, in *Mad World, My Masters*, wears both a mask and a "chin clout" or muffler. When Epicœne first appears she is wearing a mask, which is immediately removed at the request of Morose. But masks do not seem to have been extensively used either in disguises or the acting of regular women's parts. Quince's promise to Flute that he may save his young beard by playing Thisbe's part in a mask perhaps is meant to reflect Flute's ready wit rather than any general custom of the stage.

The actor's face, in case there was no covering provided for it, might be changed in hue or feature in order to make the disguise effective. Rosalind gives her face the tanned complexion of a country boy by smirching it with "a kind of umber" (I, 3). In the *Blind Beggar of Bednal Green* (III, 2) Canbee and his companion, before undertaking new rogueries, wash off "that gypsy color." There is a touch of verisimilitude in *Look About You* when Robin Hood is to

[19] Masks in the Greek theater were used, not to conceal the face, but to give it character, thus serving the purpose of make-up. Naturally the characters represented were stereotyped in feature, twenty-eight types for tragedy, and forty-four types for the New Comedy (Haigh, 221, 237). It seems strange that these conditions did not encourage frequent uses of dramatic disguise in Greek drama even before the New Comedy. Although actors played numerous parts in a play, this was done for stage convenience, and not to produce mistaken identity, except in the rare cases noted in Chapter III.

disguise as Lady Fauconbridge. She says: "Be wary, lest ye be discovered," and Robin replies: "Best paint me, then be sure I shall not blush." Brainworm as an old soldier wears "a smoky varnish" (III, 1). Edgar in *King Lear* (II, 3) planning to disguise himself as a madman, says "My face I'll grime with filth." Sir John Frugal in Massinger's *City Madam* (1619) is disguised like an Indian from Virginia — the first American Indian disguise in English drama [20] — and speaks of washing off his paint before he will be recognized.

It must be remembered that all these references imply a more or less careful change of facial make-up between scenes. Sometimes the making up took place before the audience. Skink in *Look About You* disguises himself as a drawer by smearing stage "blood" over his face, the business being performed on the stage. In *May Day* (III, 2) Angelo helps Lorenzo with his chimney-sweep disguise. He enters with a "pot of painting" and gives the impatient lover the proper complexion of a chimney sweep.

A false nose is worn by the rogue in the *Blind Beggar of Alexandria* whenever he appears as the usurer Leon. This stage property is referred to in various places in the text.

Pretended blindness was another stratagem of disguise. In the *Blind Beggar of Alexandria* and the *Blind Beggar of Bednal Green* the heroes make up as blind. In Jonson's *New Inn* Lady Frampul disguises by playing blind in one eye. She doubtless wore a patch. I do not know just how the "Beggars" were made up. Fitzwater in the *Downfall of Robert, Earl of Huntington* (III, 2) pretended blindness by merely closing his eyes; but that stratagem would not really make him less liable to recognition.

[20] In Tomkins's *Lingua* (1603–04) Tobacco is represented as an Indian; Beaumont and Fletcher's *Triumph of Time* (1608) presents Plutus with a troop of Indians; but these are not cases of disguise.

The wearing of patches was a common device for disguising the face. Brainworm as an old soldier wears "three or four patches" (III, 1). Skink in *Look About You* and the rogue in the *Blind Beggar of Alexandria* wear patches as part of their disguises. Aspatia in the *Maid's Tragedy* wears artificial scars, which she refers to as "these few blemishes" (V, 4). At the end of the *London Prodigal* Flowerdale, who is disguised as an old sailor, reveals himself with the words: "Look on me better, now my scar is off."

False hair and beards are so often mentioned in the disguise plays that references are unnecessary here. Sometimes disguises are effected by removing the beard, the character making the operation seem real by speaking of "shaving." Friscobaldo thus disguises himself as an old servant by "shaving" (*II Honest Whore*, I, 2), and Face resumes his part as butler by "shaving" (*Alchemist*, IV, 4). It is interesting to see how the playwrights strove for verisimilitude by making the boy actor appear not like a boy, but like a girl disguised as a boy. Julia, instead of saying she will cut her hair, says she will "knit it up in silken strings with twenty odd-conceited true-love knots" (II, 7), and when Second Luce at the end of the *Wise Woman of Hogsdon* reveals herself "she scatters her hair." The actor had, in a sense, a double make-up. Outwardly he appeared to be a boy. When this disguise was discovered he looked like a girl, but this too was a make-up.[21]

The change of costume and facial appearance did not

[21] There is an interesting example of disguise within disguise in Brome's *Northern Lasse* (V, 8). When Pate's doctor disguise is removed he proves to be a minister; when the minister disguise is removed he proves to be Pate, the witty servant. A symbolical disguise within disguise occurs in Field's *Woman is a Weathercock* (V, 2). When Nevill removes his parson's disguise he stands in a devil's robe and shows what "knavery a priest's cloak can hide." See also Calderon's *Amor, Honor, y Poder*, described in Chapter III, page 54.

complete the disguise. It was also important that the voice and manner of speech be disguised. Vocal mimicry gave the actor an opportunity to display his talents. This elocutionary change was not so necessary in the case of a female page, for the voice of a boy is about the same as that of a young woman. But in some of the other disguise situations the demands on the actor were more severe. When Kent enters disguised he evidently casts a critical glance over his costume and remarks: "If but as well I other accents borrow, That can my speech diffuse, my good intent May carry through itself." There was a "varying accent" in Brainworm's speech while he was disguised as a soldier (III, 2). An interesting stage direction in the *Malcontent* (I, 1) reads: "Bilioso re-entering, Malevole shifteth his speech." This indicates that the disguised duke speaks in feigned voice except when speaking with Celso, his confidant.

A peculiarity of speech sometimes had to be imitated. For example in *Look About you* Skink exchanges costumes with the stammering Red Cap and, of course, has to imitate his stammer as well. Then when Skink-as-Red-Cap exchanges with Gloucester, the latter has to assume the stammer. The stammering motive is also used effectively in the doubles situation in *What You Will* (see Chapter VIII, page 186).

Foreign languages and dialects also were imitated. Disguised characters speak Spanish in the *Alchemist*, broken Italian in *Rare Triumphs of Love and Fortune*, pseudo-French in *Old Fortunatus*, Dutch in the *London Prodigal* and in the *Shoemaker's Holiday*, to mention only a few examples. Irish, Welsh, and similar insular dialects are often used to emphasize a disguise.

The fourth theatrical change necessary in disguise situations was the change in physical bearing and general stage business. Imitative business was a good opportunity for histrionic exhibition on the part of the ambitious actor. Shakespeare liked to have his characters specify this part of their mimicry. The roguish lord in *The Shrew* says: "I know the boy will well usurp the grace, Voice, gait, and action of a gentlewoman." Portia turns "two mincing steps into a manly stride," and Rosalind bears a "swashing and a martial outside." Duke Vincentio demands instruction so that he "may formally in person bear me Like a true friar," and Imogen is instructed to act with "what imitation you can borrow from youth of such a season."

Sometimes physical peculiarities have to be imitated, as, for example, in the *Fair Maid of the Exchange*, where Frank has to act like the cripple, in order to win his lady love.

The desire to attain probability in histrionic presentation of the doubles situation would lead, strictly considered, to a realist's dilemma. If two characters did not look alike, how could there be a confusion of identity? and if they did look exactly alike, how could the audience keep from being confused? On the Roman stage absolute identity of doubles was easily produced by the use of masks. It was perhaps easier to make two masks alike than different.[22] But the audience kept the doubles apart by means of a conventional badge supposed to be invisible to the persons in the drama. An echo from the Latin [23] is seen in the Prologue to the *Birth of Hercules* where Mercury says: "But that you may knowe us asunder, I will were in my hatt a piece of a feather for a difference; and the same difference shalbe betwixt my father and Amphitruo, which none els shall perceaue but you." This precaution in the *Birth of Hercules* is, of course, not

---

[22] Although it is said that masks were not used in the Roman theater before about 115 B.C. (Teuffel, I, 25), we must remember that the doubles situations of *Amphitruo* and *Menæchmi* were originally composed for the Greek theater, where masks were regularly used.

[23] See the Prologue to *Amphitruo*.

really necessary, for the Elizabethan actors of the parts did not appear exactly alike. Perhaps the audience was expected to imagine that a badge was necessary to distinguish one actor from the other.

Ben Jonson did not think the *Amphitruo* plot was practicable before a sophisticated London audience. He told Drummond (*Conv.* XVI, 29) that he had "ane intention to have made a play like Plautus's *Amphitrio*, but, left it of, for that he could never find two so like others that he could persuade the spectators they were one." With this in memory it is interesting to compare a passage from the *Sad Shepherd* (II, 1). The witch of Paplewick intends to assume multi-impersonation and says to her daughter: "Douce, because ye may meet me in many shapes to-day, where'er you spy This broidered belt with characters, 'tis I."

As a matter of fact there was no real dilemma in the acting of doubles, for on the Elizabethan, as on the contemporary, stage, it was no more necessary that the disguised Viola should look exactly like her brother than that the actor of Rosalind should speak his lines in the real forest of Arden.[24]

This chapter has aimed to show the various values of disguise as a factor in dramatic structure, and its quadruple theatrical opportunities in stage presentation. These two aspects of the disguise motive have been set forth with some completeness in order to enable the reader to grasp the full dramatic and theatrical import of the situations discussed in the following chapters.

[24] It is interesting to note that in such an early interlude as *Jack Juggler*, where the make-up of actors was doubtless very crude, Jenkins endeavors to create conviction of resemblance through mere wordy assertion. He says that Jack is like him in head, cap, shirt, knotted hair, eyes, nose, lips, cheeks, chin, neck, feet, legs, hips, stature, height, and age!

Enthusiasts sometimes talk about the Elizabethan drama as though it were only the tragic or comic struggle of passion set forth in poetic language. They imply that the dramatist, soaring loftily in the heights, condescended reluctantly to mere devices of stage representation. We gladly agree that the poetry and spiritual conflicts in the Elizabethan drama are of imperishable beauty, and we would not minimize their fame. But the voice, mimicry, pantomime, and external physical auxiliaries, or technically speaking, the tricks of reading and impersonation, costuming, stage business, setting, and stage properties, all of which perished with the performance, were by no means scorned by the poets, for they were playwrights, too. The evidences that the Elizabethans did everything in their power and knowledge to make stage representation realistic to eyes and ears, are palpable to the scholar, and should not be ignored when discoursing on the poetic drama of Shakespeare and his contemporaries.

CHAPTER III

THE ORIGIN AND EXTENT OF DRAMATIC DISGUISE

This poet is that poet's plagiary,
And he a third's, till they end all in Homer.
And Homer filched all from an Egyptian priestess,
The world's a theatre of theft.
— *Albumazar.*

I

In the previous chapter we have tried to show the technical functions and values of disguise from the point of view of the writer who is constructing a dramatic plot, and of the stage manager who is producing the play. It will now be interesting to glance at the history of dramatic disguise, to see how writer, stage manager, and audience gradually learned to appreciate and desire these dramatic and theatrical values of disguise. We shall see scattered and crude examples in Greek drama, more practical and skilful use of disguise in Roman comedy, and well-established traditions of the motive in Italian drama.

Disguise as we have defined the device is almost totally absent from Greek tragedy, occurring only in four plays out of thirty-three. One is by Æschylus, one by Sophocles, and two by Euripides. In three of these four plays the disguise is merely incidental to the plot, and in the fourth the disguise, although basic, is of slight value.

Æschylus heads the list with his *Choephori*. In this play Orestes, after identifying himself to his sister Electra assumes the disguise of a stranger and speaks "the Parnassian speech copying the accent of a Phocian tongue."

31

Thus disguised he meets his mother Clytemnestra and tells her of the pretended death of himself. Later he slays Clytemnestra and Ægisthus. That there was some theatrical advantage in changing mask and costume is possible; but that the plot structure does not necessitate any such change is made evident by comparison with the *Electra* of Sophocles, a play which contains the same characters and the same general situations, but does not contain this disguise of Orestes.

Sophocles uses disguise, but to no great advantage, in *Philoctetes*. The problem in this play is to get the famous arrows away from Philoctetes, a stratagem which is accomplished through the guileful conversation and representations of Neoptolemus, while his friend, disguised as a merchant, appears on the stage briefly and in an auxiliary capacity. Equally episodic is the disguise which Euripides uses in *Rhesus*. Dolon, in a wolf's skin, goes forth to spy on the enemy; but Dolon's death, which defeats his purpose, is not a dramatic consequence of the change of dress.

The most dramatic disguise in extant Greek tragedy occurs in the *Bacchæ* of Euripides, but even here the situation is not skilfully handled. Bacchus, in the form of a mortal, and posing as a Bacchanalian devotee, is determined to compel King Pentheus to recognize Bacchus as a god. The king treats the supposed mortal with contempt and finally orders him imprisoned, whereupon the god exerts his supernatural power and wrecks the prison, almost killing Pentheus. The god further exerts his power and causes the king to become partly insane. He induces him to don woman's clothes in order to spy on the Bacchæ, a band of Bacchic revellers near the city. At the end of the play a messenger relates how the Bacchæ had treated the disguised Pentheus as an intruder, and how the king had finally been torn limb from limb by his own mother who insanely mistook him for a beast of the chase.

Technically the play is weak in that the female disguise of the king does not lead to much complication; furthermore, neither the king's disguise nor his undisguising produces the dénouement, his death. However, there is a good dramatic effect in the mistake of Pentheus, who even denies the existence of the god Bacchus, a mistake of true tragic irony accomplished by the concealed identity of the hero. But playwrights of a later age could have improved upon this dramaturgy of Eupirides and produced greater theatrical value from the situation given. Especially would this have been true at the end of the play. It is surely a weakness in plot that the king is never informed of the real identity of his tormentor.

It is difficult to generalize concerning the slight material in the four tragedies just treated. However, we observe that the situations under discussion do not resemble each other. We shall see presently that they are also unlike those in the comedies of Aristophanes. That is to say, we have no evidence that traditional disguise situations developed in Greek drama.

When we turn to Aristophanes we find that, although disguise played a considerable part in his comedies and, in one or two cases, may have been effective on the stage, it is not structurally basic anywhere. Let us remember that we use the word basic in a special sense; in no play of Aristophanes does a particular disguise produce both the complication and resolution of the plot.

We shall pass over a very incidental disguise in the *Acharnians* and note the plot of the *Ecclesiazusæ*. Three Athenian women disguise themselves in their husbands' clothes and are about to enter the assembly to legislate woman's rights by stratagem. What now takes place off the stage is related by one of the outwitted husbands, who tells his wife (who listens with comic irony) that the assembly has voted that the state shall henceforth be ruled by women. The rest of the play does not involve the disguise. We note the theatrical insignificance of the motive in that the disguise action is not represented, but only reported as having taken place, that there is no undisguising before the audience, and that the stratagem is never discovered.

Aristophanes produced a more theatrical situation in the *Thesmophoriazusæ* where Mnesilochus, disguised as a woman, is instructed to enter the assembly of the Thesmophoria, and to plead for Euripides, who has been accused of speaking ill of women. But the mimic ability of Mnesilochus fails, for, although he is instructed to "talk like a woman in your voice, well and naturally," he is discovered and arrested. Now this complication is solved rather cleverly by a second disguise. Euripides, disguised as a procuress, succeeds in entertaining the guard by a dancing girl. The supposed procuress offers to keep the prisoner while the guard and the girl are away and thus effects the rescue of Mnesilochus. These two situations are fundamentally comic and could be made very effective by skilful actors.

Aristophanes produced another good situation in the laughable exchange of costumes in *Frogs*, a situation, however, which, as far as the main plot is concerned, is really detachable. Dionysus, disguised as Heracles, goes to Hades to bring back Euripides. When he gets there a literary contest between Euripides and Æschylus takes place, with the result that the latter is chosen to ascend to earth with Dionysus. Such is the main plot. But when the hero first enters Hades a great deal of fun is produced by his exchanging costume and rôle with his slave, doubtless one of the earliest uses of the exchange motive. The reason for this exchange is that Dionysus, mistaken for Heracles, is vituperated in Hades by those who owe Heracles a grudge. The master gives his Heracles costume to the slave. But curiously enough the costume when worn by the slave draws the sweetest welcome of maidens. Dionysus now resumes the disguise and is immediately abused again as Heracles. Therefore he again commands his slave to wear the "lion's skin and club." This time the supposed Heracles is arrested and condemned, but offers his "slave" (Dionysus) to be tortured in his place. When the flogging is about to begin Dionysus declares his identity. This scene was no doubt funny, but if we examine the whole action we find that the situation is incidental to the main plot.

We have thus seen that disguises in Greek tragedy and Old Comedy are infrequent and isolated; and that the situations, although more effective theatrically in the comedies than in the tragedies, are nowhere structurally basic or of great organic value.

II

What the practice was in the New Comedy of Greece must be inferred by looking backward from Plautus and Terence. Menander used disguise in one plot out of the seven or eight we can attribute to him. He furnished the plots for Plautus's *Bacchides, Stichus,* and possibly *Cistellaria;* and for Terence's *Andria, Heautontimorumenos, Adelphi,* and *Eunuchus.* Of these plays only *Eunuchus* contains disguise. The fragments of Menander which have come down to us reveal no further use of the motive.[1] Philemon wrote the originals for *Trinummus,*[2] *Mercator,* and possibly *Mostellaria* by Plautus. None of these three plays contain disguise. Diphilus fur-

---

[1] See the edition by Professor Capps of Menander's four plays, the *Hero, Epitrepontes, Periceiromene,* and *Samia.*

[2] *Trinummus,* as well as *Epidicus,* has a misrepresentation of identity which I do not classify as disguise because there is no change of costume.

nished the prototype for Plautus's *Rudens*, which contains no disguise, and for *Casina* with its boy bride situation so often imitated in later comedy.

We cannot therefore make any positive general assertions for the three dramatists, Menander, Philemon, and Diphilus. But that there were some good disguise plots in that period is clear from *Eunuchus*, and *Casina*, already named, and from *Miles Gloriosus*, *Captivi*, and *Amphitruo*, whose sources cannot be definitely indicated.

From whatever source Plautus drew, it is evident that he was fond of disguise; he established the motive as a dramatic device, giving it strength, as it were, for a flourishing career, in the comedy of the Renaissance. Terence has one disguise plot, *Eunuchus*. Seneca has none at all.

Plautus sometimes used incidental disguises to help carry on intrigues. This is the case in *Pseudolus*, *Asinaria*, and *Persa*, plays which we shall not pause to discuss. He introduces disguise with fundamental functions in the four plays treated below.

Amphitruo is the oldest plot in which disguise is basic in our special sense of the word. Jupiter's impersonation moves and controls the machinery of the plot. His disguises and those of his servant Mercury clearly initiate the action, and develop it; the revelation of identity by removing the disguise finally resolves the complication. Besides this architectural value, the disguise possesses great theatrical value to the comedians who present the laughable confusions of identity together with farcical cross-purposes and amazements. With *Amphitruo* disguise sprang into full power as a dramatic motive. Further, the play resulted in a dramatic tradition — a long column of lovers disguised as supposedly absent husbands.[3]

No less influential was *Casina* with its farcical boy bride

[3] *Amphitruo* and its influence is discussed in Chapter VIII.

situation. The disguise in this play, though not basic, was of great constructive value.[4] A clever scene in *Miles Gloriosus* is the prototype of similar ruses in Renaissance drama extending at least as far as Molière's *Médicin Volant*. The braggart's captive girl one day entertains her lover, who has entered through a secret passage from a neighbor's house. A servant of the braggart happens to see them and is distressed at the intrigue. But he is convinced by the lover's servant that he had seen, not the captive girl, but her twin sister who lodged next door. This twin was, of course, fictitious, and it now becomes necessary for the captive girl to play two parts, which she does, much to the confusion of the servant, by changing dresses quickly and by using the secret passage so that she may appear from either house according to the character she wishes to maintain. The opportunities for clever acting in this situation are obvious; structurally the disguise is important because it adds comic suspense to the fundamental problem of securing the girl's freedom. The disguise, however, is not basic, and is never discovered. The girl is finally able to escape with her lover, thanks to a trick of a different character played by the intriguing servant on the braggart.

In *Captivi*, a play of quiet humor and irony, disguise initiates, though it does not resolve, the main action. A nobleman and his servant have been made prisoners of war by Hegio. The servant agrees to impersonate his master, who in turn impersonates his servant and is in that capacity sent back to his country to negotiate for the release of Hegio's son, who is held by the enemy. When Hegio discovers the deception which caused him to send away the very man he intended to hold as a hostage, he wreaks vengeance on the disguised servant. The servant pleads for mercy on the ground that his duty lay in loyalty to his master rather than

[4] *Casina* is discussed in Chapter V.

in truthfulness to his captor. But no mercy is shown and
the slave is loaded with heavy chains and dragged off to
the stone quarries. In the end the noble returns with the
ransomed son of Hegio, and also with evidence that the
impersonating slave is really the long lost younger son of
Hegio.[5]

Perhaps the resemblance between the exchange motive
just described and that in the *Frogs* of Aristophanes has
been noticed by the reader. If there were more such resemblances among the disguise situations in Greek and
Roman drama we might make a sort of classification and
draw some conclusions in regard to literary relations. But
the reader can tell by glancing back at the plots described
in this chapter that traditional motives, so easy to trace in
Renaissance drama, may in certain cases have their source
in classic drama, but had not become familiar or traditional
there. Thus we shall see how the boy bride motive in
Casina prevails and develops in Italian and English drama.
The disguised lover who impersonates the husband like Jupiter in *Amphitruo* or a servant like Chærea in Terence's
Eunuchus, often makes his entrance in Renaissance literature. The fictitious twin appears again and again using
much the same methods as the girl in *Miles Gloriosus*. The
exchange motive is frequently employed. But the most important motive of all, the female page, has no predecessor
in classic drama.

We have now seen that in classic drama disguise had
been tested and found valuable as a dramatic motive, especially in comedy. It only needed new conditions of stage
representation, new dramatic stuff, and the tastes of a later
and different civilization to produce numerous new situa-

[5] In Nash's *Unfortunate Traveller* (1594) the Earl of Surrey and Jack
Wilton agree to exchange names and ranks while traveling on the
continent.

tions, and to develop the old and the new alike until they became generally accepted as dramatic stock in trade.

III

The great vogue of disguise in Italian drama was due partly to the impulse given by Roman comedy, and partly to the influence of *novelle*. The situations borrowed from these sources were wrought into plots far more elaborate than anything produced by Plautus or Terence. Disguise was eagerly employed apparently because it facilitated the construction of highly involved plots of confusions and cross-purposes — intricate structures that are illustrative of dramatic taste in the Renaissance of Italy. The Plautian disguises are so frequently combined with disguises from *novelle*, especially with the female page situation, that we cannot proceed to the examination of the Italian plays until we have first explored the *novelle* and other early sources of dramatic stuff. After having gathered up our materials we can study the fixing of types, and incidentally the evolution of dramatic technic.

Mr. R. Warwick Bond, in discussing the difference between Italian and classic drama,[6] makes some valuable remarks on the Italian heroine. He says: "The chief change is in the position of the heroine. In Greek and Roman comedy, the scene being always in a public place, respectable unmarried girls could take no part. . . . But Italian custom, equally with classical, forbade the appearance of citizen's daughters in the streets; so that the drama would have lost, not gained, by the change in young men's taste, but for the device, introduced from the *novelle*, of presenting girls in male disguise."

To find the ultimate source of this motive would be a

[6] *Early Plays*, xxxix.

difficult problem in comparative literature; but a little
investigation shows us that women disguised as men, often
unrecognized by their husbands, are to be found earlier
than the *novelle* in French romances, and earlier than the
romances in Hindoo tales.[7] It is interesting to see that
these early instances deal with married women, and that
gradually in the *novelle* and in the drama the situation was
shifted so as to involve unmarried girls, sometimes in intrigues, but often in romantic love affairs, as in the case of
Shakespeare's Julia, Rosalind, and Viola.

The *Twelfth Night* plot, a typical female page motive,
contains four elements, or narrative units. First, the disguised heroine seeks her husband or lover; second, she
serves this man unrecognized; third, she acts as love messenger to a rival mistress; and fourth, some lady who believes that the disguised person really is a man becomes the
victim of a mistaken wooing. These four elements may be
found scattered through half a dozen stories which ante-
date the *novelle*.

In a Hindoo story[8] by Somadeva, who flourished in the
twelfth century, Kirtisena, the heroine, escapes from her
cruel mother-in-law, flees disguised in male attire, and seeks
her husband. In the course of adventures at a foreign court
she finds her husband, reveals herself immediately, and lives

[7] A still earlier case of a girl disguised as a boy occurs in the Sanskrit
play *Viddha-s'āla-bhañjikā* by Rājas'ekhara, who lived about 900 A. D.
(Schuyler, 11). A girl comes to a foreign court dressed as a boy.
The Queen, thinking "he" really is a boy, disguises the stranger as a
girl. The King falls in love with the newcomer, and the Queen en-
courages the marriage, hoping to play a joke on her husband. At the
wedding the supposed mock bride turns out to be a real bride.

This, it will be seen, is a different type of plot from that of the female
page following her lover; the chief difference being that the girl in the
play is passive throughout.

[8] Story of Kirtisena, · Brockhaus, 125.

happily ever after. Somadeva's story, together with the French *Le Liure du tres Chevalereux Comte d'Artois et de sa Femme*, and two Icelandic sagas (probably from French originals), have been cited as sources or analogues [9] of the ninth tale of the third day of the *Decameron*.[10]

The romance of *Comte d'Artois* is perhaps only a little older than the *Decameron*. It relates how Philip I. leaves his wife because they have no issue, and imposes severe conditions for his reunion with her. She follows disguised as a man, becomes his servant, wins his confidence, arranges for him a meeting with a princess, substitutes for her rival at this rendezvous, and finally bears him a son, thus fulfilling one of the conditions.

The Icelandic *Magus saga* and *Mirmans saga* go back to 1300 or earlier. The disguise situations (alike in these two stories)[11] tell of an emperor's abandoning his wife and imposing severe conditions of a reunion. The wife disguises as a knight and fights as an ally of her husband. The trick which later results in cohabitation need not concern us here. But the emperor does not learn of his wife's adventures until she relates her story and presents his son.

A simple but effective female page disguise is used in the romance *Du Roi Flore et de la Belle Jehane*, a thirteenth century adaptation of an older romance in verse.[12] In this story Jehane, disguised as a squire, follows her departed husband and serves him seven years without being recognized. A more interesting situation develops in the romance of *Tristan de Nanteuil* (sometimes called *Gui de*

[9] Landau, 145–150; Lee, 101–108.

[10] Boccaccio, however, disguises Giletta as a female pilgrim. Painter follows the Italian closely. Shakespeare in *All's Well* evidently means to represent his heroine in female garb. At any rate there is no dramatic confusion of any consequence in any of these three stories.

[11] Cederschiöld, lxxxvi; Kölbing, 218.

[12] Landau, 136.

Nanteuil),[13] which probably dates at the beginning of the thirteenth century. Tristan disguises his bride, Blanchandine, as a knight, and she accompanies him on adventures. At the sultan's court, a woman falls in love with, and marries, the supposed knight. Blanchandine (who thinks that her husband Tristan is lost) avoids the revelation of her sex for several days and then prays God to save the situation by changing her into a man. The prayer is heard and the metamorphosis accomplished.

It would doubtless be possible to multiply these examples by searching farther into medieval French romance. But we have already examined enough to see that the motive of the female page following her lover was known in Europe before the time of the Italian *novelle*.

The fascinating situation of the lovelorn or venturesome heroine disguised as a page was frequently used in the prose tales of Boccaccio, Fiorentino, Salernitano, Straparola, and Bandello, ranging in time from 1358 to 1554. Boccaccio has a well-known parallel to *Cymbeline* in the *Decameron, II, 9*.[14] He has an unusual disguise story in the *Decameron, II, 3,* which was translated by Painter in the *Palace of Pleasure* (Tome I, 34). A gentleman falls into the train of a beautiful young abbot who is on his way to the pope. At an inn the gentleman is forced to occupy a small room adjoining the abbot's chamber. During the night the abbot calls in the young man and reveals herself as a woman, the daughter of the King of England. The youth and girl-abbot are married on the spot — the princess performing the religious ceremony herself.

Fiorentino in *IV, 1*, of the *Pecorone* (begun in 1378 though not published until 1558), wrote a story which is closely paralleled in the *Merchant of Venice*. *Pecorone, III, 1*, has a disguise situation which results in mistaken wooing. A

[13] Meyer.   [14] *Cymbeline* is discussed in Chapter IV.

lady disguised as a friar accompanies a priest, who, however, is not aware of his companion's sex. The two lodge with a widow, whose daughter mistakenly woos the girl-friar. The consequent happenings bring about the revelation of sex.

Salernitano, in his *Novellino* (pr. 1476), has half a dozen *novelle* which show his interest in the female page disguise. *Novella 11* tells of a shoemaker, who is so jealous of his wife that he takes her out only in the disguise of a medical student. The male apparel, however, only makes it easier for the wife to meet her lover. *Novella 33*, a version of the *Romeo and Juliet* story, has a heroine setting out in the costume of a friar. However, no mistake of identity ensues. In *Novella 39* Susanna, disguised as a man, takes service with a shipmaster, and follows her lover, whom she is eventually able to free from slavery. *Novella 40* is a very ingenious story of a gallant who cuckolds a man by disguising the wife as a youth and bringing her on board ship in the presence of the husband, who knows that the disguised person is a woman but thinks all the while that she is a neighbor's wife and not his own.[15] *Novella 43* relates how a girl, condemned to death by her father because of a love affair, is set free by servants and escapes disguised as a man. She takes service with a nobleman but eventually returns and marries her lover. In *Novelle 27* and *35* women disguise as men, but there seems to be no confusion of identity.

A situation which reminds us of *Philaster* is found in Straparola's *Tredeci Piacevolissime Notti, IV, 1* (pr. 1550). Costanza, an athletic girl, seeking adventures in the disguise of a man, takes service at a royal court. The queen falls in love with the girl-man and makes advances, which,

---

[15] Chapman's *May Day* (IV, 7 and 8) has an ironical situation similar to this. *May Day* was adapted from Italian, as we shall indicate below.

however, are resisted. Eventually Costanza's identity and
the queen's misbehavior are revealed. The queen is burned
and Costanza becomes the new queen. An interesting discovery made at the end of the story is that the queen's waiting maids are really men — her paramours.

Bandello's novels published in 1554 contain a plot (*II, 36*)
which seems to be indirectly a source of *Twelfth Night*.
However, Bandello was himself indebted to an Italian play,
Gl' Ingannati, for the plot. He uses a similar disguise situation in *I, 18*, and a very simple disguise in *II, 27*.

From the medieval romances and novels, as we have seen,
came the most popular disguise motive in English drama.
The disguised heroine was transferred from the novel to the
stage by the methods learned from Plautus and Terence,
dramatists who had shown how theatrically effective analogous disguise situations could be. The novels also contributed the disguised spy, as well as the female page, to
dramatic literature. The disguised spy is more important
in English, than in Italian drama, and will be discussed in
Chapter VII. Medieval narratives also presented disguised
lovers, men dressed as women, and exchanges of costumes,
but these motives in non-dramatic literature are interesting
to us only as analogues to the situations inherited by dramatists directly from Plautus.

Italian drama then has a double inheritance. It derives
dramatic stuff from romances, *novelle*, and other tales, as
well as from classic drama; it borrows technical methods
from Plautus and Terence. From this inheritance it develops
a distinctive practice of its own. The Italian method is
to combine materials and to elaborate the action. Thus any
given play might consist of various disguise situations spun
together into a highly intricate plot of much confusion, cross
purpose, and involution. Although we realize that this
type of plot does not allow character growth or portraiture,

or comic emphasis on any one situation, and besides has
a tendency to descend into farce, yet we must admit that it
results in intricate action accelerated by many surprises and
guaranteeing against dull moments while the play is in
progress.

Nowhere is the Italian method of elaborating a plot
better illustrated than in Dovizi da Bibbiena's comedy
La Calandria, acted in 1513 (Bond, xvii). The ground-
work is the *Menæchmi* situation. But the playwright has
made the twins brother and sister. Then he has multiplied
the Plautian confusions by introducing disguise, enabling the
girl to appear as a boy, and the boy as a girl. The consequence is a mistake of sex as well as of person. Santilla,
posing as a boy, and using her brother Lidio's name, has
had an insistent offer of marriage before the play begins;
and during the play is constantly mistaken for her brother.
The latter disguises as a girl while engaged in an intrigue
with a married woman by the name of Fulvia; and Fulvia's
husband, Calandro, is head over heels in love with this
supposed girl. To make matters still worse Fulvia is part
of the time disguised as a man, and Santilla's servant is
part of the time disguised as a woman. When we remember
that the twin motive is in itself sufficiently confusing, we
can realize how much more intricate the plot becomes when
involved with a female page, disguised lovers, and a male
mistress situation.

The play just described is, so far as I can discover, the
earliest Italian play containing a female page. A twin
brother and sister, the latter disguised like her brother,
appear again in an influential and much discussed play,
Gl' Ingannati, which was acted in 1531. This play has
been translated by Thomas Love Peacock (*Works*, 1875,
vol. 3), and synopses of the plot are not hard to find among
discussions of *Twelfth Night* and its sources. We shall con-

tent ourselves here with showing in what respects it is more complicated than *Twelfth Night*.

In *Twelfth Night* Viola enters the action without any initial entanglement. She has not even seen the duke. *Gl' Ingannati* opens with Lelia in danger of being married off to old Gherardo. She is in love with Flaminio, who, however, has forgotten her. (Flaminio corresponds to Shakespeare's duke.) He is in love with Isabella, who is the daughter of old Gherardo, Lelia's confident suitor. This triangular relation between Lelia, Gherardo, and Isabella has no corresponding complication in *Twelfth Night*.

Lelia dresses as page, serves Flaminio as love messenger to Isabella, is mistakenly wooed by Isabella, and hears herself denounced by Flaminio, who, of course, does not recognize his page. This, owing to the love affair which had begun before the play, is somewhat more complex than *Twelfth Night*.[16]

Another complication not in *Twelfth Night* is the result of supposed disguise. Gherardo, the old suitor, and Virginio, the father of Lelia, have both heard of her disguise. Consequently, when the twin brother appears on the scene, they, (thinking he is Lelia disguised) chastise him by locking him up with Isabella! The subsequent confusions completely mystify the two fathers, Isabella, and her servant, Lelia's nurse, and the lover Flaminio.[17]

The influence of *Gl' Ingannati* through the novels of Bandello and Montemayor; through the Italian plays *Gl' Inganni* and *Il Viluppo;* through Lope de Rueda's

[16] Some of these scenes in *Gl' Ingannati* are rather closely paralleled in the *Two Gentlemen*. See Chapter IV.

[17] Note that the presence of two extra suitors in Shakespeare's play, namely, Sir Andrew and Malvolio, does not really produce much additional complication. The scenes they appear in are character comedy rather than plot comedy.

Engaños, and Calderon's *Española de Florencia;* through French translations and the Cambridge Latin play *Lælia*, and many other adaptations was wide and persistent. It would require considerable time and skill to analyze and study those plots thoroughly, and to ascertain their relations with *Twelfth Night*.[18] These plays are all skilful variations of the *Menæchmi* situation, the Plautian effects being intensified by substituting the girl disguised as a boy for one of the twins.

In fact it is evident that all Italian plays containing girls disguised as boys are in causal relation with each other in varying degrees. But we must dismiss this disguise temporarily, merely appending in a footnote a few more titles to prove the popularity of the motive.[19]

Thus we have seen how familiar the disguised heroine following her lover had become in Italy in the sixteenth century. This disguise, as we have pointed out, was not inherited from classic drama. We shall now turn to a motive which came to Italian literature directly from the *Casina* of Plautus. The farcical situation of a sinewy youth dressed as a girl and married off to some amorous fool is not uncommon in Italian drama.

[18] For bibliography see Anders, 70; and Rosenberg, xviii–xxviii. See also the discussion of *Twelfth Night* in Chapter IV.

[19] Female pages, in most cases involved with other interesting disguise situations, occur in the following Italian plays in addition to those already mentioned: Dolci's *Ragazzo* (1541); Aretino's *Talanta* (1542); Piccolomini's *Alessandro* (1550), the source of Chapman's *May Day;* Ruzzante's *Anconitana* (1551); Calmo's *Travaglia* (1556); Parabosco's *Fantesca* (before 1557); Piccolomini's *Ortensio* (1560); Cecchi's *Pellegrine* (1567); Secco's *Interesse* (1581), to which Molière's *Dépit Amoureux* is indebted; Grazzini's *Parentadi* (1582); Cinthio's *Arrenopia* (before 1573), a reworking of his own novel which served as the source of Greene's *James IV;* Cecchi's *Rivali* (before 1587); Guarini's *Pastor Fido* (1585); Giusti's *Fortunio* (1593); and della Porta's *Cintia* (1606), the Italian version of the Cambridge Latin play, *Labyrinthus*.

In 1501 Girolamo Berrardo produced *Cassina*, an adaptation of Plautus's play. He retained the Plautian farcical stuff, and made a considerable improvement in technic by bringing the maiden in question actually upon the stage. He also knit the plot somewhat more firmly by making the rival lovers father and son. In Machiavelli's *Clizia*, produced 1525, this latter change was adopted. But Clizia, like Plautus's Casina, does not come out upon the boards. In fact, Machiavelli narrates all of the disguise situations instead of really acting them. Thus, in act V, scene 2, after we have already been told a number of times that old Nicomaco is being gulled by a boy bride, the old man comes out and tells us in an extended speech how he had gone to bed with the supposed Clizia and, after much trouble and violence, had been shocked and shamed to discover that he was dealing with a man servant in disguise.[20]

Berrardo and Macchiavelli served as intermediaries between Plautus and Dolce, whose *Ragazzo* (1541) presents an old man and his son in love with the same girl. The intriguers palm off a disguised youth on the father, while the son joins the heroine.

Farcical meetings between a bridegroom and a boy bride occur in Aretino's *Marescalco* (pr. 1533), and in della Porta's *Fantesca*, which we shall analyze below. Mistaken wooings of disguised boys are presented in Bibbiena's *Calandria*, the plot of which has been indicated above; also in Parabosco's *Fantesca* (before 1557), and in della Porta's *Cintia*, whose Latin adaptation is analyzed in the following chapter.[21]

It often happens that gallants in furthering their intrigues

---

[20] Symonds makes the remark (II, 187) that Gelli in his *Errore* "closely followed the *Clizia*." This is a mistake, for, as Reinhardstöttner has shown (383–384), there is practically no resemblance in the plots.

[21] See page 81.

employed female disguises, as in *Calandria*, in order to reach their mistresses unmolested. In the form of chambermaid or duenna the lover attracted no attention and hoped to enjoy the fullest protection. Disguised lovers are frequent in Italian drama. I have found them in twenty-five plays, and it would probably not be very difficult to find twenty-five more.[22]

A number of other types of disguise appear somewhat less frequently than the three we have already discussed. For example, Ruzzante's *Moschetta* (1551) presents the spying husband. A husband, disguised as a student, tempts his own wife. She yields; but when she discovers the identity of her intended paramour she declares that she had known him from the beginning. Other spy motives occur in Grazzini's *Gelosia* (1550–1566), and in Bentivoglia's *Geloso*, which is indebted to Grazzini.

Let us finish our account of the Italian drama by analyzing della Porta's *Fantesca*, published in 1592, thus contemporary with the *Two Gentlemen of Verona*. It combines a number of traditional motives,[23] and illustrates, moreover, the intricate involution which we have noted as a distinctive quality of the Italian drama of intrigue.

Fantesca

ACT I. Essandro, disguised as a maid, calling himself Fioretta, serves Cleria, with whom he is in love. Cleria does not suspect "Fioretta's" sex. "Fioretta" has told her of a "twin brother," and, posing as this "brother," has wooed Cleria. Cleria sends "Fioretta" to the "twin

[22] See references to these plays in Chapter VIII.

[23] We find the following traditional motives in the order named: male maid, disguised lover, twin, mistaken wooing, supposed girl locked up with a girl, doubles, beard, beating, and recognition.

brother" saying she is willing to flee with him. This action is planned by Cleria in order to escape marrying Cintio, her father's choice. Meanwhile, Cleria's father, Gerasto, is in love with "Fioretta."

ACT II. Essandro, posing as the "twin brother," arranges with Cleria to enter her chamber secretly. Meanwhile, Gerasto (Cleria's father) talks during an amorous dream about "Fioretta." His wife immediately locks up "Fioretta" together with Cleria, where the lover reveals himself to his lady. But Cintio, the favored suitor, is still an obstacle. His father, Narticoforo, is expected any day to make arrangements with Gerasto for Cleria's marriage. In order to cross this negotiation, Essandro plans to disguise a servant as Narticoforo and an ugly dwarf as Cintio, hoping thus to incur Gerasto's disapproval of Cintio as a son-in-law.

ACT III. But when the supposed Narticoforo presents his supposed son, whose vile smell and dwarfed and impotent body make him absolutely repulsive as a husband, Gerasto declares that his daughter shall have him nevertheless. Now the real Narticoforo and son are announced, and Essandro tries another counter-plot. He himself disguises as Gerasto, and the dwarf disguises as Cleria, and, thus prepared, they receive the strangers. The supposed Gerasto presents his supposed Cleria, explaining that, besides her unattractiveness, she is physically unable to serve in the capacity of a wife. The representations disgust Narticoforo and his son, and the trick promises to be successful. Meanwhile Gerasto continues wooing "Fioretta."

ACT IV. Presently the real Narticoforo meets the real Gerasto. Each (having met impersonators) insists that the other is an impostor. These deceptions have already involved a number of other characters, and much confusion of the *Amphitruo* and *Suppositi* type follows. A comedy duel is fought, or rather threatened, by braggart Spaniards acting as proxies for the two fathers. "Fioretta" is still pursued by Gerasto.

ACT V. Gerasto relates that when he tried to embrace "Fioretta" he felt the moustache of a vigorous youth, who kicked him in the abdomen. After revelations of identities and recognitions of lost relatives the play ends. Essandro wins his Cleria, and Cintio receives her younger sister.

Such is the plot of a typical Italian disguise play. The reader may observe for himself that numerous old situations are combined and that the action is elaborated by sharp turns and ingenious windings.

From the regular Italian drama traditional motives, such as disguise, were borrowed freely by the *commedia dell' arte*. This species of comedy with its fixed types of character very naturally depended on fixed situations, and, through great popularity, helped to crystallize and perpetuate many disguises, especially the female page and the disguised lover. What the influence of the elusive *commedia dell' arte* was upon English is now difficult to determine. Miss Smith has shown[24] that Ben Jonson is indebted to a *commedia dell' arte* for the mountebank scene in *Volpone*. Perhaps many English plays are indebted to *commedie dell' arte* which have not survived. We shall not go into these matters in detail, but shall simply give in a foot-note a classification of some fifteen disguise plots in this interesting department of Italian drama.[25]

[24] *Commedia dell' Arte*, 187.

[25] A number of disguises occur in the scenarios of *commedie dell' arte* published in the Scala Collection, 1611. Female pages appear in *La Fortuna di Flavio*, Gior. II (see summary by Miss Smith in *Mod. Phil.* VIII, 567); *La Finta Pazza*, Gior. VIII; *Il Marito*, Gior. IX; *La Sposa*, Gior. X; *Il Capitano*, Gior. XI; *Il Pellegrino Fido Amante*, Gior. XIV; *La Travagliata Isabella*, Gior. XV; *La Specchio*, Gior. XVI; and *Li Tre Fidi Amici*, Gior. XIX. See also a slight female page

We have thus glanced at the rise and development of the disguise motive through classic drama, medieval romances, Italian *novelle*, and Italian drama into the age of Shakespeare. It will be seen in the following chapters that English playwrights were heavily indebted to their predecessors or contemporaries in Italy. But it will also be noted that, despite this indebtedness, much originality and independence was shown, not only in reshaping old situations, but in producing new devices for dramatic effects.

IV

But before going on to the study of English plays we may profit by glancing at the disguise plots in a few other literatures.

The Italian influence on French drama deserves a word or two here. French drama of the sixteenth century is not of much consequence. The most noted playwright during that period in France was Pierre Larivey, who died in 1611, He wrote nine comedies. Four of these are disguise plays, and all four are either translated or adapted from Italian.[26] *Le Laquais* contains the female page and male mistress motive of Dolce's *Ragazzo*. *Le Morfondu* borrows the spy

motive in *Li Tragici Successi*, translated by Miss Smith in *Mod. Phil.* VII, 217–220.

Lovers disguised as doctors may be found in *La Finta Pazza*, Gior. VIII; *Li Due Capitani Simili*, Gior. XVIII; and in *Li Due Fidi Notari*, Gior. XX. Lovers disguised as women are found in *Il Marito*, Gior. IX, and in *Il Doctor Disperato*, Gior. XIII. Other lover disguises are used in *Il Vecchio Geloso*, Gior. VI, and in *Il Pellegrino Fido Amante*, Gior. XIV.

There is a male mistress motive in *La Creduta Morta*, Gior. VII, besides the two resulting in the cases of the lovers disguised as women.

The above information is based on analyses kindly loaned me by Dr. Winifred Smith.

[26] Macgillivray, 26–39.

and lover disguise from *La Gelosia* of Grazzini. *Le Fidelle* is from Pasqualigo's *Fedele*, which was translated into English by Anthony Munday under the title *Fidele and Fortunio*. And *Les Tromperies* is a translation of Secchi's *Inganni*, which contains a female page and mistaken wooing.

Larivey is typical of his period and shows that the traditions of disguise situations in French plays came from Italy. The native medieval drama evidently did not use the motive. I have found only one disguise plot[27] in the three collections of farces published by Fournier, Lacroix, and Mabille respectively.

The use of disguise in Spanish literature was no less popular than in Italian. It would be an endless task to discuss all the various disguise plays in Spanish. But we shall at least put the student of drama in the way of seeing for himself the wide use of the effective intrigue motive which forms the subject of our special study in English drama.

Montemayor's romance *La Diana* seems to be the source of Shakespeare's *Two Gentlemen*. Cervantes's novel, *Las Dos Donzellas* was adapted by Fletcher as *Love's Pilgrimage*. We have already mentioned Lope de Rueda's play *Los Engaños*, an adaptation of *Gl' Ingannati*. In *Medora* (before 1566), another play by Rueda, we have a boy masquerading as a girl. Cristobal de Virues's tragedy *La Gran Semiramis* presents the heroine in male attire. Cervantes's comedy *El Laberinto de Amor* is a veritable maze of disguises. In this play Julia and Porcia first disguise as shepherds, then as students. Porcia next appears as a peasant, then as a peasant girl (at the desire of Anastasio, thus constituting a "retro-disguise," since he thinks she is a

[27] *La Farce de Munyer*, by André de la Vigne. A priest poses as the cousin of a dying miller, and pretends to comfort the miller, but incidentally feasts with the wife.

peasant boy). Presently she exchanges clothing with a princess. Porcia thus appears in five different disguises. Since the men also are disguised the play becomes a tangle of mistaken identities.

Overingenuity of plot evidently pleased the Spanish audiences as much as it did the Italian.   If we look at Calderon's *Española de Florencia*, mentioned above as a play in the *Ingannati* cycle, we shall find Lucrecia serving her fickle lover as page, carrying messages to a rival mistress, who falls in love with the page — all this as in *Twelfth Night*. But we shall find increasing bewilderment. Lucrecia-page convinces the rival mistress that she (the page) is really the twin brother. Next Lucrecia impersonates the rival mistress in a meeting with her master and lover. Resuming her rôle as page Lucrecia suggests to her lover that he woo his page as though "he" were Lucrecia. This, by the way, reminds us of the mock marriage in *As You Like It*. In the next act Lucrecia divests herself of man's apparel, with the result that when the twin brother actually does appear every one thinks it is Lucrecia back in disguise again. Before the end of the play the heroine, disguised as a fortune-teller, tells her own story of love and suffering, and reveals herself only when her lover has become sufficiently impressed by her story.

Calderon uses the disguised heroine in many other plays. For example, in *La Vida Es Sueño* Rosaura, the heroine of the underplot, appears in man's clothing. In *Amor, Honor y Poder* Flerida, the Infanta, appears veiled, and in a night-dress above man's clothing — a subtle disguise! In *La Devocion de la Cruz* Julia is dressed as a man. In *La Gran Cenobia* Irene appears disguised as a peasant. *El Joseph de las Mugeres* presents Eugenia disguised as a man. She is tempted by Melancia, who thinks her a young man. Eugenia-man escapes, and her temptress, like Potiphar's wife, accuses her;

but the charges are reduced to absurdity by the revelation of sex.

Tirso de Molina (Tellez, G.) was another seventeenth century dramatist who delighted in the disguise motive. Schack (III, 413) says that the disguised damsel serving her fickle lover as page was a favorite character with him. The plays he mentions as typical are *Don Gil de las Calzas Verdes*, *El Amor Medico*, and *La Huerta de Juan Fernandez*.[28]

Lope de Vega has a large number of plays in which disguise is used as the basic motive. With him too the disguised heroine was popular. In one play, *Las Batuecas del Duque de Alba* (1618), a female page wanders by accident into the domain of the Batuecas, a fabulous people. A maiden woos her, but is discouraged in her suit by the fact that the female page one day gives birth to a child. The Batuecas believe they have discovered a specimen of a strange race whose men are able to bear children. In *El Alcalde Mayor* (1620) the disguised Rosarda plays a rôle somewhat like that of Portia in the *Merchant of Venice*.[29]

The lover disguised as a gardener is a device of which the Spanish dramatists never tired.[30] It is found in Calderon's *Selva Confusa;* in Tirso de Molina's *Quien Hablo, Pago,* and in his *Huerta de Juan Fernandez;* also in Lope de Vega's *Soldado Amante,* and in his *Hidalgo Bencerraje.* The lover appears as dancing master in Lope's *Maestro de Danzar,* and as private tutor in *El Domine Lucas.* A romantic love mo-

---

[28] Bourland (xv) says that the following plays of Tirso also contain female pages: *Averigüelo Vargas, La Mujer por Fuerza, La Villana de la Sagra,* and *La Villana de Vallecas.*

[29] See Hennigs, 57. Other plays by Lope de Vega, which contain traditional female page situations are *Las Burlas y Enredos de Benito* (1600), *El Ingrato Arrepentido* (1600), *El Ginoves Liberal* (1614), *La Gallarda Toledana* (1616), *Quien Mas no Puede* (1616), *El Hidalgo Bencerraje* (1621), *Las Ramirez de Arellano* (1641), and *Mas Pueden Celos que Amor* (undated).   [30] Northup, 176.

tive occurs in Lope's *Ilustre Fregona* (adapted from Cervantes's novel of the same name). In this play a cavalier falls in love with a beautiful serving maid and, in order to woo her, exchanges position with his own servant. The wooing is successful and the play ends happily by the discovery that the maid really is of noble birth.

Disguised spies may be seen in Lope's *Bella Mal Maridada* (1600), *Ausente en el Lugar* (1617), and in *El Mejor Alcalde el Rey* (1635). The latter play is a version of the *Measure for Measure* plot.[31]

A very familiar stage business in Spanish drama was the muffling of the face by a cloak, or, in the case of ladies, by a veil. This temporary concealment of identity, however, did not usually affect the progress of the plot. It was merely a bit of acting characteristic of the cloak-and-sword comedy.

Perhaps this allusive account of Spanish plays will suffice to emphasize the general thesis that disguise was a basic, well-worn device in Renaissance comedy. England in literature, especially with respect to this one particular motive, first rivalled Italy whence she drew her cultural inspiration, and then Spain whom she respected as a once formidable enemy. In all three nations the comedy of romantic intrigue was absorbing the energies and interests of playwrights and playgoers; and, however the three literatures differed in method, they had in common one feature, the use of dramatic disguise.[32]

With the above brief survey of the origin and extent of

[31] See synopsis in Wurzbach, 159.

[32] Professor Jackson has pointed out interesting disguise plots in Sanskrit drama from the first half of the seventh century to the tenth century. In studying the plays indicated by him I have found considerable resemblance to Occidental drama. The Viddha-s' ālabhañjikā of Rājas'ekhara is a curious parallel to the complicated plot in Jonson's *New Inn*. (See Chapter IV, page 88). This Sanskrit play has been mentioned above (page 40) as probably the first drama to

dramatic disguise we shall close the preliminary investigation and proceed to a more intimate study of the English plays before 1616. Our special interest is not in determining where the Elizabethan playwrights got their disguise situations, but in tracing out the career of these motives in a limited but busy period of the London drama. Let us therefore merely summarize the acknowledged foreign debt of English dramatic disguises. Ovid furnished the basis of the disguise plot in *Gallathea*. Spanish novels contributed the disguises in the *Two Gentlemen* and in *Love's Pilgrimage*. Italian novels are the ultimate sources of the *Merchant of Venice, Cymbeline*, and *James IV*. Italian plays were adapted or drawn upon for the *Supposes, Twelfth Night, May Day, The Shrew*, and *Albumazar*. *Amphitruo* is adapted in the *Silver Age* and the *Birth of Hercules;* and the influence of Plautus is strong in *Jack Juggler, What You Will*, and *Epicœne*.

The reckoning of the total score against English drama can never be made because of the large number of non-extant English plays that were doubtless heavily indebted to Italian. Furthermore, there are probably a number of lost Italian plays to which both extant and non-extant English plays were indebted. It is my hope that the considerable number of parallels brought together, or indicated, in this volume may be of definite value to those scholars who are interested in tracing out the literary ancestry of plays, not only in English but in other languages as well.

present a girl disguised as a boy. Mock marriages to boy brides occur in the play just mentioned, and in *Mālatī and Mādhava* by Bhavabhūti. The love intrigue in Sri-Harsha Deva's *Ratnavali* presents a doubles situation that reminds us of similar motives in Latin and Renaissance drama. The king has planned an assignation with a lady who was to come to a bower disguised as the queen. The queen by chance comes to this bower first and is mistaken as the disguised lady. This results in confusion and disclosure of the intended amour. Political spying occurs in *Mudrā-rākshasa* by Vis-ākha-datta.

But the Elizabethan dramatists did not always borrow their disguises. A strong evidence of their interest in the disguise motive is furnished by the numerous cases where they borrowed a plot which did not contain disguise and enriched its dramatic and theatrical value by the addition of that complication. Thus Whetstone added the female page and spy motives to a plot borrowed from Cinthio. Greene used disguises in *Orlando Furioso*, and *Friar Bacon and Friar Bungay* which he did not find in his sources. Marston's multi-disguise in the *Dutch Courtesan* is his own contribution to a rogue who inherits other gifts from Painter's *Palace of Pleasure*. Chapman showed considerable skill in altering a story from Petronius by introducing disguise. Beaumont and Fletcher brought disguise to the Spanish story they used in the *Coxcomb*, and Fletcher's *Monsieur Thomas* has a disguise not contained in the sources. And Shakespeare, though he usually found his disguise plot all ready for him, seems to be independent of his sources in the Kent motive of *King Lear*, in the Don Pedro disguise of *Much Ado*, and in the spying father of the *Winter's Tale*. Many other plays, as for example, *Soliman and Perseda*, *Patient Grissil*, the *Dumb Knight*, and the *Widow*, contain disguises not found in their sources.

Yet these plays are not entirely original in the disguise situations introduced, for when we study them in the various settings of similar contemporary plays it will be seen that, although the dramatists were independent of the direct sources of their plots, they were usually dependent on the traditional disguise situations which were being successfully presented on the stage during that period.

When it comes to the question of absolute originality it is dangerous to make any positive assertions. Some of the important disguise plays for which I have found no sources are *Sir Clyomon and Sir Clamydes*, *Soliman and Perseda*, the

Wise Woman of Hogsdon, *Philaster*, *London Prodigal*, and the *Malcontent*. These plays seem to have evolved out of suggestions in other English plays which preceded them by a short time. The four curious multi-disguise plays discussed in Chapter VI have as yet not been related to any definite parallels.

As specimens of English originality in disguise motivation I have already[33] suggested two things, the surprise motive, and the combination of surprise and retro-disguise, situations which come in for detailed discussion in succeeding chapters.

Although the arbitrary terminus of our special study is 1616, we shall glance at many other plays before the closing of the theaters. The career of the disguise motive in England subsequent to 1642 is not especially fascinating. It seems to be used more or less as an outworn convention. The female page appears, for example, in Dryden's *Rival Ladies*, in Otway's *Caius Marius*, and in Wycherly's *Country Wife* and *Plain Dealer*. Congreve's *Double Dealer* has a spying husband, and his *Mourning Bride* contains some rather interesting disguises. There is a disguised spy in Steele's *Tender Husband*. Disguised lovers may be found in Addison's *Cato;* in Steele's *Funeral, or Grief à la Mode*, and in his *Conscious Lovers;* in Sheridan's *Scheming Lieutenant*, and in his *Critic*. A ridiculous use of the lover disguise is in *Three Hours After Marriage* by Gay, Pope, and Arbuthnot, where two lovers gain access to their mistress, disguised respectively as a mummy and a crocodile.

In the contemporary theater we have recently seen two interesting uses of disguise with a symbolic function. In Kennedy's *Servant in the House* the leading figure, Manson, is disguised as a servant from a foreign land. The concealment of identity, however, is of slight importance compared with the fact that Manson is carefully conceived to look,

[33] See Chapter II, page 12.

think, and talk like the Son of Man. As a counterpart to this drama Molnar's *Devil* exhibits Satan embodied as a shrewd and wily man, the friend of a couple on the verge of sin. In this play, too, the symbolism is paramount to the disguise. Strictly speaking there is no disguise at all, for the man never changes his appearance.

For the serious drama of our contemporary stage the device of disguise unaided by symbolism seems perhaps too slight a thing to alter the state of a play. Besides we are selling our imagination for a mess of realism. The masters of the factitious give us stage fixtures which are genuine as those actually used in real life, or, if not genuine, are at least most cleverly imitated. Therefore the average critical taste of today encounters a dilemma in a doubles situation. Unless the impersonation is real enough to deceive it is not convincing. And if it is perfectly deceiving it is likely to victimize the audience as well as the people in the play and is therefore not ideally entertaining. Furthermore, we, the auditors of today, demand that the people in a play shall have as good eyesight and powers of perception as we. We insist that our wives and sweethearts could not for any noticeable length of time make us believe that they were schoolboys or Russian generals, and we would lose sympathy with any one else who could be easily gulled.

If we turn from the photographic realism of the modern social play and seek out the "ten, twenty and thirty cent" melodrama, we may find some detective in picturesque disguise; or if we look to the romantic improbabilities of light opera or musical comedy we may find a lover or lady fair concealing their identities in tinselled masquerade; but somehow it all seems tawdry. Perhaps the playwright and auditor alike have lost the naïveté and the unquestioning imagination which inspired the poetic product of English genius in the spacious days of Queen Bess.

CHAPTER IV

THE FEMALE PAGE

Dost thou think, though I am caparison'd like
a man, I have a doublet and hose in my disposition?
— *As You Like It*

I

STARTING from medieval French romance, and threading
her way through the novels or plays of Italy, the heroine
in hose and doublet at last reached the England of Shakespeare, where she became the most graceful and charming
figure on the stage.[1] Perhaps in real life, too, the female
page sometimes wandered through merry England. Queen
Elizabeth herself once listened to an ambassador who offered
to convey her secretly to Scotland, dressed like a page, in
order that she might under this disguise see Queen Mary.
Elizabeth appeared to like the plan, but answered with a
sigh, saying "Alas! If I might do it thus!"[2] At any rate
we shall see that as a literary tradition, in the novels and on
the stage, the disguised heroine was already established in
England when Shakespeare wrote his *Two Gentlemen of
Verona*.

By that time the female page had often appeared in non-
dramatic literature in English. Rich's *Apolonius and
Silla*, the second novel in his *Farewell*, had used substantially the plot of *Twelfth Night* as early as 1581. The eighth

[1] Some illuminating remarks on the disguised heroine as a character
are made by Marie Gothein in *Die Frau im englischen Drama vor Shakespeare, Jahrb.*, xl., 35.

[2] Melville, 106.

61

novel, entitled *Phylotus and Emelia*, has the same female page plot as the anonymous comedy *Philotus*, which was printed in 1603, but which may be as early as Rich's novel.[3] Sidney's *Arcadia* in 1590 told of Zelmane-page following Pyrocles unrewarded. And in the same year Lodge's *Rosalynde* presented the disguised heroine whom Shakespeare adopted. The prototype of Julia could have been found a decade earlier than the *Two Gentlemen* in the manuscript of Yonge's translation of Montemayor's *Diana*. A dozen of the ballads published by Percy or Child sing the fortunes of the lady disguised in male attire. Some of these too must have antedated and influenced the drama of Shakespeare and his contemporaries.[4]

In order to show to what extent Shakespeare was influenced by stage traditions in choosing and elaborating the Julia disguise, we shall examine a number of female page plays produced in England before the *Two Gentlemen*. We shall see that Shakespeare profited by the weaknesses as well as by the merits of these plays. If he borrowed the potency of certain disguise situations, he invariably improved their dramatic efficiency.

As early as 1569–70 a Latin play, *Byrsa Basilica*,[5] had presented a girl in the apparel of a boy. The disguise is quite incidental, merely affording the heroine a method of escape from an awkward predicament.[6]

George Whetstone's *Promos and Cassandra*, which was printed in 1578, but was never acted, contains perhaps the earliest female page situation in the vernacular drama. Cassandra enters "apparelled like a page" (Part I, III, 7),

---

[3] See Chapter V, page 113.

[4] Züge, 6, 71.

[5] Churchill and Keller, 281. We cannot say where this play was acted.

[6] A brief summary of the plot is given in Chapter V.

soliloquizes a few lines and goes out to keep her appointment
with Lord Promos. She never reappears, nobody sees her,
and no complication results from the disguise. It is worthy
of note that this disguise is not in the novel on which Whetstone based his play.[7] He was thus the first of many Englishmen who added disguise to plots borrowed from other
literatures.

Sir Clyomon and Sir Clamydes,[8] although not printed until
1599, may have been written as early as *Promos and Cassandra*. It contains the romantic elements of the disguised
girl serving her lover as page incognito, and mistakenly
wooed by some other woman. It has in addition such motives
as the sentimental farewell, the girl's giving a jewel as a love
token, her apology for wearing boy's clothing, and her expression of weariness from travelling — dramatic effects
that recur in Shakespeare's plays. In technic *Sir Clyomon*
with its loose and rambling plot reminds us of a medieval
romance. The author, whoever he was, had only partially
realized the dramaturgic value of disguise.

What we have just remarked may be illustrated by a
summary of the play. Clyomon bids farewell to Princess
Neronis, receiving her jewel as a love token, and departs
to fight a combat. After he has gone Neronis is kidnapped,
but escapes by disguising herself as a page. She gets employment as a shepherd's boy, and the first complication comes
when the country lasses fall in love with "him." One day
while strolling along she finds a dead body, decorated with
Clyomon's sword and shield. She concludes that her love
is dead, and attempts suicide, but "Providence," who is
apparently on the watch for this opportunity, puts out his

[7] Giraldi Cinthio, *Heccatommithi, VIII 5*.

[8] The date and authorship of *Sir Clyomon and Sir Clamydes* cannot
at present be determined. Suggestions as to date vary from 1570 to
1584. See Schelling, I, 199.

hand and thwarts her fell purpose. Investigation proves
that the body is that of the villainous kidnapper. Some
time after this experience, Neronis-page accidentally gets
service with her lover Clyomon, whom she presently recognizes. She remains incognito, and is sent ahead as his
messenger to Denmark. At the Danish court she is finally
revealed to him as his lady love and quondam page.

The plot of such a play suffers when compared with the
firmer weaving in Lyly's *Gallathea* (entered in 1585[10]). There
the disguise, suggested by one of Ovid's *Metamorphoses*,[11]
results in many mistaken wooings and cross purposes. The
action is very compact, and the dialog is full of ironical
subtlety. Gallathea and Phillida have been disguised as
boys in order to escape Neptune's demand for the sacrifice
of a virgin. Each falls in love with the other, whom she
believes to be a boy. The two girl-pages next join Diana's
train, where they are wooed by three nymphs. Each girl-
page pretends in jest that the other is a girl and woos her.

[9] The attempted suicide of Neronis upon mistaking the dead body
for that of her lover perhaps offered a suggestion for act IV, scene 2 in
Cymbeline, a situation which editors usually attribute to Shakespeare's
invention. See also Forsythe (M. L. N., April, 1912) who suggests that
the Cloten situation may have been borrowed from the Alcario impersonation in *I Ieronimo*.

[10] Feuillerat, 576.

[11] Bk. IX. Iphis, a girl, had been presented to her father as a boy
and thus reared by her mother. The father promises his supposed son
in marriage to Ianthe. Iphis, in spite of herself, falls in love with
Ianthe. In answer to the prayers of Iphis and the mother, Isis trans-
forms Iphis to a boy.

Lee, in discussing the sources of the *Decameron* (page 292), tells
of two cases of pretended metamorphosis where lovers disguised as
women pretend that some deity changes them into men. In the curious play *Philotus* (see Chapter V, page 113) a lover disguised as a girl
pretends that the heavenly powers change him into a man. *Tristan
de Nanteuil* presents an interesting metamorphosis. See Chapter III,
page 42.

Each of the two girls presently suspects the other's sex. Meanwhile, Cupid, the disguised intrigant, has been captured by Diana, and Neptune promises to waive the sacrifice of a virgin if Cupid is released. Gallathea and Phillida are then revealed as girls, but, since they are by this time truly in love with each other, Venus promises to transform one into a boy — which one, she will not say until they reach the church door.[12]

A technical defect, to which we have alluded in Chapter II, is inherent in this intricate tangle of cross-purposes and mistaken wooing; the plot does not contain within itself the power of resolution. The knot cannot be untied. Revelation of disguise does not lessen the central difficulty, and the resolution can be brought about only by Venus, the *dea ex machina*, who guarantees the metamorphosis.

Lyly, who was always fond of stylistic subtlety, put much comic irony into the dialog of *Gallathea*. Note, for example, Phillida's remarks to Gallathea (both being in page costumes): "It is a pretty boy, and a fair, he might well have been a woman" (II, 1); "It is pity you are not a woman" (III, 2), and, "I have sworn never to love a woman."

Shakespeare later used similar involved dialog and seems to have been directly influenced by Lyly. In *Gallathea* (III, 2) occurs the passage:

"*Phil.* Have you ever a sister?
Galla. — — — I pray have you ever a one?
Phil. My father had but one daughter, and therefore I could have no sister."

These lines are similar to Viola's reply to the Duke (II, 4), "I am all the daughters of my father's house, And all the

[12] An interesting inverted parallel to this situation is found in Fletcher's *Loyal Subject*. Olympia is very fond of the supposed girl "Alinda," and when "Alinda" proves to be a boy Olympia admits love for him and they go off to church.

brothers too." In act IV, scene 4, Phillida says to Gallathea, "Seeing we are both boys and both lovers, — that
our affection may have some show, and seem as it were love, —
let me call thee mistress." We are reminded of these lines in
As You Like It (III, 2), when Rosalind-page tells Orlando of
a fictitious youth who "was to imagine me his love, his mistress; and I set him every day to woo me." We shall presently give a number of examples of Shakespeare's subtle
dialog. He had learned it from Lyly, but the felicity of the
pupil surpasses that of the master.

Soliman and Perseda, mentioned in the Stationers' Register
in 1592, but possibly written about 1588 (Boas, *Kyd*, lvii),
has a female page situation which seems to be original. At
least it is only remotely suggested in Wotton's *Courtlie
Controuersie*, the probable source of the play. But the closing incident may have had some influence on Beaumont and
Fletcher's *Maid's Tragedy*, and will be discussed in that
connection.[13] Perseda's male apparel only brings her to
death; but in another play of Oriental color, the *Wars of
Cyrus*, the heroine cleverly utilizes a page's costume in order
to escape her royal captor. This play was printed in 1594
and had probably been acted by the Children of Her Majesty's
Chapel by 1590.[14]

Lælia, a Latin adaption of *Gl' Ingannati*, was performed at
Cambridge in 1590, and revived in 1598. The problem of
this play's relations to Shakespeare's *Twelfth Night* has not
received a solution. Churchill says (*Jahrb.*, xxxiv, 286) that
no evidence forces the conclusion that Shakespeare knew
Lælia. Schelling, on the contrary, says (II, 77) that *Lælia*
was the "undoubted immediate source of Shakespeare's
Twelfth Night." But it is interesting to note that this play,
whether Shakespeare ever borrowed from it or not, had the
most complicated female page plot in England before 1590.

---

[13] See below, page 92.   [14] Keller, *Wars of Cyrus*, 9.

Greene's *James IV*, printed in 1598, but written perhaps as early as 1590,[15] contains a number of similarities to other female page situations both earlier and later. The essential disguise elements in the story are the queen's fleeing "disguised like a squire," her adventures which bring her to the care of Lady Anderson, the latter's mistaken wooing of the "squire," and the "squire's" fainting when hearing bad news about the king.

Greene did not fully realize the dramatic and theatrical opportunities of his situation. By omitting the female squire motive from the dénouement he departed from his source, a novel by Cinthio[16] in which the heroine comes to her husband's camp and is called the Unknown Knight. In the novel the heroine is brought before her husband still disguised, and some dialog takes place before the revelation. Greene omitted this part of the action, thus losing a chance for a theatrical undisguising, and an opportunity for the piquant and equivocal language which was used so successfully by Lyly and Shakespeare.

These early plays, *Byrsa Basilica, Promos and Cassandra, Sir Clyomon and Sir Clamydes, Gallathea, Soliman and Perseda*, the *Wars of Cyrus, Lœlia*, and *James IV*, are evidences that English theater audiences were familiar with the female page by 1590. Playgoers had seen the heroine apprehensive lest her male garb seem immodest; weary from travel through forests; patiently following her lover to serve him unknown, or leaving him to carry his messages to a rival lady; wooed by that lady who was misled by outward appearance; wittily alluding to her real identity in veiled

---

[15] According to Fleay (*Biog. Chron.*, I, 265) although Collins (II, 79) is not convinced.

[16] *Heccatommithi, III, 1*. In *Arrenopia*, a play which Cinthio based on his own novel, the heroine appears on the battlefield dressed as a knight, calling herself "Agnoristo." See Klein, V, 348.

language; swooning like a woman, or fighting in man's harness, and dying like a soldier.   The same playgoers may have heard similar events recited in the ballads, or may have read of them in English novels.

Yet these plays, novels, and ballads were by no means the only contemporary plots containing female pages.   Plays especially were perishable.   The number of non-extant plays before 1592 is much greater than the number of extant. They must have done their part in popularizing disguise. We may surmise that the lost play *Felix and Philomena* (Philismena?), 1584, contained the female page story from Montemayor's *Diana*, and that it may have been the immediate source of Shakespeare's *Two Gentlemen*.   The extant plays described above are less important for their individual contribution than for the proof they give that the female page was by 1592 a well-established personage on the stage, and already endowed with distinct characteristics and functions in the drama.

II

Although the traditional disguises in the *Two Gentlemen*, the *Merchant, As You Like It, Twelfth Night,* and *Cymbeline* are all borrowed, they are all bettered.   Either by new combinations of old materials, by stricter dramatic economy, by focusing the attention on the female page as a character, by the heightening of theatrical values, or by infusing poetic subtlety into the dialog, Shakespeare made his female page plays superior to those of his predecessors or rival contemporaries.

Shakespeare's skill in building a play around a disguised heroine is clearly exhibited in the *Two Gentlemen of Verona,* produced perhaps as early as 1591.   Montemayor's novel *La Diana* seems to be either directly or indirectly the source of the Proteus-Julia-page story.   But in Montemayor the love episode ends by Felismena's telling Don Felix that she had served him as page two years before. That method is undramatic. The undisguising should take place before the audience and should be an organic element in the dénouement; Shakespeare made it so in the *Two Gentlemen*. There the revelation of disguise is precipitated by a swoon, and identity is verified by the rings, the swoon and the rings both having been suggested by earlier plays. Thus three different dramatic motives are combined in one dramatic moment.

Such combination of material is dramatic economy. Economy is further shown in the construction of the serenade scene (IV, 2). In Montemayor the Host wakes Felismena to hear a serenade. She listens and recognizes the voice of Don Felix in praise of a rival mistress; but, although watching until dawn, Felismena is unable to distinguish her false lover in the group. Montemayor shows us only the Host and Felismena, while Shakespeare's staging presents the Host, Julia, Proteus, Silvia, and others simultaneously. Thus the scene is made compact and effects multiplied by introducing in disguise the person most vitally concerned in the action, an action which could not proceed if that person's identity were known. Even when the subject of discussion is Julia herself, she participates with subtle speech.

A good theatrical effect in the *Two Gentlemen* is the swooning of the disguised heroine. Shakespeare may have borrowed this from Greene's *James IV*, where Dorothea, upon being informed that the king is "dreading death" because of the reported death of the queen, feels a sudden qualm at the heart and is revived with "licor" (V, 1). The business of swooning has more dramatic occasion and theatrical effectiveness in the *Two Gentlemen*. In the last scene Proteus threatens to assault the resisting Silvia. Valentine arrives just in time to rescue her, and Proteus becomes surprisingly penitent, whereupon Valentine immediately forgives him, and, to show that there is no ill will, offers to surrender his sweetheart into the bargain. Julia-page promptly swoons and her identity is revealed within a few moments.

The action in that scene is further enriched by the use of the rings. This motive, borrowed perhaps from *Sir Clyomon and Sir Clamydes*,[17] is an accompaniment of disguise in *Two Gentlemen*, the *Merchant*, and *Twelfth Night*. All possible dramatic use of the rings is made in the *Two Gentlemen*. When Proteus and Julia have their farewell scene they exchange rings. At court Proteus sends Julia's ring to his new love, the love messenger being the disguised Julia herself. Then Silvia refuses the token, which leaves Julia in possession of two rings — the one she received from Proteus at Verona, and the one she gave him in exchange. The last use of the rings effects the dénouement. In the excitement of hearing Valentine offer Silvia to Proteus, Julia swoons. She retains enough presence of mind, however, to present the wrong ring and begs forgiveness for not having delivered it to Silvia.

Shakespeare's method in this play varies significantly from the method of the Italian dramatists. We have seen how they produced great complexity of plot by a process of combination. But they intensified their action without concentrating the attention on any single character. Shakespeare differed from them by focusing the attention on a

---

[17] In *Sir Clyomon* the hero receives a jewel from Neronis when he bids her farewell; but no dramatic use is made of it. In *Soliman and Perseda*, Erastus gives his lady a ring, and receives a carcanet in return. The familiar ring story in the *Merchant of Venice* may have been borrowed from Fiorentino's novel. Did Shakespeare know that story early enough to get a hint for the ring motive in the *Two Gentlemen*?

single character, making that the axis of the plot.[18]   In the
Two Gentlemen the disguise of Julia is not, for example,
counterbalanced by the disguise of Proteus as a woman —
that would have been the Italian way — but is enhanced
by combination with subordinate motives, such as the rings,
and is dwelt upon until full dramatic emphasis results.

Shakespeare's development of the female page motive
gives this type of disguise greater individual importance in
England than it had in Italy.   In *Twelfth Night* Viola has
more dramatic individuality than the corresponding heroine in
Gl' Ingannati, whose twin brother is almost equally involved
in the action.   In *As You Like It* there is slight intrigue
but much comic emphasis on the ironical situation of Rosalind.   In the *Merchant* and in *Cymbeline* simple disguise
incidents possess very great dramatic, theatrical, and
stylistic value.   And in each case the disguise complication
stimulates our admiration for, or sympathy with, the disguised person; thus the playwright directs our attention
to the character and makes the disguise situation something
more than a mechanical device.

In the *Merchant of Venice* disguise and the ring motive are
used in combination with the casket story and the pound
of flesh story.   Whether these four elements had existed
together in the non-extant play the *Jew*, which Stephen
Gosson alludes to, we cannot say.   From the slender evidence in Gosson we may assume that only the last two elements were combined in the *Jew*.   Fiorentino combines the
wife-lawyer disguise with the pound of flesh story in a
novel which Shakespeare's play, except the Gratiano-Nerissa
part, parallels at every step.

The female page, though only a subordinate motive in
the *Merchant*, has considerable dramatic value.   It resolves

[18] To a certain extent Greene has the same method in the delineation of Dorothea in *James IV*.

one part of the action, and simultaneously initiates a new set of complications, which are in turn resolved by the revelation of identity. These last complications constitute a felicitous postlude to a tragic action timely averted.

As You Like It is practically all drawn from Lodge's *Rosalynde*. Shakespeare has altered the story by focusing our attention on Rosalind. He has endowed her with a charming femininity which is only emphasized by disguise. The plot, which we need not recall, frequently reveals this femininity. Rosalind swoons, like other disguised heroines before her, but, after a brief dramatic suspense, takes heart and tries to be a man, insisting that her swooning was only counterfeit. Later, when her identity is known, she mitigates the apparent immodesty of appearing in man's apparel by declaring that she has no doublet and hose in her disposition. Similar apologies had appeared earlier in *Sir Clyomon* and in *Gallathea*. In the *Two Gentlemen* Julia fears that the world might make her "scandalized" for undertaking so "unstaid" a journey. And at the end of the play she speaks the pertinent words: "It is the lesser blot, modesty finds, Women to change their shapes, than men their minds." Rosalind further reveals her true character by her expression of weariness after travelling through the forest. She says she could cry like a woman were it no disgrace to her male apparel. Such speeches had been made before by Neronis in *Sir Clyomon* and by Dorothea in *James IV*.

Shakespeare further concentrated our attention on the disguised heroine by emphasizing the comic irony in Rosalind's situation, especially in the mock marriage of Orlando with Rosalind-"Ganymede"-pretending-to-be-Rosalind and in the mistaken wooing by Phebe — both situations borrowed from the novel.[19] This comic emphasis is more clearly felt

[19] The disguises in *As You Like It* are echoed in Shirley's *Love Tricks*. Margaret in Lamb's *John Woodvil* is reminiscent of Rosalind.

in the dialog which Shakespeare gave to Rosalind. Thus
the bold relief of the female page is heightened positively
by the dramatic means already noted, and negatively by
subordinating the other characters, even Orlando, to Rosalind.

In *As You Like It*, as in nearly all the English female-
page plays, the heroine is a more pastoral figure than the
typical disguised heroine in Italian drama. Her travels
take her through forests, and in these forests part of the
action is represented as taking place. It is so in *Sir Clyomon*, *Gallathea*, *James IV*, *Two Gentlemen*, *Twelfth Night*,
Cymbeline, *Philaster*, and in a long succession of similar plays.
This pastoral element, due to various influences upon English
writers, helps to give a distinct personality to the female
page in their plays. The Italian drama of intrigue, where
the heroine in the costume of a boy appears more frequently
than in the pastoral drama,[20] presented the action tradi-
tionally on the street outside two or three neighboring houses.
This staging necessarily prevented the romantic atmosphere
of the woods characteristic in English comedy.

Shakespeare's method of individualizing the character
without losing any of the structural functions of the female
page is clearly illustrated in *Twelfth Night*. We have already shown that *Gl' Ingannati*, the ultimate source of
Shakespeare's plot, is a more complicated play than *Twelfth
Night*.[21] Perhaps Shakespeare borrowed directly from Rich's

The mock wooing is paralleled in Calderon's *Española de Florencia*.
See Chapter III, page 54.

[20] The disguise in *Pastor Fido* is slight. In *Aminta* there is no
disguise.

[21] See Chapter III, page 46. For early analogues see Anders,
67–71; also Luce, *Introd.* to *Apolonius and Silla*.

Reminiscences of the disguise situation in *Twelfth Night* may be
found in Ford's *Lover's Melancholy*, Shirley's *Grateful Servant*, Massinger's *Bashful Lover*, and in Wycherly's *Plain Dealer*. Aaron Hill
in *Henry V* (II) introduces a female page like Viola who tells a tale of
her "sister."

novel, *Apolonius and Silla*. No matter what his source, Shakespeare suppressed or simplified those complications which involved the twin brother, thus gaining opportunity for greater emphasis on the disguised heroine. Yet, while subordinating the twin brother, Shakespeare did not fail to utilize him with the fullest theatrical value when necessary. He improved the traditional plot considerably by adding the forced revelation resulting from the simultaneous entering of the doubles.[22] Shakespeare had used this method of revealing identity earlier in the *Comedy of Errors* and in the *Taming of The Shrew*.

Structurally disguise is basic in *Twelfth Night*. It produces the many complications in the main plot, and the entire entanglement is happily resolved by the undisguising. There is a gradual involution and deepening irony of the action up to the end. The duke employs a love messenger who unwillingly and unconsciously perverts the import of the messages. Olivia makes a serious mistake in sex for which no one could blame her. Sebastian finds a set of complications all ready for him when he arrives on the scene. Viola, in the heat of the struggle of outward circumstance, has an inner conflict of her own. It begins in act I, scene 4, when the duke asks her to woo Olivia for him. Viola replies:

> "I'll do my best
> To woo your lady: (*Aside*) yet, a barful strife!
> Whoe'er I woo, myself would be his wife."

The structural firmness of the play resides in the fact that none of these complications would have come about except for Viola's disguise; that the revelation of her identity would have removed them at any time, and that the final revelation is a complete and satisfactory dénouement of the whole play.

[22] See Chapter II, pages 10–11.

These four plays show that Shakespeare recognized the female page as a valuable element in romantic comedy, and that, while skilfully utilizing borrowed disguise effects to the fullest dramatic value, he managed to concentrate attention on the individual person in disguise. It remains to illustrate how Shakespeare obtained valuable dramatic effects in the dialog of the disguised person. In Chapter II we alluded to the subtlety of disguise dialog and its relation to acting. Let us be.more specific here. When we examine the irony or veiled meanings in the lines quoted below, we remember that their dramatic value can be fully appreciated only when they are spoken on the stage. When Viola tells the Duke that she will never love any woman, that, in fact, she will never love anybody but her master, the reader gets a double meaning from her speech, but the spectator gets a dramatic effect in the pantomime which the reader misses. If the scene is so staged that the Duke is not facing Viola when she speaks the words, she may indulge in a bit of acting which emphasizes the humor in these hidden meanings. This side play is often directed to the audience, but it may produce the same effect by being directed to a third person on the stage. The first method, though not high art, has frequently been employed on the English stage.

This type of subtle dialog is employed abundantly in Lyly and Shakespeare. We shall quote a few typical examples from Shakespeare. In the serenade scene of the *Two Gentlemen* (IV, 2) Julia-page makes several equivoques on the music of Proteus who "plays false." But most noteworthy is the elaborate veiled allusion in act IV, scene 4, where Julia-page tells Silvia that she knows Julia almost as well as herself. She veils her own situation in every word of her little fabrication about the pageant where "trimm'd in Madam Julia's gown" she

> ". . . did play a lamentable part.
> Madam, 'twas Ariadne, passioning
> For Theseus' perjury and unjust flight;
> Which I so lively acted with my tears
> That my poor Mistress, moved therewithal,
> Wept bitterly."

To make the allusion complete Silvia replies: "I weep myself to think upon thy words." Montemayor's novel contains something like this, and may have suggested to Shakespeare the theme which he introduced here in Lylyan fashion, and improved in Viola's tale of a sister.

In the *Merchant of Venice* there is comic irony in Bassanio's declaration to Antonio: "Antonio, I am married to a wife . . . I would lose all, ay, sacrifice them all, here to this devil, to deliver you." To this Portia replies: "Your wife would give you little thanks for that, If she were by to hear you make the offer."

Portia's and Nerissa's clever twittings of their husbands in the last scene of the play are so well known that quotation is unnecessary. The general idea might have been suggested by Fiorentino's novel. His sentence "And I can swear, says the lady, with as much solemnity, that you gave the ring to a woman," may have suggested Shakespeare's line, "I'll die for't but some woman had the ring." But all the rest, a hundred lines, is of Shakespeare's own composition and in his characteristic vein.

Rosalind upon reviving from her swoon insists that it was counterfeit. Oliver says: "Well then, take a good heart and counterfeit to be a man." Rosalind replies: "So I do; but, i'faith, I should have been a woman by right."

In *Twelfth Night* veiled meanings are numerous. The duke speaks an unconscious equivoque in act I, scene 4, when he tells Viola: "Dear lad . . . they shall yet belie thy happy years That say thou art a man." And he is nearer the truth than he knows when telling the page in detail how "all is semblative a woman's part." In act II, scene 4, the duke says to Viola: "thine eye Hath stay'd upon some favor that it loves; Hath it not, boy?" Viola replies that she loves someone of "your complexion" and "about your years, my lord." Later in the same scene Viola veils her wooing in the poetic fiction beginning: "My Father had a daughter lov'd a man, As it might be, perhaps, were I a woman, I should your lordship." [23] When this charming history of the "sister" who never told her love is finished, the unseeing duke comments: "But died thy sister of her love, my boy?" and Viola answers enigmatically: "I am all the daughters of my father's house, And all the brothers too." [24] In act III, scene 1, Olivia woos the page so persistently that "he" finally declares that "he" has one heart "And that no woman has; nor never none Shall mistress be of it, save I alone."

In *Cymbeline* we see that Shakespeare to the last felt the theatrical and poetic value of subtle dialog. When Imogen sees the hospitality of Guiderius and Arviragus (her brothers, though she does not know it) she says aside: "Would it had been so, that they Had been my father's sons" (III, 6). A little earlier Guiderius had observed to the fair page: "Were you a woman, youth, I should woo hard." In the last scene of the play when Cymbeline is introduced to Imogen-page he says: "I have surely seen him; His favour is familiar to me. Boy, Thou hast look'd thyself into my grace, And art mine own." But he does not really recognize his daughter, even though

---

[23] An inverted parallel occurs in Glapthorne's *Hollander* (1635), where Popingay, disguised as a woman, woos Dalinea in a veiled allusion beginning, "I had a younger brother." See also above, page 76.

[24] A parallel to this answer has already been noted in *Gallathea*. See above, page 65.

they converse apart for a few moments. This comment on the page's features shortly before the revelation of identity is very much like the duke's comment in *As You Like It* just before Rosalind reveals herself: "I do remember in this shepherd boy, Some lively touches of my daughter's favour," a line which had been suggested by Lodge's novel. A great many more such speeches of irony or double meanings might be quoted, but we have perhaps sufficiently illustrated Shakespeare's method of enriching the dialog in a disguise situation.

While Shakespeare was producing *Twelfth Night* and earlier disguise plays, other dramatists used the female page motive incidentally in a few plays which we shall glance at for purposes of comparison. In Marston's *Antonio and Mellida* (1599) the heroine disguised as a page escapes her father's wrath and goes to join Antonio in the forest. She reveals herself to her lover almost immediately and is presently captured by her father. This disguise has little value except for a bit of dialog, when Mellida-page, bent on escape, dances before her father. The father says: "Sprightly, i'faith. In troth he's somewhat like My daughter Mellida." Heywood perhaps meant to burlesque female page disguises in his *Four Prentices of London* (1594). The heroine disguises as page and serves her lover intimately but incognito, the situation amounting to a *reductio ad absurdum* because of the alleged fact that the page was her lover's bedfellow for a year without his discovering her identity or sex.[25]   An incidental disguise somewhat like that

---

[25] Compare Carliell's *Deserving Favorite* (1629), where a female page and her lover, a disguised duke, spend the night in a hermit's lodge without recognizing each other. The "page" keeps her doublet on in order to avoid revealing her sex. In Fiorentino's *Pecorone*, *III, 1*, a lady disguised as a friar shares a bed with a priest for some time without revealing her sex.

of Shakespeare's Jessica occurs in William Haughton's *Englishman for My Money* (1598). A Portuguese usurer living in London has three daughters whom he desires to marry off to rich foreigners. The girls prefer Englishmen, and Laurentia, dressed in the garments of their tutor, escapes from her father's home and marries her lover.

Incidental uses of disguise such as we have just named serve to emphasize the fact that during the last decade of the century Shakespeare alone was able to construct successful comedies upon the disguise of the heroine.

Shakespeare's technic might be called traditional technic raised to the highest power of efficiency. The weaving of his disguise plot was simple and direct; from that he never varied. A disguise was assumed, deception produced, and final revelation made in a traditional way which amounted almost to a formula. Other dramatists at the beginning of the seventeenth century began to play variations on the disguise theme. Heywood in the *Wise Woman of Hogsdon* disguised his heroine as page and then let some deceived person retro-disguise her as a lady, thus getting a double complication. Jonson in *Epicœne*, and Beaumont and Fletcher in *Philaster*, introduced persons so well disguised that even the audience was deceived until the end of the play. Yet, although some fourteen female page plays with various novelties intervened between *Twelfth Night* and *Cymbeline* (1610), the latter play represents no new method of presenting disguise. Shakespeare's last use of the female page was in his seasoned and successful, but nevertheless conventional manner.

Far from deceiving the audience Shakespeare in *Cymbeline* (III, 4) discusses Imogen's disguise at length, "doublet, hat, hose, all That answer to them," and, with his accustomed alertness to histrionic considerations, he instructs Imogen to practice her part "with what imitation you can borrow

From youth of such a season." The traditional apologies for male apparel appear in Imogen's remark, "Though peril to my modesty, not death on't, I would adventure." The familiar speech about weariness is found in scene 6 of act III, where Imogen, who has slept on the ground for two nights and is half starved, decides that "a man's life is a tedious one." All this keeps the audience constantly aware of the fact that the page is Imogen in disguise.[26] And they can sympathize thoroughly with the heroine in her adventures which end in a bit of tragi-comic irony when Posthumous strikes the "scornful page" to the ground only to learn the next moment that the "page" is his wife long supposed dead.

III

While certain playwrights, including Shakespeare, were using hackneyed forms of disguise action others were exerting themselves to get novelty and variety. Some of these interesting experiments in technic are bound up with the history of the female page disguise. Retro-disguise and complete surprise in disguise plots have been defined and discussed somewhat abstractly in Chapter II (pages 11–14). We shall here analyze a few plots, which are dominated by these motives separately or in combination. Let us repeat that if some person in a play believes that a female page really is a boy and then disguises that page as a girl, we have a retro-disguise and the possibility of a new set of complications. Such complications impose a special kind of action at the end of the play, which produces a double dénouement. First, a certain group of characters has to discover that the female-page-girl is a page disguised as a girl, and, second, all the characters have to discover that the page

[26] See Schulz, 42–44, for a comparison between Imogen's disguise and that of Genevra in Bocc. *Decam.*, *II, 9*.

who had been disguised is really a girl, although some of
the principals in the action had been unaware of this fact.

Just how early or frequently retro-disguise occurs outside
of England I cannot say. I have found it, for example, in
the Sanskrit drama.[27] Italian drama sometimes presents
this situation and was doubtless the teacher of the English.
The motive appears, for example, in Parabosco's *Il Viluppo*
(*II, 2*), where Viluppo reminds Valerio of the day when he
disguised his supposed page as a lady.[28] Another Italian
play, *La Cintia*,[29] by G. B. della Porta, was adapted into a
Latin comedy called *Labyrinthus*, which was printed in 1636.
It had been acted at Cambridge as early as 1599 (Churchill
and Keller, 309).

The plot of this play is very labyrinthine but we shall tell
enough to illustrate our discussion. Lucretia tells her servant that she has been reared as a boy, that she loves
Horatius, and is serving him in male disguise as a pretended
love messenger. She further reports that, on the pretense
of bringing about an assignation between him and a certain
"Lepida," she has really filled "Lepida's" place herself.
Meanwhile another woman is mistakenly wooing Lucretia-
page. Horatius becomes suspicious about his page, and
next insists on seeing "Lepida" himself. Lucretia-page
now dresses herself as "Lepida" and again deceives Horatius in the amour. A bit of information soon complicates
the plot, for the supposed lady "Lepida" is really a boy.
And those that know this, jeer Horatius whenever he boasts
of having enjoyed "Lepida." But when Horatius learns
of the deception practiced on him he declares he is in love
with the unknown lady who favored him, whoever she may

[27] See my article in *M. L. N.*, xxvii, 92.
[28] See Klein, IV, 790.
[29] *La Cintia* is itself indebted to Piccolomini's *Ortensio*. See Klein,
V, 650.

be. Eventually Lucretia-page reveals herself and admits that she is the one who spent the nights with Horatius.

The retro-disguise situation in *Labyrinthus* is not very skilfully constructed. However, it shows the girl masquerading as page and then dressing as girl again before revealing her sex. An incidental use of this motive is exemplified in Heywood's *Four Prentices of London*, acted about 1594. In Heywood's play the French lady disguises as page and serves her lover intimately for a year without being recognized. Meanwhile the lover falls in love with Bella Franca (his own sister, though he does not recognize her). Presently the French Lady-page, who is jealous of the rival, disguises herself as a girl and becomes the servant of Bella Franca. But the next time the lover sees his lady he recognizes her. Dramaturgically Heywood made no profit out of the second disguise of the female page. The action was simplified rather than amplified.

Perhaps 1599 was too early a date to expect successful variation of the traditional devices. Heywood essayed retro-disguise again in the *Wise Woman of Hogsdon* (1604). This time he produced a plot of considerable ingenuity. He used the retro-disguise motive to lead up to a marriage supposedly farcical, but eventually real.[30] The plot is briefly as follows: Second Luce, disguised as a page, and pursuing her lover Chartley, overhears him planning a secret marriage with Luce at the Wise Woman's. Thereupon she becomes page to the Wise Woman, who, never suspecting the sex of her page, plans a trick on Chartley. By a ruse Second Luce-page, retro-disguised as a girl, is substituted for Luce in a marriage to Chartley. The bridegroom, who has thus really married Second Luce, but thinks he has

---

[30] Farcical marriages to a boy bride are discussed in the next chapter, where it is shown that the situation is borrowed from Plautus directly or through Italian literature.

married Luce, plans coolly to marry Gratiana. Now comes
a highly involved screen scene, in which these three girls —
the real wife, the supposed wife, and the intended wife — appear together with Chartley and several other characters. In
this scene the Wise Woman reveals her substitution trick
and jeers Chartley at having married a boy bride. But the
Wise Woman is herself deceived, for the supposed boy bride,
Second Luce, "scatters her hair" and proves that she is
Chartley's first love and a real bride.

This play illustrates a successful use of retro-disguise.
The jeering at Chartley because they think he has married
a boy bride constitutes a sort of false dénouement. But
the counter-revelation is a surprise even to the wise old
intrigante.[31]

But Heywood's play by no means exhausts the possibilities of involving a female page situation. We might
analyze these possibilities in four steps. First, a girl disguises as a boy. Second, some one, believing that this really
is a boy, disguises "him" as a girl. Third, the supposed
boy temporarily disguised as a girl is married off to some
young man. The witnesses jeer at the supposed boy bride,
who suddenly turns the laugh by revealing herself as a real
girl and a real bride. Fourth, the three steps are reproduced
as stated, but even the audience is deceived, for they have
not been taken into confidence. Such a surprise dénouement
of a retro-disguise situation is presented in the *Widow*.
But we shall defer the examination of that intricate play
until after we have described the surprise motive as another

---

[31] An interesting retro-disguise situation may be seen in Shirley's
Doubtful Heir (IV, 2). An example of retro-disguise resulting in a
supposed mock marriage is fundamental in Hausted's *Rival Friends*.
See also Glapthorne's *Hollander*, where a chambermaid disguised as a
man is married to a gallant disguised as a woman. Thus a supposed
mock marriage turns out to be a real marriage.

innovation, or perhaps an invention, in the early years of James's reign.

The decade 1600–10 was of great significance in the development of structure in disguise plays. We have already noticed the perfect use of the accepted romantic material in *Twelfth Night*, and the variation of disguise intrigue in the *Wise Woman*. But somewhere near the end of this decade came a new method which made a significant contribution to dramatic technic. The new motive, which, so far as I know, had never before been employed in any drama, is the unforeseen resolution of a plot by the revelation of a disguise which was unknown to the audience.[32]   According to the old method playwrights had kept the audience very closely in touch with the disguise action. The characters had informed us that they were going to disguise themselves, had discussed their dual rôle in soliloquies, had sometimes told us how they were going to act, and what they were going to wear, and while in disguise had made many references to their real identity in equivoques and veiled allusions. But by the new method the audience was completely deceived during the play and surprised at the end. This necessitated a complete absence of veiled allusion, and an entirely new motiving of the action; for the audience must not even suspect that there might be disguise.

Who is to be accredited with this invention? Jonson in *Epicœne?*   Or Beaumont and Fletcher in *Philaster?*   *Epicœne* was acted in 1609 (Thorndike, *Infl.*, 16, 67; Cf. Henry, *Epicœne*, xxii). *Philaster* was certainly written before Oct. 8, 1610, and it may have been written as early as 1608 (Thorndike, *Infl.*, 64, 65). The *Widow*, another play containing the surprise motive, has also been assigned to a date of 1608–9 by Bullen (*Middleton*, I, lxxxvi). There is evi-

---

[32] Compare the two surprise motives of classic drama, the *deus ex machina* and the discovery of family relationship.

dence that Jonson wrote the disguise plot in this play.[33]
Hence even if *Epicœne* did not precede *Philaster*, Jonson may
still have been the originator of the surprise motive.

Epicœne is full of comic action which victimizes Morose.
He hates noise but gets more than he can bear and resorts
to a humiliating means of escape.[34] The plot has a well-
motivated beginning, middle, and end. That there was disguise in the play no one could suspect. There has been
no hint of it in the dialog[35] and the most searching critic of
plot motivation could find no need of it. It comes as a
complete surprise. The dénouement is complete, and when
referred back to the events of the play makes them all seem
more ridiculous.

Philaster has a similar dramatic surprise. Here an in-
tense tragic action is built up on a false charge against the
heroine and a page. The audience knows that the page is not
guilty, but are in suspense as to whether the hero can be
convinced of the innocence of the lady and the page. After
a long series of tragic actions it is suddenly proved that the
accusation could not possibly be true, for the page is found
to be a girl in disguise.[36]

This play of Beaumont and Fletcher is so crowded with
incidents that any satisfactory synopsis would be too lengthy
here. But if we read[37] the play carefully we observe that

[33] See below, page 88.

[34] See an analysis of *Epicœne* in Chapter V.

[35] I do not think that the etymology of the word "epicœne," meaning common gender, was sufficiently clear to the audience to let out
the secret of the play. See Chapter II, page 13, for evidence that the
intriguing companions were themselves deceived.

[36] See the surprise female page disguise in Middleton's *Anything
for a Quiet Life* (1619) for some resemblance to *Philaster*.

[37] It is sometimes difficult for a reader to appreciate a surprise disguise, because the list of *dramatis personæ* gives the secret away; sometimes the real name of the character is attached to the dialog, or is

the audience cannot know that Bellario is a disguised girl.[38]
The suspense of the spectator is not a speculation whether
Bellario is a girl or a boy, but whether Philaster can be
convinced of Arethusa's innocence or not.   And as to the
latter question the suspense is perfectly motivated regard-
less of disguise.   When the disguise is revealed, it is a
complete surprise, but it is also a complete dénouement.[39]
Disguise in a play of this type is an organic but hidden
motive which performs the important function of resolving
the plot.

This new method of plot construction has its advantages.
It was a novelty to the blasé theatergoer, to whom the expository type of play had told in advance most of the events
to be enacted.   But it had also its disadvantages, as we have
already pointed out in Chapter II (page 13).   It was too
obviously a *coup de théâtre*.   It victimized the audience as
well as the people in the play, and it did not permit appre-
ciation of ironical situations or dramatic misunderstandings.
For example, in *Philaster* one could not realize at the first
performance the irony in Dion's false accusation of a page
who was really his own daughter and because of sex could
not be guilty of the charge made.   Again in the forest it
followed by the stage direction "disguised as a page."   See below,
page 89.

[38] In act I, scene 1, Dion alludes to his daughter who had undertaken
a tedious pilgrimage.   In the next scene Philaster describes Bellario in
the speech, "I have a boy," etc.   But there is no hint that Dion's
daughter is identical with this boy.   Dion himself is completely
deceived.

[39] Many students of *Philaster* will not agree with me that the surprise was complete.   They may support their case by Dion's speech,
which I have discussed, by Bellario's suspicious affection for Philaster, and by the *prima facie* possibility that on the Elizabethan stage
any page might turn out to be a girl.   However, even if these things
are to be looked upon as clues, we observe that the action continually
puts the audience on other trails.

is Dion who is most vociferous in laying a new crime on the page (his daughter). In fact neither the fundamental cause of the tragic action nor the pathetic situation of the love-lorn and unrewarded maiden at every turn of the play could be more than half appreciated by one who did not know of the disguise.

This new technic had many devotees,[40] while the old method of carefully forewarning the audience held its own. A compromise, good dramaturgy I should think, is to drop a few hints in the course of the dialog, so that the more alert of the spectators, if not all of them, may suspect disguise, and anticipate the dramatic effect of a discovery. Such is Chapman's method in *May Day*, printed in 1611, but doubtless acted several years earlier.[41] In that comedy the dénouement is a surprise to many spectators. Others, however, have been led to suspect the existence of disguise by hints made in the dialog. The source of *May Day* is Alessandro Piccolomini's comedy *Alessandro*. In that play the female page has an expository soliloquy in which the disguise and the reason for it are explained to the audience. Chapman, in reworking the Italian play, omitted the expository passage and chose not to forewarn the audience definitely, but merely to let them suspect that a certain page was a girl in disguise.

In act III, scene 5, Quintiliano, commenting on Leonoro's page Lionel, says: "Afore heaven 'tis a sweet-faced child, methinks he should show well in woman's attire." The hint is broader in act IV, scene 6. Here Leonoro plans to disguise his page as a woman in order to gull an innocent youth. The master says: "Come, Lionel, let me see how naturally thou canst play the woman," and when he has

---

[40] See Chapter V, pages 117-18.

[41] Prof. Parrot has concluded (II, 731) that *May Day* was produced in 1601 or 1602.

gone out Lionel speaks the words: "Better than you think for." The intended gulling does not advance far in the May day masque at the end of the play, for the female page-girl is recognized by her lover. We find this type of suspected disguise frequently in later plays. For example, in Ford's *Lover's Melancholy* (1628), where the disguise situation is slightly reminiscent of *Twelfth Night*, the audience is given strong hints in act II, scene 1, that the page Parthenophill is really Eroclea in disguise. Thus also the audience is partly taken into confidence in Shirley's *Love in a Maze* (1632) and in his *Grateful Servant* (1639).

We have already remarked that when surprise and the retro-disguise are combined they constitute the acme of plot involution. There must have been a great desire some-time during the years 1608–11, perhaps during a single theatrical season, to get as much novelty as possible in disguise situations. The most intricate plot of all is found in the *Widow*, a play attributed by the printer to Middleton, Jonson, and Fletcher. This play was acted perhaps as early as 1608.[42] Jonson's part in this play has been disputed, but there seems to be internal evidence that he had a hand in it. The disguise part of this plot comprises the retro-disguise (by this time a well-established motive) and the supposed farcical wedding. The situation is further involved by the use of surprise. Now these combinations re-appeared in a very close parallel by Jonson in the *New Inn*, so that unless we accuse Jonson of borrowing a plot in the *New Inn*, we may infer that he was a collaborator in the authorship of the *Widow*.[43]

[42] Bullen (*Middleton*, I, lxxxvi) attributes the play to Middleton alone and assigns 1608–9 as the date of production.

[43] See Tennant, *New Inn*, xliii. Also for an interesting parallel between these two plays and a Sanskrit play see my article in *M. L. N.*, xxvii, 92.

Koeppel (64) and Baxmann have pointed out Boccaccio's *Decam.*,

The Martia plot of the *Widow* is as follows: Martia, disguised as a man, is robbed and stripped to her shirt (III, 1). In this sorry plight she seeks admittance at the door of a house where Philippa awaits her lover. The maid mistakes Martia-man for the lover and gives "him" a suit of her master's clothes (III, 2). When Philippa meets the supposed young man she solicits "him," but Martia-man begs off by postponing the affair and gets away. Philippa realizes too late the danger to her honor when this "young man" is seen in her husband's clothes. In another scene the husband meets Martia-man and accuses "him" of being a robber. Martia-man again seeks refuge in Philippa's house, and the amorous wife conceives the plan of disguising Martia-man as a girl in order to conceal from her husband the intended intrigue (V, 1). Now a certain Francisco falls in love with Martia-man-girl, much to the amusement of Philippa and her maid, who think their refugee is a young man. This supposedly farcical courtship leads to a marriage between Francisco and Martia-man-girl, at which all the witnesses hold their sides in laughter. But jest turns to earnest, for a gentleman standing by takes his cue and dramatically recognizes the supposed boy bride as his daughter. Bride and groom are happy, but Philippa has to continue her life of prosaic fidelity.

As we read this summary we must remember that the theater spectators were victimized as much as Philippa and her maid, for nothing in the lines informs the listener of the original disguise. The dénouement is a genuine surprise revelation. The reader of the play is likely to forget this because the stage directions call Martia by her real name and furthermore say "disguised as a man."

II, 2, as an analogue to the Martia-robber plot. But it is very important to note that Boccaccio does not use disguise, since his story is that of a merchant who is robbed and stripped, and afterwards entertained by a widow with whom he spends the night.

During the decade when so much ingenuity was exerted on disguise plots there were also a number of plays that used the female page in the traditional manner, very incidentally and without much dramaturgic skill. For the sake of completeness and to emphasize the extensive use of the female page disguise we shall mention a half dozen such plays. In the Latin comedy *Zelotypus*, acted at Cambridge about 1600–1603, Lavinia disguises as a man in order to follow her husband, who has been exiled from Venice. The husband has gone no farther than the beach, where he is disguised as a fisherman. Fate so orders it that he is able to rescue Lavinia-man from drowning. He does not recognize her at first and she declares she is a Sicilian slave, but finally husband and wife are revealed to each other.

In 1604 the female page disguise was used incidentally in the anonymous *Fair Maid of Bristow*, and in Middleton and Dekker's *I Honest Whore*. In both plays the disguise is discovered almost immediately and does not affect the action.

Edward Sharpham's *Fleire*, entered in 1606, contains two female pages of minor importance. In this comedy of London manners two girls disguise as boys in order to interfere with their lovers' attentions to a pair of courtesans. The pages fail to secure services with their lovers, but are employed by two noble suitors to the courtesans, and in this service are able to frustrate a poison plot against their own lovers. The plot complication is slight and the disguise does not enter into the resolution. These disguises might have been worked into several dramatic situations but the author failed to realize his opportunity for dramatic effect.[44]

The Dumb Knight by Markham and Machin, probably acted in 1607, illustrates a minor but interesting use of male

[44] For other aspects of the *Fleire* plot see Chapter VII, page 154.

disguise for a lady. Mariana, who is in love with the imprisoned Philocles, visits him and helps him escape by means
of the time-worn device of exchanging costumes.[45] She
remains disguised as Philocles but is soon discovered.

In *Love's Cure, or the Martial Maid* by Beaumont and
Fletcher, probably acted between 1605 and 1609, and afterwards revised by Massinger (Thorndike, *Infl.*, 74), Clara,
the martial maid, having served her father as a squire in the
wars, makes her appearance in man's attire. But her identity
is not concealed, and she wears female habit during the rest
of the play.

IV

Our discussion has now covered the development of female
page plots up to the theatrical season of 1608–9. The thirty
or more plays which appeared before or by that year illustrate a variety of situations and methods that left little to
be accomplished in the way of originality in technic in the
plays which were written after 1608–9. Between forty and
fifty plays used the female page disguise during the three
decades which followed. But they did not add much to the
stock of material nor to the skilful methods already initiated. Nevertheless we shall notice a few of the most interesting of these plays, especially those falling well within the
period chosen for this treatise.

Disguise was comparatively uncommon in tragedies; but
we do find it occasionally. For example, we have already
alluded to the female page disguise in *Soliman and Perseda*.
Beaumont and Fletcher used a similar situation in the *Maid's
Tragedy*. The same authors used a situation in *Cupid's*

[45] In England it had already appeared in the *Wars of Cyrus, Thomas
Lord Cromwell, George a Greene, Knack to Know a Knave, Look About
You, I Sir John Oldcastle,* and *Blurt, Master Constable.* See also chapter
III, pages 34 and 38.

Revenge which resembles the Pyrocles and Zelmane-page story in the *Arcadia*. Both of these tragedies were performed by 1611 (Thorndike, *Infl.*, 66, 69).

The fifth act of the *Maid's Tragedy* owes a sensational climax to Aspatia's employment of male disguise. Her betrothed lover, Amintor, has abandoned her to marry Evadne, a union of tragic consequence. Aspatia, who has not been heard from since her cynical speech in act II, scene 2, enters in disguise in the last scene of the play and introduces herself to Amintor as "brother to the wrong'd Aspatia." She challenges him to single combat and fences so badly that she is slain by the false lover. Her dying words reveal her identity.

The plot of this play has been generally considered the invention of the authors, but it cannot be said that they were entirely original in the scene just described. The female page's presenting herself as her own brother is a detail already used in the *Maid's Metamorphosis*. And the general tragic method of the dénouement is a parallel to the theatrical effects in the last act of *Soliman and Perseda*, where Perseda in male disguise introduces herself to Soliman as "A gentleman, and thy mortal enemy," and challenges him to single combat. She is slain and reveals her identity in her dying words. The parallel must not be pushed too far, but there is certainly evidence of a reminiscence of the earlier play in the *Maid's Tragedy*.

The female page situation in *Cupid's Revenge* is not organically a part of the main plot. The main events would have taken their course and arrived at exactly the same resolution without the disguise. Consequently we may assume that the playwrights introduced the tragic episode to add theatrical effectiveness to the last act.[46] Without taking time to sum-

[46] Jacobi (24) thinks that the playwrights' purpose was to show a contrast between the devoted Urania and her unprincipled mother.

marize the plot [47] let me indicate the state of things in act V.
Prince Leucippus has fled to the forest because Queen Bacha,
now his stepmother and formerly his mistress, desires to
kill him.   The queen's daughter Urania would inherit the
throne in case of the prince's death.   But the simple-hearted
Urania, scorning political honors, disguises as a boy and,
hunting out Leucippus, offers herself to him as a page.
Leucippus tries to dissuade the "boy" by calling attention
to his inability to reward any service.   But the "boy" remains, and when a false courtier enters with drawn sword
and lunges at the prince, Urania-page jumps between and
receives the blow.   The prince still does not recognize her.
Finally she reveals her identity thus:

> "*Ura.*   I am Urania.
> *Leuc.*   Dullness did seize me!   Now I know thee well:
> Alas, why cam'st thou hither?
> *Ura.*   Feth, for love:
> I would not let you know till I was dying;
> For you could not love me, my mother was
> So naught.   (*Dies.*)"

So far as I know, the only other female page in preceding
English drama who served her lover unrewarded is Euphrasia
in *Philaster*.   That character naturally bears a relation to
Urania, but there was an earlier inspiration for both of these
pages.   It has recently been pointed out [48] that the apparent
source of the Leucippus and Urania-page episode is the
Pyrocles and Zelmane-page story in Book II of the *Arcadia*.
A quotation from that book will establish the parallel pretty
clearly.   Zelmane, daughter of Plexirtus, disguises as a page
and serves Pyrocles devotedly for about two months.   But
she becomes ill largely through "griefe for Plexirtus fault."
And as she dies she reveals herself to Pyrocles and adds:

[47] A good summary is given by Ward, II, 685.
[48] Herbst, 63.

"I know you would never have loved me (and with that she wept) nor, alas, had it bene reason you should, considering manie wayes my unworthines."

Let us now instance a couple of plays to show how certain traditional female page elements were worked into new plots, sometimes resulting in a strange mixture of ingredients. The mixture of romantic material with realism may be seen in Lodovick Barrey's *Ram Alley*, which was printed in 1611. It is a comedy of manners in the Middletonian vein but it is quite romantic in the use of the disguise. The very first lines of this play are of the traditional romantic tone:

> "*Constantia.*   In this disguise, ere scarce my mourning robes
> Could have a general note, I have forsook
> My shape, my mother, and those rich desmesnes,
> Of which I am sole heir; and now resolve
> In this disguise of page to follow him,
> Whose love first caus'd me to assume this shape.
> Lord, how my feminine blood stirs at the sight
> Of these same breeches!"

The apology for male costume in the last sentence goes back as early as *Sir Clyomon*. Constantia-page now serves her lover, and instead of discovering a rival lady as in earlier idealistic plays, she is able to spy upon his "punk" and the play soon turns into a series of vulgar intrigues and episodes. In the course of the play the lover pays ardent court to the widow Taffeta (II), while the widow's maid falls in love with Constantia-page and expresses her desires in the frankest language. This mistaken love of a woman for a female page was also, as we have seen, a traditional complication.

In act V when the lover hears that the widow is about to marry some one else, he immediately regrets having neglected Constantia, throws his purse to the page (Constantia), and hangs himself on the spot without a moment's hesitation. Constantia-page runs crying for help and the lover is rescued.

Presently Constantia-page offers to get Constantia for the lover "If he but swear to embrace her constant love." The page goes out and soon the young heiress Constantia returns. This happy ending, though not imitative in detail, reminds us of the way in which Rosalind-page offers to get Rosalind if only Orlando "will have her when I bring her," and then goes out to return as herself.

Curious reminiscences of detail crept into plays, sometimes perhaps unconsciously. In Nathaniel Field's *Amends for Ladies* (1611) the Ingen and Lady Honour-page story has been declared independent of other plays.[49] However, there are one or two slight borrowings. For example, the stage direction, *"Enter Lady Honour, like an Irish Footboy,"* in the scene where she presents her lover with a letter from herself (II, 3), is rather an unusual specification of disguise. It seems reminiscent of *"Enter Antonio like an Irish Footman,"* in act II, scene 1 of the *Coxcomb* (1609–10), where Antonio presents his wife with a letter from himself. Field was the chief actor in the *Coxcomb*, whence it is not strange if he caught a hint. Another influence on Field is shown in the surprise motive. This was doubtless inspired by *Epicœne*, another play in which he acted. The audience is kept ignorant of the fact that the "Irish Footboy" is Lady Honour until act III, scene 2, when she drops a hint in an aside.

Fletcher returned to the use of surprise, but employed it ineffectively, in the *Night Walker* (1614). In this play a very active and ingenious young lady named Alathe disguises herself as a boy and becomes her own brother's partner in roguery, neither the brother nor the audience knowing that the "boy" really is a girl. Then after posing as a ghost,

[49] Fischer (*Amends for Ladies*, 36) says: "Für den Teil der Handlung, — lässt sich kein Vorbild finden; dies ist vermutlich eigene Erfindung des Dichters."

pedlar, angel, and so forth, she succeeds, through a number of improbable adventures, in winning back the love of her betrothed, whose affections had wandered. It is not until the last scene that the audience is aware of this roguish "boy's" sex and identity. But the effect of this surprise is not especially successful. It does not seem that anything was gained by witholding the information from the audience.

Sometimes the incidents in Jacobean disguise plays are bizarre and improbable. In Fletcher's *Love's Pilgrimage*, which is only an adaptation of Cervantes's "exemplary novel" *Las Dos Donzellas*, we find two girls in pages' costumes, both seeking the same faithless lover. The party is captained by the brother of one of the girls, all three people having met by accident. After adventures with robbers, and other excitement, they find the faithless lover in a water front brawl. He is rescued and on his supposed death-bed repents of his infidelity to the two girls, and agrees to marry one of them,— the one accompanied by her brother. The other girl conveniently gets the brother.

Interest is gained in the same way by a number of sensational happenings in the *Faithful Friends*, where a female page goes to the firing line with her lover, an officer, but is unrecognized by him. In the heat of battle she rescues him from capture by the enemy and in quieter moments reveals herself to him.

Two other plays appearing just before 1616 we shall merely name. Middleton's *No Wit, No Help Like a Woman's* is a comedy of intrigue involving the heroine's disguise as a gallant. R. Tailor's *Hog Hath Lost His Pearl* contains a romantic underplot in which the female page disguise and the hermit disguise are essential. But both of these plays seem rather strange and improbable. They represent a strained seeking after novelty.

One way of producing a novel effect upon an audience

that has looked long on a given motive is to turn that motive inside out, as it were. This can be accomplished by pretending disguise where there is none. It not only gives a new plot but it serves as a good-humored burlesque of the old situation. The familiarity of the female page situation enabled playwrights to introduce a variation of that theme by letting the people in a play suspect disguise when there was none at all. This happened as early as 1605. In *Volpone* Lady Would-Be, seeing her husband with a young man, becomes suspicious and her jealousy turns suspicion into assurance that the young man is a courtesan in disguise. She berates her husband bitterly for being a patron of a "female devil in a male outside" (IV, 1). In the next scene the truth is discovered and her anxiety relieved.

Suspicion of disguise where there is none amounts almost to a burlesque in *Honest Man's Fortune*, by Fletcher, and perhaps Massinger, acted in 1613. In this play Laverdine persists in believing that the "loving and loyal page" Veramour is a woman in disguise. One of the maids also does "most dangerously suspect this boy to be a wench." Presently Veramour says to the insistent Laverdine (IV, 1): "Well, I perceive 'tis vain to conceal a secret from you; Believe it, sir, indeed I'm a woman." Veramour proceeds to support this declaration by disguising as a woman (V, 3) and mock heroically saying to his old master: "I am a poor disguised lady, That like a page have followed you long For love, God wot." Veramour further informs us that he "took example by two or three plays, that Methought-concerned me." But the fact of the whole matter is that Veramour is really a boy, who roguishly decided to humor Laverdine in his suspicion of disguise. This explanation of the affair is made clear in the last fifty lines in the play.[50]

[50] A surprising mistake is made by K. Richter in his dissertation (32, 33, 42). He misses the fun of the piece and thinks that Veramour

Evidently Fletcher was again fooling the audience accustomed to the popular *Philaster*.

We have now discussed more than forty English plays containing the female page disguise. In this brief examination we have seen a traditional disguise blossom into maturity and show the first signs of decay.[51] Shakespeare, observing the popularity of this motive, borrowed his materials and his methods and wrote immortal plays. Heywood, Jonson, Beaumont and Fletcher introduced or invented new tricks of technic, but all their virtuosity could not save them and their plays today experience no popularity and only rare revival. The cause of such failure is no secret. Mere mechanism of costumes, disguises, speeches, and replies do not alone carry a drama to the hearts of an audience. The human element, the character, the femininity of the dis-

really is a woman in disguise. He even speculates on the source of this situation (42), "In Veramour haben wir den verkleideten Mädchenpagen, eine ganz geläufige Erscheinung in der Elisabethanischen Dramatik." He mentions Julia, Viola, and Imogen and proceeds: "Dass die Verfasser diese Figur aus der zeitgenössischen Dramatik, meiner Ansicht nach aus Shakespeare, ganz bewusst entnehmen, zeigt eine Stelle unseres Stückes selbst: Akt V, Scene 3." Evidently Dr. Richter refers to the lines which I last quoted.

[51] It may be worth while to set down a partial list of the female page plays which were produced between 1616 and 1642. They are: Fletcher's *Pilgrim* (1621); Middleton's *Anything for a Quiet Life* (1619–23), and *More Dissemblers besides Women* (1622); the *Witch of Edmonton* (1621) by Rowley, Dekker, and Ford; Heywood's *Fair Maid of the West* (1622) and *Challenge for Beauty* (1635); Jonson's *New Inn* (1629); Ford's *Lover's Melancholy* (1628); Shirley's *Love Tricks* (1625), *Wedding* (1626), *Grateful Servant* (1629), *Maid's Revenge* (1639), *Doubtful Heir* (1640), the *Imposture* (1640), and the *Sisters* (1642); Massinger's *Duke of Milan* (1620), and *Bashful Lover* (1635); Brome's *Damoiselle* (1637), *Mad Couple Well Matched* (1636), and *English Moor* (1636–7); May's *Heir* (1620); Carliell's *Deserving Favorite* (1629); Hausted's *Rival Friends* (1631); Glapthorne's *Hollander* (1635); Marmion's *Antiquary* (1636); and Harding's *Sicily and Naples* (1638).

guised heroines which no disguise, however masculine, could conceal, that is the element which makes the Rosalinds, and Portias, and Violas endearing. Their male apparel not only does not conceal, but it actually reveals their feminine charm. Therein lies the art of Shakespeare. When we turn to retro-disguises, surprises, sensational episodes, and burlesques we may get a certain startling effectiveness, to be sure, but it is only a momentary brilliance and not the steady radiance of greater genius.

CHAPTER V

THE BOY BRIDE

By gar I am cozoned. I ha married oon Garsoon.
— *Merry Wives of Windsor*

THE popularity of the female page was never equalled by
the reverse disguise, that of a boy dressed as a girl. Even
in Italian drama the farcical boy bride of Plautian origin was
never as frequent as the female page.[1] In English sword
plays and morris dances the familiar grotesque and farcical
character "Bessy" was acted by a man dressed in woman's
clothes.[2] The conception of a man dressed as a woman is
always farce. This perhaps explains the comparative un-
popularity of the boy bride. We have seen that the disguised heroine became an important, if not essential, part
in romantic comedy. A romantic comedy situation could
be spun out for hours without seeming to pall on the spectators. But farce must by its nature be quick, flashing and
momentary. It cannot easily be sustained for any great
length of time. That is the important reason why the disguise of a man as a woman is not generally found as the basic
cause of main complications. There are, however, three or
four exceptions, the most notable being Jonson's *Epicœne,
or the Silent Woman.*

[1] See Chapter III, page 48, for mention of Italian adaptations of
Plautus's *Casina.*
[2] An influence of this character is shown in the masque in act IV,
scene I, of the *Thracian Wonder,* 1598 (Fleay, *Biog. Chr.,* I, 287), where
the clown is "dressed like Maid Marian."

101

Another fact may help to explain the difference in popularity between the boy bride and the female page. We have suggested in the previous chapter that the use of boy actors may have added piquancy to the part of the disguised heroine. Perhaps the fact that the performer of a boy bride part was really a boy had a dampening effect. Women's parts were, of course, always played by boys dressed as women. Consequently there was no real difference in acting the part of a woman character and the part of a boy disguised as a woman. Hence there was no novelty in the latter situation and no special appeal to the spectator's imagination. It did not have the whimsical attractiveness of a female page part acted by a boy.

The various cases of men or boys disguised as women may be catalogued in three classes. The first includes the simple disguises which did not lead to any further complication. The second type we may call the male mistress situation. It includes cases where the disguised boy was mistakenly loved and wooed by some man. Most of the plays we are to consider fall into that class. But the best complication resulting from a man's use of feminine garb is where the person so disguised becomes the bride of some braggart gallant or old dotard much to the joy of the intrigants. This type, which we may call the boy bride situation, is exemplified in *Epicœne*.

We have already seen in the preceding chapter that when Shakespeare produced his female page plays he was following a fashion and putting on the stage the type of plot which had already met with the frequent favor of the London audiences. It is not easy to think of Jonson as following anybody in England, but we shall see that in many of his disguise plays he was to a certain extent influenced by his English predecessors or contemporaries. The dependency of *Epicœne* may best be determined by giving an account of all the male mistress plays which preceded it in England. The results will show that when *Epicœne* was produced the London playgoers had already laughed at a considerable number of plays in which boys were disguised as girls.

But before going on to a discussion of *Epicœne's* predecessors, let us remind ourselves of the elements in the disguise situation of Jonson's play. The components are: a boy dressed as a woman; the wooing of this male mistress; the disguised boy's mingling intimately with ladies; a braggart's confessing that he has had an amour with the male mistress; the old man's marriage to the disguised boy, and the jeering when the boy bride is undisguised. The serious purpose of the stratagem is to get money from the victim. Finally, a distinctive feature of the play is that the whole disguise intrigue was a complete surprise to the spectators, who had not been led to suspect the sex of "the silent woman."

A boy disguised as a girl appears in the Latin Cambridge play, *Byrsa Basilica* (1569–70. See Chapter IV, page 62), the earliest use of the motive in plays composed in England. The plot was perhaps of no great influence on succeeding plays, but we shall nevertheless give a brief summary. Emporius woos Virginia. A rival wooer, Cap-a-pé, is advised to get Emporius intoxicated, and then to carry off Virginia. The drinking duel of the two rivals results in Cap-a-pé's becoming swinishly drunk; and in this condition he reaches Virginia's house where he goes to bed. Virginia escapes in the clothes of Cap-a-pé, who is forced to wear Virginia's clothes when he departs. In this costume he is offered to Emporius on the pretense of being Virginia, but his identity and that of the real Virginia are disclosed before other complications can arise.

We do not find another case of a boy disguised as a girl until fifteen years after this Latin play, in Lyly's *Gallathea*, where Cupid disguises as a nymph. The love god uses this

device — so he says (II, 2) — in order that he may better
exercise his power over the virgins of Diana. Cupid is captured and threatened with punishment for his mischief, but
is finally released. This is only a simple use of disguise. It
might have been elaborated into a male mistress situation
by having Cupid mesmerize the pastoral swains into love
with him as nymph only to plague them by revealing his
identity as a boy.

Such a mistaken wooing was soon presented on the public
stage. It was used incidentally in two plays which were
both printed in 1594, and both acted possibly as early as
1588.[3] These plays are the *Wars of Cyrus* and the *Taming
of A Shrew*. In act II of the *Wars* the heroine Alexandra
escapes personal danger by exchanging costumes with her
page Libanio. Libanio-as-Alexandra is held captive and put
under the care of Dinon. The keeper, misled by the costume and dissimulation of Libanio, makes love to his captive,
who pretends to favor the suit and lulls Dinon to sleep with
a sweet song, only to slay him and escape. Libanio reaches
the home of the heroine and is rewarded. The Inductions
to *A Shrew* and *The Shrew* are familiar to all. Let us only
observe one or two points in the structure. In *A Shrew* the
roguish noblemen tell Sly that his lady has come to congratulate him on his safe return. This "lady" is a boy in
woman's attire. But Sly is deceived and says: "Come sit
down on my knee, Sim, drink to her, Sim, For she and I
will go to bed anon." Just then the players are announced
and the boy-lady is sent as a messenger to tell them to begin
their comedy, a rather inappropriate errand for a person
supposed to be a real lady. Thus the episode ends rather
abruptly and no further allusions are made to the "lady."
Shakespeare's chief improvement of this episode consists in

[3] See Keller, *Wars of Cyrus*, 9; and Tolman, *Shakespeare's Part*,
210.

letting Bartholomew-girl by clever argument dissuade Sly from his amorous desires. The ending, though abrupt, is poetical:

"Come, madam wife, sit by my side,
And let the world slip: we shall ne'er be younger."

But neither Shakespeare nor his predecessor made very skilful use of this disguise. Both plays lose dramatic value in not revealing the sex of the supposed lady; for, as the case stands, it is a practical joke which is never made known to the victim.

Horse-play was necessary to please one element of the Elizabethan audience, and was easily furnished by the farcical male mistress situation. Two bits of buffoonery which were especially frequent seem to go back as far as Plautus's *Casina*. In that play an armor-bearer is disguised as a girl and substituted for Casina, the bride to have been. When the husband kisses "her" he feels a rough beard, and in a moment the supposed bride gives him a vigorous trouncing. The joke about the beard and the violent beating of the victim were both continued in Elizabethan plays.

Greene in his *Orlando Furioso* added a farcical disguise situation to the original story (Schulz, 3). Orlando's page dresses up the clown as Angelica, not bothering about shaving his beard, for he knows that the mad Orlando will not observe it. The trick works ill to the clown, however, for Orlando mistakes him for his betrothed and supposedly false Angelica, and beats him off the scene. The purpose of this disguise digression in the play is merely to raise a laugh from the groundlings. It reminds us of a similar bit of farce in Munday's *Downfall of Robert, Earl of Huntington*, where the Bishop of Ely attempts to escape disguised as an old woman, but is recognized immediately because of his beard.[4] Dramatically the disguise had no value in the plot, but there was theatrical point in the ludicrous case of the bishop. Shakespeare has a similar bit of farce in the *Merry Wives*. When Falstaff, disguised as the Witch of Brentford,[5] is hustled roughly out of doors the Welsh parson evidently pierced the disguise, for he says: "By yea, and no, I think the o'man is a witch indeede: I like not when a o'man has a great peard; I spie a great peard under his muffler."[6] In Fletcher's *Monsieur Thomas* (after 1610)[7] when Hylas kisses Thomas, who is disguised as a girl, he notices the beard, but stupidly remarks: "Her lips are monstrous rugged; but that surely Is but the sharpness of the weather."[8]

The other farce motive which has become a literary tradition was the violent beating administered by the supposed lady. In Lyly's *Woman in the Moon* such a scene occurs when Stesias, disguised as his wife, encounters the three lovers who had appointments with her and gives each one a lusty beating.[9] We find a similar comic action in Chapman's *May Day*, where the supposed lady accompanies his

[4] This disguise is supposed to be historical. See Hart's *Merry Wives*, 176.

[5] Professor Brander Matthews (*Molière*, 261) has compared Falstaff's escape with that of the hero in *M. de Pourceaugnac*.

[6] The boy bride in the last act of *Merry Wives* will be discussed below, page 112.

[7] See below, page 118.

[8] The incongruity of a man's bearded face in a woman's part seems to have been a standing joke. When Flute is asked to play the part of Thisbe he objects: "Let not me play a woman; I have a beard coming." It is related that Charles II, one day annoyed by a delay in the theater, sent for Davenant, the manager, and asked him why the play did not begin. Sir William replied: "Please you, sir, the queen is not yet shaved."

[9] A similar scene occurs in *Pidinzuolo*, an anonymous Italian farce, played in 1517. A lover has a rendezvous with a lady, but, instead of the lady, her brother in female disguise comes and whips the lover.

revelation with a sound trouncing of the wooer. Chapman borrowed part of the male mistress situation from the Italian play *Alessandro*, of which *May Day* is an adaptation, but the violent ending of the scene is the English playwright's addition. In *Monsieur Thomas* Thomas, disguised in his sister's clothes, is mistaken for the sister by the father, who orders her back to the house. But Thomas responds by knocking his father down. The beating motive is especially effective in *Philotus*, as will be seen below. It also occurred in a great number of plays after the period which I am considering.

But to furnish the mere claptrap of acting was not the worthiest function of disguise. A real, constructive value was the motivation of comic entanglement. The exchanging of costumes by a young man and a girl in order to facilitate the escape of one of them often resulted in comic complication for the man in female costume. We have already discussed the situations in *Byrsa Basilica* and in the *Wars of Cyrus*. In *George a Greene, the Pinner of Wakefield* we have another male mistress complication resulting from the exchange of costumes. This farce motive, as well as the other disguise motives in the play, are taken with no important variation from the prose romance, the *Famous History of George a Greene*. A part of the plot may be summarized here. Wily on his own initiative conceives a stratagem for bringing the lass Bettris to his master George a Greene. Disguised as a "semster's maide" he presents himself at the home of Grimes with the fiction that he is bringing work to Bettris, the daughter of the house. Grimes, meeting the disguised Wily on the doorstep, is immediately charmed by the supposed sempstress, who manages to escape into the house. Presently Bettris, having put on the apparel in which Wily entered, passes Grimes safely, although he again wants to make love. This happens in act III, and in the last act the identity of the "sempstress" is still unrevealed. Grimes gets consent of George and the King to marry "her." But Wily, a bit frightened, reveals herself with the words: "Witnesse, my Lord, if that I be a woman; For I am Wilie, boy to George a Greene, Who for my master wrought this subtill shift." [10]

The simple disguise episodes are uninteresting, but they should be taken account of, because every situation containing a boy disguised as a woman would tend to make that disguise a stock device before Jonson's comedy appeared. In Haughton's *Englishmen for My Money, or A Woman Will Have Her Will* (1598, Henslowe) Walgrave, disguised as the neighbor girl Susan, enters the home of his beloved Mathea. Her father falls in love with the supposed girl, makes amorous suggestions, and temporizes (as he thinks) by sending Susan to bed with Mathea! Four other plays dating from about 1595 to 1606 presented men disguised as women, with little complication resulting therefrom. In Heywood's *Brazen Age* Hercules serves Omphale a while clad in woman's garments. But there is no mistake in identity and no complication. In Armin's *Two Maids of Moreclacke* the lover is told that he may claim his bride when he "has been from himself a woman." He satisfies the demand by disguising as a nurse. An interesting scene occurs in the last act of Day's *Law Tricks*, where the page Joculo attempts to play the rôle of a long lost daughter returned. At first he seems certain of success, while the real daughter who is actually present is considered an impostor. But a rigid cross-examination finally reveals the fraud. In Dekker and

---

[10] In Markham and Machin's *Dumb Knight* is an exchange of no consequence. Philocles gets out of prison by exchanging costumes with his lady love who has just come to visit him. The trick is successful, but Philocles, after speaking a couple of lines, goes out and no further dramatic use is made of the device.

Webster's *Westward Ho* the suspicious Justiniano disguises himself as his own wife and meets a gentleman whom he suspects of alienating his wife's love. Justiniano discovers that his wife is faithful.

A unique situation is developed in *Look About You* (printed 1600) when Robin Hood plays the part of Lady Fauconbridge. Sir Richard Fauconbridge has been tricked by his own wife, who has made love to him under the character of a "merchant's wife." He so far forgets his marital vows under the spell of the "merchant's wife" that he makes an assignation with her in his own home. A very funny scene ensues when Robin Hood, disguised as Lady Fauconbridge, and Lady Fauconbridge herself, disguised as the "merchant's wife," keep Sir Richard bouncing between his desire to maintain outward respectability and his eagerness for an amour. Finally both Robin Hood and the lady throw off their disguises and Sir Richard can only resort to the familiar explanation that he had known his wife all the time.

It may have seemed unconvincing to some playwrights to expect that a youth old enough and large enough to take the part of a hero should be able to disguise himself successfully as a girl. Hence a certain verisimilitude was obtained by disguising the hero as an amazon. In Sidney's *Arcadia* Pyrocles had disguised himself as an amazon,[11] and in *Antonio and Mellida* the hero had utilized the same disguise.[12] Day employs an amazon disguise as a basic motive in the *Isle of Gulls* (1605), a play which is reminiscent of the *Arcadia*.[13] The result is an involved situation of much

[11] The Pyrocles-amazon disguise is borrowed from *Amadis of Gaul*, Book XI. See H. W. Hill, 12.

[12] A later amazon disguise occurs in *Swetnam, the Woman Hater* (1618). In Shirley's *Arcadia* (1633) Pyrocles is disguised as an amazon.

[13] See Hill, 32.

comic irony. Lisander disguises himself as an amazon and comes to woo the duke's daughter Violetta. In the course of things the duchess herself falls in love with Lisander-amazon, for she suspects that he is really a man. The duke, on the other hand, believing Lisander a woman, falls in love with "her." He plans to gull his wife by encouraging her delusion (as he supposes it) concerning Lisander-amazon's sex. So he tells the duchess that Lisander really is a prince in disguise come to woo Violetta (which is the truth, although the duke does not suspect it). The duchess woos Lisander and the eavesdropping duke thinks it a capital joke. Lisander now arranges a secret appointment with the duchess, and in his amazon character he promises to meet the duke at the same place. He complicates matters still further by disguising a courtier in his own amazon dress and sending him to the double rendezvous. Finally, after much comic worrying by the duke and the duchess, the ruse is discovered.

There are only a few plays in which the male mistress motive is a fundamental cause of complication. One we have just described. Another is the Latin comedy *Labyrinthus*, described in the previous chapter. Let us glance at the plot again, this time fixing our attention on the male mistress. Lepidus, disguised as a girl "Lepida," carries on a love affair with a lady. Horatius has fallen in love with "Lepida" and employs his page (Lucretia in disguise) to make an assignation for him. Lucretia is practical enough in her love for Horatius to substitute herself for "Lepida." Horatius, now madly in love with "Lepida," insists on seeing "her" next time. Again Lucretia-page outwits her lover and substitutes for "Lepida." Now whenever Horatius speaks of having enjoyed "Lepida" (which is somewhat like the braggart assertions of La Foole and John Daw), he is ridiculed by those who know "Lepida's" sex. In the end, however, after he has heard of the substitute trick, he marries Lucretia.

We have mentioned earlier in this chapter that the disguise in *Epicœne* was engineered in order to trick Morose out of his money. A bit of cozenage in Marston's *What You Will* (printed 1607) bears a remote resemblance to this purpose in *Epicœne*. A certain page declares he "will convey, crossbite, and cheat upon Simplicius," and executes his threats by disguising Pippo as a "merchant's wife," introducing this creature to Simplicius as an attractive lady of open mind toward affairs of love. The page first explains to his victim that the lady's fool has a strange habit of demanding rapiers, purses, and trifles, but that this must be humored, for the property is always returned. Of course the fool is impersonated by the intriguing page himself, and Simplicius, who falls madly in love with the male lady, is neatly relieved of his hat, cloak, rapier, and purse.[14]

A similar but more daring scheme for obtaining money by means of the male mistress disguise is worked out in Middleton's *Mad World, My Masters* (printed 1608). Follywit, who has often duped his grandfather, learns that the old gentleman has a "quean." So he disguises himself as the courtesan and gains access to an inner chamber which contains a chest of jewels. On the way to this chamber the disguised grandson is beset by the butler, who woos the supposed courtesan as he has often wooed the real one. This time the "courtesan" promises a meeting and the butler is overjoyed. When the old gentleman finds his casket rifled he is furious but decides gamely that his lechery has been fairly punished. By some irony of fate Follywit marries the very courtesan he had impersonated, and when the

---

[14] In Nash's *Unfortunate Traveller* (1594) Jack Wilton disguises himself as a "half crown wench" and cozens a Swiss captain out of six crowns.

grandfather sees his own rubies on her hands he is only confirmed in the belief that the courtesan had robbed his casket. The truth is never revealed to the old man.

Let us now summarize briefly the significance of the twenty-odd plays which we have just examined. Our study of these plays has proceeded on the theory that those disguise plays produced in London which used the theme of a boy disguised as a girl would in the course of time make the boy mistress situation a stock device in England, and that Jonson's *Epicœne* was an unusually successful application of this stock motive. By 1608 theatergoers had already seen twenty or more plays in which some boy or man had masqueraded in the clothes of the opposite sex. In ten of these plays the disguise of sex had led to a mistaken wooing by some man who suffers ridicule because of his mistake.

Even the victim's marriage to the boy bride had been seen in English plays before *Epicœne*. The situation had been used in the eighth novel of Riche's *Farewell*. The same story had constituted the comedy *Philotus*, printed in Edinburgh in 1603. And a boy bride had been dimly limned in no less a play than Shakespeare's *Merry Wives*. Therefore Jonson may just as fairly be charged with borrowing from English as from Italian or Latin drama.

In the *Merry Wives* Anne Page has promised to meet Slender at the masque of fairies, dressed in green. She has also promised to meet Dr. Caius, in white. Both Slender and Caius are gulled, for they carry off boys who had been disguised as girls, dressed respectively in the colors agreed upon, and supplied with code words. Dr. Caius rages: "Ver is Mistris Page: by gar I am cozoned. I ha married oon Garsoon, a boy."

The eighth novel in Riche's *Farewell* is the tale of *Phylotus and Emelia*, and, as far as the disguise plot is concerned, the comedy *Philotus* presents no substantial difference. Whether

Riche's novel is older than the comedy or vice versa, or
whether the two plots have a common source cannot at
present be said.[15] The story is briefly as follows: The
father of Emelia wishes to marry her off to old Phylotus.
But her young lover Flavius helps her elope with him, escap-
ing from home disguised as a young man. "Now it fell
out" that Phylerno, Emelia's brother and double, who has
just returned, is captured by the father and Phylotus, and
naturally enough is mistaken for Emelia-in-disguise. The
brother plays up to the joke, "admits" that he is Amelia,
sends for her clothes, and goes home with old Phylotus to
live as his daughter until the marriage. Fate is kind to the
young man, for the old dotard puts Phylerno-girl in the same
chamber with his own daughter Brisella. This results in a
happy union for them.[16] When the wedding day comes
Phylerno-girl goes to church and is united in holy matri-
mony with Phylotus. At night the bride and groom
have a tilt to determine who shall have the mastery.
Phylerno-girl pummels the blood out of Phylotus's face
and forces the old man to accept terms of peace. The
terms are that the bride shall come to his bed only once a
month and that it shall be in the dark and no word spoken.
The ingenious Phylerno sends a street walker to fill his place
while he goes to his Brisella. This arrangement is soon
interrupted, for it so happens that Emelia's lover Flavius
had been at church and had seen the wedding of Phylotus
to Phylerno-girl. He mistook the bride for his own mistress
Emelia; and the next time he sees Emelia he drives her into
the street. The distracted girl goes home and confesses all
to her father, finally revealing the true state of things.

This completes our consideration of the male mistress

[15] See the preface (viii, ix) to Riche's *Farewell, Shak. Soc.*, 1846.

[16] The preliminary to this union is a pretended metamorphosis of
sex in answer to Phylerno's prayer. See Chapter IV, page 64.

and boy bride plays which preceded *Epicœne*. Now it may be admitted that the resemblances between Jonson's play and the preceding disguise plays are by no means close parallels. But it must then be observed that there is no closer parallel between *Casina* and *Epicœne;* yet Plautus's play is usually given as the source of Jonson's disguise plot.[17]

The story of *Casina* tells of a married man who is in love with Casina and wants his bailiff to marry her, so that he may himself safely carry on an amour. The wife discovers the plan and substitutes an armor-bearer in disguise for the bride. When the bailiff and the lover come to embrace the bride they are respectively welcomed by sound thrashings. The theme common to this play and *Epicœne* is the marriage to a disguised youth instead of a girl. But the reasons for this disguise trick, the results of it, and the theatrical representation of the situation in *Casina* have no counterparts in Jonson's play. The truth of the matter is, it seems to me, not that Plautus was the direct source of Jonson's play, but that Plautus was the ultimate source of a number of Italian plays, which inspired a number of English plays, which established a certain tradition, which culminated in *Epicœne*.

In this culmination we admit that there was more of creation than of borrowing. The lady love or wife who turned out to be a man in disguise was, as we have seen, a stock situation. But in presenting this old situation Jonson with great skill, as we shall see, made a radical departure from traditional methods in technic. We have already expressed our views in Chapters II and IV [18] that surprise is not good dramaturgy because it victimizes the audience.

---

[17] Miss Henry in her edition of *Epicœne* (xxxiv) follows Koeppel (*Quellen Studien*) in saying that Plautus's *Casina* was the source of the disguise in *Epicœne*.

[18] See Chapter II, page 13, and Chapter IV, page 86.

However, to Jonson and certain fellow dramatists the motive seemed desirable for some reason, perhaps as a novelty in contrast with the old expository methods. The fact that Jonson decided to make the boy bride situation a complete surprise to the audience gave him a new problem in comedy structure. For, since the spectators were not to be informed of the disguise, they could not look upon that motive as the cause of any humorous complication. In other words, the spectators, not knowing of the disguise, would not realize until the end of the play that certain incidents were dramatic complications. Consequently Jonson used another dramatic cause to give meaning and humor to the incidents throughout the play. From a story by Libanius he got the idea of Morose's "humour," the peculiar aversion to all sorts of noise. This "humour" in the play impels the action so naturally and completely that the plot would have been considered good even if the last two pages of manuscript had been lost and we had never known that this noisy bride was really a boy in disguise.

The double operation of these two motives is the distinguishing feature of the play. One motive, the aversion to noise, is known to the audience at the beginning of the play and operates forward. The other motive, the presence of disguise, is not suspected and therefore must operate backward in the spectator's recollection of the scenes which have just been performed. Let us analyze the technic of *Epicœne* by arranging the incidents of the play in two groups according to the motive upon which they depend chiefly for dramatic value.

(a) *Incidents that are comic because of Morose's objection to noise:* 1. The first scenes develop Morose's "humour." His aversion contrasts well with his own talkativeness. 2. Epicœne speaks so low as to be almost inaudible. 3. The parson can be heard only with difficulty except when he

coughs. 4. Epicœne berates Morose for being angry with
the parson. 5. Boisterous congratulations of Morose.
6. Truewit's noisy burlesquing of Morose's curses. 7.
The collegiate ladies demand festivity. 8. Cleremont's
introduction of drums and trumpets, banqueting and
drinking, the quarreling collegiates, the fighting Mr. and
Mrs. Otter, etc. 9. The noisy woman drives Morose to
talk of divorce. 10. A garrulous divorce proceeding.

(b) *Incidents that appear doubly comic when the audience
has discovered that the bride is really a boy*: This would include nearly all the incidents of the first group, in addition
to the following: 1. John Daw courts the "silent woman."
2. Epicœne kisses the collegiate ladies. 3. Daw hints that
he has been intimate with Epicœne. 4. Epicœne requests
certain "excellent receits" from the collegiates. 5. Epicœne
and the collegiates indulge in amorous secrets. 6. John Daw
and La Foole both confess that they have enjoyed Epicœne
before she became a bride. 7. Morose confesses to impo-
tency in order to get his divorce. 8. But Epicœne declares
that no cause will separate her from her husband. 9.
Dauphine is promised inheritance of Morose's whole estate
providing he can cancel the match. He proceeds to do so
by taking off Epicœne's wig.

This unexpected disguise revelation adds a new comic
aspect to the whole play and imposes the necessity of a
second reading or witnessing of the play before it can be
fully enjoyed. The comic stuff resides in the relations
which the supposedly silent woman bears to Morose, to the
braggart fools, and to the collegiate ladies respectively. The
discovery of the disguise serves not only as a complete
dénouement which resolves every complication, but as an
intensifier of the whole comedy; for the various relations
just mentioned seem doubly funny when it is remembered
that the noisy "silent woman" is of the male sex.

The stage history of *Epicœne* is curious. The play enjoyed considerable popularity until Garrick's production in 1776.[19] Some critics thought that the play then failed because the part of Epicœne was acted by a woman. This theory, however, does not seem tenable, for the part had been successfully acted by women ever since 1664.[20] The real reason, as Miss Henry suggests, is that the eighteenth century was too "genteel" to appreciate inelegant and coarse humor. As for the surprise ending, there seems to have been no serious objection until recently. Prof. Gayley says, "Not by reason of, but in spite of its dénouement, was the popularity of the *Silent Woman* achieved."[21] The proposition as stated might be difficult to prove in a law court, but it no doubt voices the opinion of many contemporary critics.

We must remember that Jonson was experimenting, as we have shown in the previous chapter. He and Beaumont and Fletcher seem to have become tired of the conventional technic whereby the audience had the plot pretty clearly explained to them before it ever happened. Consequently these playwrights made a radical departure in the surprise ending, a trick of technic which frequently recurred in succeeding plays. Jonson used an incidental surprise in the *Alchemist* (1610), where Surly masquerades as a Spaniard for three scenes before the audience learns of his real identity. In the *New Inn* (1631) father, mother, and daughter are in disguise, but the audience does not know of it until the very end of the play. In the *Staple of News* (1625) Jonson accompanies the surprise motive with a criticism of the shock of surprise. Pennybody has been spying in disguise on his prodigal son until the end of act IV, when he

---

[19] Henry, xxv.
[20] Henry, xxiii.
[21] Gayley, II, 121.

suddenly reveals himself. Expectation, one of the gossips
making running comments on the play, says: "Absurdity
on him, for a huge overgrown play-maker! Why should he
make him live again, when they and we all thought him
dead?" [22] In Fletcher's *Night Walker* (1614) the female page
is a surprise.[23] In Fletcher's *Loyal Subject* (1618) the audience does not know until the end that "Alinda" is young
Archas in disguise. Other interesting plays containing surprise revelations of disguise are Massinger's *Bondman* (1623)
and *Bashful Lover* (1635), Shirley's *Wedding* (1626), and his
Sisters (1642), Goffe's *Careless Shepherdess* (1623), Brome's
City Wit (1629), Carliell's *Deserving Favorite* (1629),
Hausted's *Rival Friends* (1631), and Marmion's *Antiquary*
(1636). These plays and others that might be named show
that the *Epicœne* and *Philaster* type of dénouement exerted
considerable influence on later dramaturgy.

To return to the main subject of this chapter let us glance
at two or three plays that followed *Epicœne* and were inspired, if not by the details, at least by the general situation
in that play. It cannot be said that there was any close
borrowing on the part of these followers. But it is interesting to note how they carried on the tradition of the male
mistress and boy bride disguises.[24]

Fletcher's *Monsieur Thomas* (produced after 1610) [25] contains a boy bride situation in the last two acts. Thomas
dons his sister's clothes in order to carry out a love intrigue,
the incidents of which we shall not now narrate. But the

[22] Compare Truewit's remark at the end of *Epicœne*; see Chapter
II, page 13.

[23] For a description of the *Night Walker* see Chapter IV.

[24] Miss Henry (*Epicœne*, lvii) calls Jasper Mayne's *City Match* and
P. Hausted's *Rival Friends* "literary descendants" of *Epicœne*. Yet
neither of these two plays uses the male mistress motive.

[25] See Stiefel, *Zur Quellenfrage*, 242.

young man is mistaken for his sister by a number of people, among them his father, whom he knocks down. Another victim of the disguise is a certain Hylas. Thomas-girl roguishly receives the caresses and kisses of Hylas, who is so stupid that he imputes the bristling roughness of Tom's lips to the "sharpness of the weather." Soon Thomas-girl is married to the eager Hylas, who somehow loses track of his bride for a few hours. When he sees Tom's sister Dorothy he naturally claims her as his wife, and she, of course, thinks he is mad. Hylas soon sees through the trick that has been played on him, but finally gets Dorothy after all.

Scholars have cited Whetstone's *Heptameron, IV, 1*, and Boccaccio's *Decameron IV, 2*, and *VIII, 4* as sources of the scenes which we have just summarized.[26] But these novels, although they have some resemblance to *Monsieur Thomas*, do not contain the boy bride or the male mistress disguise. Yet Fletcher here fell in line with contemporary London tradition; from English plays, as we have seen, he might have borrowed the male mistress, the boy bride, the joke about the beard, and the beating motive.

An incidental boy bride situation occurs in W. Smith's *Hector of Germany* (printed in 1615). Old Fitzwaters is affianced to Floramel and young Fitzwaters is in love with her. She prefers the son, and with the help of a steward contrives to substitute a disguised page at the wedding. As he leaves the church old Fitzwaters learns that he has been gulled. Meanwhile Floramel and her lover have put to sea.[27]

An incidental male mistress motive occurs in Daborne's *Poor Man's Comfort* (1613). In a mad-scene Sigusmund thinks that the clown Catzo is a woman, and solicits "her"

[26] See Guskar, 23.

[27] Marriages to boy brides occur in *Love Tricks* (1625) and in *Love in a Maze* (1632), both plays by Shirley.

amorously. In so far as Catzo is a clown disguised as a woman, and the victim of the deception is mad, we have a resemblance to the farcical scene in Greene's *Orlando*, where the hero mistakes the disguised clown for his betrothed Angelica.

We have now brought the tradition of the male mistress disguise up to 1616. In our comparison of the various plays studied in this chapter we have made the observation that the disguise of a boy in woman's clothes resulting in the wooing, or farcical marriage of the supposed lady, was an old and familiar theme in England when Jonson produced *Epicœne*. We have also seen that, although none of the male mistress or boy bride plays stand slavishly near to Plautus, his pleasant shadow hangs over them all. But *Epicœne* is interesting more for its technic than for its material. We have shown by a detailed analysis just how the surprise discovery of disguise differed dramaturgically from the conventional motivation of disguise action. The new technic, like recent revolutionary practices in painting, may have been extreme, but there is no doubt that it helped to place dramaturgy on a more sophisticated level and to direct its appeal to an audience no longer naïve.

CHAPTER VI

THE ROGUE IN MULTI-DISGUISE

> I cane turne into all
> Coullers like the commillion.
> — *The Marriage of Wit and Wisdom*

In the previous chapters we have remarked that the appeal of the female page situations was largely due to the conditions of the stage, the fact that boys played female parts; we have also remarked that this same fact may have been one reason why the boy bride situation did not seem quite so appealing. We shall now discuss a group of disguise plays that owe their existence evidently to the presence of a "star" impersonator in the Admiral's Men. These curious disguise plays in which the chief performer makes a great number of changes with amazing rapidity may well be called "Virtuosenstücke." [1] The almost acrobatic action is as mystifying as a sleight-of-hand performance. But in spite of, or because of this, they were good "box office plays." It is a significant fact that four popular multi-disguise plays were all produced by the Admiral's Men between 1594 and 1600. I suggest that these plays were used as a vehicle for starring a single skilful performer.

Monday's *John a Kent and John a Cumber*[2] was played thirty-two times from December 1594 to July 1597. Chapman's *Blind Beggar of Alexandria* was played twenty-two times from February 1595–6 to April 1597. And the

[1] Creizenach, IV, 252.
[2] Greg endorses Fleay's theory that this is the play referred to by Henslowe as the "*Wiseman of West Chester.*"

fact that in 1601 Henslowe expended over nine pounds for properties for this play, seems to indicate that it was still going. Concerning the stage history of *Look About You*, printed in 1600, and of the *Blind Beggar of Bednal Green*, mentioned by Henslowe in 1600, we know less. But since two of the multi-disguise plays were so popular up to April and July of 1597, it seems to me very probable that the other two were produced after that time, perhaps in the next theatrical season. This theory fixes 1597 as the date *post quem* for *Look About You* and the *Blind Beggar of Bednal Green*, both of which were written by 1600.

There may have been a fifth multi-disguise play tried out by the Admiral's Men, which Henslowe calls "*The Desgyses.*" Fleay thought that this play might have been a first draft of Chapman's *May Day*. Sir Sidney Lee recently remarked[3] that a "free French metrical version by Jean Godard of Ariosto's comedy (*I Suppositi*) was printed under the title of *Les Desguisez* in 1594," and added that Henslowe's lost piece "translates, there can be no doubt, the new French recension of *I Suppositi*." What evidence beyond the titles Sir Sidney has in support of his theory he does not state. One objection to the theory that Henslowe's *Disguises* was an English translation of a French metrical version of an Italian comedy is that *I Suppositi* was not a multi-disguise play, and consequently not the kind of disguise play which Henslowe was featuring in 1595. A study of the chronological table[4] which I have transcribed from Henslowe's

---

[3] *French Renaissance in England*, 420 n.

[4] *The Wiseman*, New, Dec. 2, 1594.

Wiseman, Dec. 6, 29; Jan. 16, 23, 1594–5; Feb. 4, 12, 19, 28; April, 25, 26; May 6, 15, 26; June 4, 11; Aug. 26; Sept. 9, 29.

Disguises, New, Oct. 2, 1595.

Wiseman, Oct. 6.

Disguises, Oct. 10, 16.

Wiseman, Oct. 19.

Diary suggests to me that, after the *Wiseman of West Chester* (*John a Kent*) had proved successful, Henslowe wanted to add another multi-disguise play to his repertoire, and tried the *Disguises*, which failed after six performances, but was followed by the *Blind Beggar*, which succeeded and was kept in repertoire with *John a Kent*.

But we have at least four English multi-disguise plays extant, and upon examination of them one makes the inevitable inference that these plays were written for the Admiral's Men primarily in order to exploit some clever actor who possessed remarkable ability as a mimic and impersonator.

The nature of the plots in these plays is nearly always the same. The main character is a rogue skilful in disguising, who keeps the action moving by shifting from one costume into another, the exchange of costume taking place almost instantaneously. The result is normally a shifting from one complication into another. Hence a multi-disguise play is really a chain of incidents.[5] At any rate this type of

Disguises, Oct. 27, 30.
Wiseman, Nov. 7 (?)
Disguises, Nov. 10.
Wiseman, Dec. 30; Jan. 17, 1595–6; Feb. 4.
Blind Beg., New, Feb. 12, 1595–6.
Beggar, Feb. 16, 19, 22, 26; April 15.
Wiseman, April 17.
Beggar, April 26.
Wiseman, April 30.
Beggar, May 3, 13, 18; June 3.
Wiseman, June 8.
Beggar, June 25; July 5.
Wiseman, July 7.
Beggar, Nov. 6, 12; Dec. 2, 10, 23; Jan. 15, 1597 (sic) 25; March 14; April 1.
Wiseman, July 8, 12, 18.

[5] We have said in the previous chapter that in a farcical play disguise is usually incidental or episodic. Observe that in multi-disguise

play departs farther than other types from any rigid scheme of rise and fall, tying and untying of action, such as critics have applied as the test of a well-constructed play.

The representation of many characters simultaneously by one actor probably developed from the device of shifting rapidly back and forth from the real character to the disguised character, a dramatic motive which we have already found in Plautus's *Miles Gloriosus*.[6] Similar rapid changing occurs in da Bibbiena's *Calandria* (1513), which we have discussed in chapter III.[7] In that play Lidio and his twin sister make many shifts. Lidio appears as himself in I, 2; as a woman in III, 24; as himself in V, 1; as a woman in V, 3, and finally as himself in V, 5. Santilla appears as Lidio in II, 1; as herself in III, 24, and as Lidio in IV, 3. This shifting, however, involves only one disguise of each character, and is therefore quite different from multi-disguise where a single actor represents four or more different characters. Somewhat more like the English plays is Cervantes's *Laberinto de Amor*[8] where a girl disguises successively as shepherd, student, peasant man, peasant girl, and princess. Yet this Spanish play, although presenting many disguises, does not have quick changes in the action. Multi-disguise perhaps appeared in the *commedia dell' arte*;[9] but as far as we can judge there was no direct influence on the English drama from any of the sources we have just mentioned. However, it is probable that English actors have borrowed

plays the multiplicity and continuity of these incidents make disguise the basic dramatic motive.

  [6] See Chapter III.
  [7] See page 45.
  [8] See Chapter III.
  [9] Creizenach (IV, 252) says that the motive was very common in the *commedia dell' arte*. I am not able to corroborate his statement after an examination of fifteen *scenarii* from the Scala collection. None of the fifteen plots contained multi-disguise.

from the stagecraft of the Italian actors in the *commedia dell'
arte*. Quick changes of aspect by means of wigs, false beards,
or false noses that could be slipped on or off in a twinkling
are provided for in the English plays, and this art was
doubtless developed in Italy. Possibly masks were used in
the multi-disguise plays but we have no evidence to support
such a theory. In this connection we are reminded of
Moliére's *Médicin Volant*, said to have been derived from the
improvised comedy of Italy.[10] In that play Sganarelle disguises himself as a doctor, and by a series of lightning changes
maintains his part as servant, as well as the fictitious part
of doctor.

Anthony Munday, the "best plotter," started the fashion
of multi-disguise plays in England[11] in *John a Kent and
John a Cumber*. Two noblemen, Griffin and Powess, are in
love with Sidanen and Marian. But these two ladies are
to be married off on the morrow to Pembroke and Morton.
The two lovers determine to outwit the fiancés, and appeal
to John a Kent for magical aid. John promises assistance
but makes the mental reservation that he will

> "Help, hinder, give, take back, turn, overturn,
> Deceive, bestow, breed pleasure, discontent,
> Yet comicly conclude, like John a Kent."

He produces a false beard and disguises as a hermit fortune-
teller. In this character he directs the two ladies to wash
in St. Winfrid's well. Next he undisguises, and sends the
two lovers to the same spot. He then resumes his disguise
and brings the two lovers and the ladies together at the well.
The happy party is soon safe in a castle.

[10] Matthews, *Molière*, 59.

[11] The *Marriage of Wit and Wisdom* looks like a multi-disguise play
but is not. See Chapter II, page 19. Fraud in Wilson's *Three Lords
and Three Ladies of London* (1585) makes four changes of character.
But the disguises are symbolized.

Meanwhile, Pembroke and Morton are frantically searching for their prospective brides. By accident John a Cumber comes wandering from Scotland and offers to help the fiancés by setting up his skill in magic against that of John a Kent. He disguises himself like John a Kent, and the next morning when the two lovers are taking the air outside the castle, Cumber-like-Kent lets in the fiancés disguised like "antiques." When they have thus gained an entrance Cumber-like-Kent enters the castle and bars the gate. Presently the real John a Kent comes along and the lovers realize that they have been victimized.

This brings us to the middle of act III and from that time onward the numerous surprising incidents and sudden shifts render it useless to attempt an intelligible summary of the plot. John a Kent is assisted by Shrimp, a dexterous boy who crawls in and out through keyholes, and whose other powers are much the same as those of Ariel.

John a Kent makes six changes during the play. He disguises first as a hermit, then undisguises, then is hermit again, then himself, then disguises as John a Cumber, and finally resumes his own shape. As a hermit he wears a beard and a gray friar's gown. As himself he wears green. There is no evidence concerning his other costumes.

Munday's play resembles the three which followed, not only in general structure but in details of action and scene. The scene where the magician, disguised as a hermit, tells fortunes is imitated in the openings of both the *Blind Beggar of Alexandria* and *Look About You*. The hermit disguise is evidently used in the *Blind Beggar of Bednal Green*, judging from Bess's various uses of the word "father," and the "Beggar's" frequent reference to his cell.[12]

[12] These hermit scenes may be indebted to a similar scene in act III of *George a Greene, The Pinner of Wakefield* (mentioned by Henslowe in 1593).

Munday's play seems very complicated and full of involved circumstances when compared with earlier disguise plays, but it pales into utter simplicity beside Chapman's *Blind Beggar of Alexandria*, the multi-disguise play which the Admiral's Men produced a little more than a year later.[13] In that play the "Beggar" leads a quadruple life which requires a constant shifting of costume as well as the preservation of four distinct personalities. The most farcical complication of all is his relations with a couple of sisters. Disguised as a blind hermit he predicts whom they will marry. He then marries both in the two different characters as he had foretold, and by simply reversing these characters he becomes the paramour of each woman. After a while when the women are about to become mothers, he announces the death of one fictitious husband and lets his brother report the death of the other. Those two disguises, are then discarded forever. Finally, disguised as the new king, he sympathizes with the ladies over the deaths of their husbands.

To attempt a continuous narration of the plot would only perplex the reader. Therefore we may simply note the actions of each character while the Beggar is in that rôle. The first character is Irus, the blind hermit. His costume in that part is distinctive, the hood and perhaps dark glasses easily concealing his identity. The second character is the "mad brain Count Hermes," who dresses in a velvet gown wears a velvet patch over his left eye, and carries a pistol. The Beggar's third self is Leon, the rich usurer, who is recognized by his great nose, the frequent object of jest in the play. And finally, as his fourth self he is Duke Cleanthes, who wears a sword, and, although an Egyptian nobleman, doubtless dresses in some Elizabethan court costume.

[13] When this play was printed in 1598 the disguise was advertised on the title page by the phrase "his variable humours in disguised shapes."

As "Irus" the Beggar tells Queen Ægiale how to find her lover, Duke Cleanthes; he prophesies to Elimine that she will marry "Count Hermes"; he prophesies to Samathis that she will marry "Leon," the rich usurer; he witnesses falsely in favor of "Leon," who extorts money from a debtor, and he tells Queen Ægiale how to kill her son and her husband.

As "Count Hermes" he marries Elimine, humiliating his rival, a Spanish braggart; he witnesses falsely in favor of "Leon"; he becomes the paramour of Samathis, and he slays Prince Doricles.

As "Leon" he marries Samathis; he falsifies a note and extorts a large sum from Antistines; he becomes the paramour of Elimine; he reports the death of "Count Hermes," and finally collects some outstanding bills.

As "Duke Cleanthes" he humiliates four kings; he meets the wives of "Count Hermes" and "Leon" and sympathizes over the deaths of their husbands. Evidently also he succeeds to the throne of Egypt and presumably marries Ægiale, the Queen.

After reading such a bewildering series of incidents one is tempted to suggest that the Blind Beggar and his tribe were burlesques of the disguises used in serious comedies. But there is nothing to show that these plays were in any sense burlesques. They are deliberate farces, but nothing more.

To act the part of the roguish Beggar in his fourfold capacity would certainly require a man of much versatility. And yet the test was not the severest possible, for the four characters in the *Blind Beggar of Alexandria* are all fictitious. And, of course, when a character is fictitious there is no imitation or impersonation required. But in *Look About You* the character called Skink impersonates, first, a real hermit whom he has slain; second, a stammering porter's son; third, the Earl of Gloucester; fourth, Prince John;

fifth, an alehouse drawer; sixth, the hermit again; seventh, a falconer; eighth, the hermit; and last he is discovered as Skink. Four of the persons imitated appear at various times during the action in their real characters. The play is further complicated by the fact that six persons besides Skink employ disguises. The necessity for ready impersonation of other characters made the rôle an exacting one. I think it must have been played by the actor who had already won his spurs in the two plays just described.

In this play our attention is centered on Skink, a court creature, who has murdered Rosamund and the hermit, and perhaps others, but who is in spite of all this a pleasant villain. A German scholar has said that Skink is not a descendant of the Vice, which may be true, but to the less critical observer Skink recalls a number of roguishly vicious predecessors.[14] In the play even the victims of his tricks refer to him as "This mad-mate Skink, this honest, merry knave." Instead of summarizing the plot we shall content ourselves with narrating the incidents in Skink's career during the play. The "old king's" party has been in search of the assassin Skink for two months, while he has been safe behind the hermit's gown, "beard and counterfeited hair." One day he goes to court in his own shape and is almost pardoned by his friend, the prince, but the pardon misses fire and again Skink must become a fugitive from justice. In striving to escape the criers he exchanges clothes with the stammering Red Cap. Skink, who now has to stammer his speeches, carries a message to Gloucester, his enemy, who is a prisoner in the Fleet. Gloucester forces the supposed Red Cap (Skink) to exchange costumes with him. Gloucester now is free, but has to stammer. Skink plays the part of the Earl, but is unfortunately in prison. Prince John comes to the Fleet and the "Earl of Gloucester" (Skink)

[14] Eckhardt, 191.

plays with him at bowls, and during the game succeeds in getting Prince John's cloak, sword and hat. In this disguise Skink regains his freedom. In the garb of Prince John he meets Sir Richard Fauconbridge and borrows a gold chain from him! Sir Richard goes out, and the next minute Gloucester, now disguised as Sir Richard, comes in. Skink, as Prince John, now fears that he is under suspicion, and returns the chain to "Sir Richard" (as he supposes, but really Gloucester). This puzzles Gloucester, who thinks he is talking with Prince John. The real Prince John enters presently, but not before Skink has escaped.

In the evening we find Skink in a tavern still disguised as Prince John. He hears the voices of his pursuers below, and in a twinkling seizes the drawer's apron, smears his own face with blood, and pretends to the pursuers that Prince John has struck him. They know that the "Prince John" must be Skink, and therefore ask the supposed drawer where the scoundrel went. He directs them into an inner room and escapes into the darkness outside.

By this time matters have come to such a pass in the play that four characters, Prince John, Prince Richard, Sir Richard Fauconbridge, and Lady Fauconbridge, resolve separately to repair to Blackheath in order to get help from the soothsayer and holy hermit. This hermit, of course, is Skink, who has a merry time giving his questioners most amazing information, especially about the escapades of Skink. The listeners appear somewhat doubtful and the hermit replies in a veiled allusion:

> "Himself if he deliver not so much, before you sleep,
> Root me from out the borders of this realm."

Finally the hermit tells Prince John and Sir Richard that Skink is going to make a robbery at a certain corner. They start for the place. Immediately Skink emerges from the

cell disguised as a falconer, with a patch on his face and
carrying a falconer's lure. By talking loudly as he goes
out he gives the impression that he is taking leave of the
hermit within. Skink, now disguised as a falconer, promptly
goes out and robs Prince John and Prince Richard as he had
said he would. He also reveals himself and laughs at the
discomfiture of his victims. They immediately suspect the
identity of the hermit. And meanwhile the fates are setting
a trap for Skink. Gloucester has come to the hermit's
cell, and, finding the temporarily discarded garments of the
holy man, has decided to play the hermit himself. Hence,
when Prince John and Sir Richard go back to the cell, they
find the hermit quietly counting his beads, and consequently
decide that their suspicions were wrong. That was a bit
of good luck for Skink, but the sly old fox knows that it is
only a temporary salvation. As a last resort he gets his
other hermit suit and tries to face it out against Gloucester.
Each hermit now declares the other a counterfeit and himself real. The result is that both fugitives are exposed and
captured. After a spectacular court scene both are pardoned.

The device which forces the discovery of disguise is, as
we have said in Chapter II,[15] a good bit of technic. A common method of forcing revelation was the simultaneous
appearance of the real character and the impersonator.
But this play is original, I believe, in presenting two impersonators in identical disguises, each person insisting that
the other is an impostor.

This account by no means exhausts the disguises in *Look
About You*, but we shall not strain the reader's patience by
further synopsis. We have gone thus far because we felt it
necessary to show that this play was the acme of multi-
disguise. One might almost say it is disguise gone mad.
I do not know the origin of the plot, but it sounds like folk-

[15] See page 11.

lore.[16]   The formula is simple — a fugitive running down the road and forcibly exchanging costumes with every one he meets, to be mistaken for each in turn.   Whoever the author of *Look About You* was, it is evident that he was writing for some star of the Admiral's Men, and that he was trying to outdo the intricacy of the two older plays in the repertoire of the company.

The fourth multi-disguise play is the *Blind Beggar of Bednal Green*, which was written before May 1600 (Henslowe) by Chettle and Day.   It seems to me a safe guess that the authors wrote this play in order to cater to the same taste which had already approved of multi-disguise plays.   A hint or two and doubtless the title were derived from a ballad entitled the *Beggar's Daughter of Bednal Green*.[17]

Without narrating the plot we shall indicate the character and number of the hero's changes.   Lord Mumford, exiled as the result of a conspiracy, decides to remain in England in disguise.   First, he spies on his enemies as an old lame soldier; second, he is the "blind beggar" who lives on Bednal Green; third, he enters "like a serving man"; fourth, he is the "beggar" again; fifth, the "servingman"; sixth, the "beggar"; seventh, he appears as the "serving man," and finally he undisguises.   Some of the shifts back and forth from "serving man" to "beggar" are very rapid and remind us strongly of the plays previously considered.   But in general this plot does not possess the rapid action which was necessary for a good multi-disguise play.

---

[16] See, for example, the *Ballad of Gude Wallace* (Child, III, 273). It relates how Wallace, besieged by enemies, escapes from his mistress in the disguise of a woman.   Presently Wallace doffs the female apparel and exchanges clothes with a beggar whom he has met on the road.

[17] Percy, II.

Before dismissing the *Blind Beggar of Bednal Green* let us note the comic irony in the speeches of Bess to the "beggar," her father in disguise. These quotations are especially interesting because they belong to the very rare use of veiled allusions in the multi-disguise plays. Bess sees her father dressed as an old soldier but does not recognize him. She hands him a coin and says:

. . . . . . "Good Father take it;

. . . .

My Father was a Souldier, maym'd like thee, —
Thou in thy limbs, he by vil'd infamy."

Later Bess becomes the ward of the "blind beggar." The first sound of his voice recalls her father, but she does not recognize the "beggar." She says to him:

"I call'd thee father, ...
. . . . were my father here
Hee'd tell thee that his Daughter held him dear;
But in his absence, Father, thou art he."

In another speech she is close to the actual fact when she says:

"Within thy looks I see the presence of my reverend Father."

About 1600 the multi-disguise fashion seems to have been played out after six years of popularity. At least we do not know that any more such plays were written after that date. Perhaps the novelty had worn off. Perhaps the great impersonator had died. Or perhaps the four plays we have here studied held their place on the boards and sufficiently met the demand of the day. But whether they were kept in repertoire or not they exerted some literary influence. Their excessive disguises seem to have affected a dozen or more plays between 1598 and 1616.

Jonson probably got a hint for the tricky Brainworm in *Every Man in His Humour*. Brainworm disguises first as an old soldier (somewhat like Momford) and by a cock-and-bull story of wars and destitution succeeds in selling a worthless old rapier. Then, in the character of the soldier, he takes service with his own master. Next he indulges in a drinking match with Justice Clement's man in which he exchanges costumes with that victim. And in this second disguise he delivers a counterfeit message which helps the lovers in the play. Brainworm soon meets Matthew and Bobadil who, having a grudge against Downright, bribe the supposed Justice's man to secure a warrant for Downright's arrest. Brainworm disguises himself as a City Sergeant and makes the arrest. Finally, when the tricks are exposed, Justice Clement drinks sack to the rogue and pardons him for the "wit of the offence." [18]

In the structure of this play the main comedy is dependent on the "humours" of the persons, while the movement from one situation to another is to a great extent brought about by the disguises and intriguing of Brainworm.[19]

Two somewhat similar multi-disguises appear in later plays. In Sharpham's *Fleire* (entered in 1606) Antifront disguises as the "Fleire" in order to spy upon and protect his wayward daughters. Second, he disguises as an apothecary in order to defeat their plot when they send for poison to murder their scornful lovers. Third, when the girls and their agents are brought to trial he disguises as a doctor of laws in order to conduct the trial to a happy ending.

In Middleton's *Family of Love* (licensed in 1607) Gerardine disguises (IV, 2) as a porter and delivers a false letter which

---

[18] Compare the four disguises assumed by Crasy in Brome's *City Wit*. Also note the similarity of the names Brainworm and Crasy.

[19] Jonson planned multi-disguise in his *Sad Shepherd*, where Maudlin says that she will appear in "mony shapes today" (II, 1). In the fragment the witch appears first as Marian, then as herself, and next as Marian again.

makes it appear that Dr. Glister is father to a bastard. Next Gerardine disguises as an "apparitor" and hears the charges against Dr. Glister. Third, Gerardine disguises as a doctor of laws and pronounces Dr. Glister guilty, but promises to withhold the penalty on condition that he may marry Dr. Glister's daughter Maria. When Dr. Glister subscribes to this the roguish lover undisguises.

Sometimes the main purpose of the rogue was to get money, and the clever dodges adopted make us feel with Justice Clement that the disguised rogue ought to be pardoned for the wit of the offense. In Marston's *Dutch Courtesan* (printed in 1605) Cockledemoy, described as a "knavishly witty City Companion," one day disguises as a barber and shaves Mulligrub, a rich vintner. During the bustling tonsorial business the "barber" manages to pick the pockets of his victim. Next he assumes some other disguise and cozens Mrs. Mulligrub out of a gilded cup and a large succulent salmon. When the outraged Mulligrub gets on Cockledemoy's trail the latter drops his cloak, which Mulligrub picks up; he is forthwith arrested and put in the stocks for theft. Cockledemoy now assumes his third disguise, that of a bellman, and discovering Mulligrub in the stocks, confides with him, receives his purse for safe keeping, and promises to inform the constables of his good reputation. When the constables arrive the "bellman" makes such accusations of Mulligrub that the poor fellow is carried off to jail. Cockledemoy's fourth disguise is that of a sergeant; in this character he picks the purse of a gentleman on trial. At the end of the play the rogue promises to return the stolen goods and is pardoned.[20]

---

[20] Koeppel (29) points out that the tricks of Cockledemoy owe something to the 66th novel in tome I of Painter's *Palace of Pleasure*. But I observe that that novel, however, contains no disguise. There is also no disguise in the 24th novel of tome II, which is cited as analogous to other parts of this play.

Another play in which a persistent campaign of disguise and cozenage is waged is Middleton's *Mad World, My Masters* (1606), where Follywit victimizes his grandfather. First, disguised as "Lord Owemuch," he gets the secrets of his grandfather's will; then, masked as a robber, he and his companions rob the old man, telling him as a precaution that they have already robbed and bound "Lord Owemuch." Third, Follywit, disguised as a courtesan, gets access to the old man's chamber and carries off a box of jewels. Finally, at a feast Follywit disguises as a player and, on the pretext of needing "properties" for the comedy, gets his grandfather's chain, jewel, and watch. At the end of the play the grandfather, who had always prized his grandson's wit, forgives him.

Cozenage on a professional scale is carried on in Beaumont and Fletcher's *Beggars' Bush* (1622), where the "knavish beggars" Higgins and Prigg disguise four times each. In Middleton's *Michaelmas Term* (1604) Shortyard and False-light assist their master Quasimodo in an extensive plan for cheating Easy out of his estate. Each of the two roguish servants disguises three times as various fictitious persons, who lead Easy deeper and deeper into the toils until he is forced to sign away his lands.

Multi-disguise involving three or four changes of costume and employed for other purposes than roguery are found in the *Two Maids of Moreclacke, Westward Ho, Cupid's Whirligig, Woman is a Weathercock*, and *Faithful Friends*, all appearing before 1616; but we shall not take the time to discuss these plays.[21] Shakespeare himself employed multi-disguise on a small scale in *King Lear*. Edgar disguises first as

---

[21] In Fletcher's *Pilgrim* (1621), based on Lope de Vega's *Peregrino en su Patria*, Alinda disguises as a boy, "she-fool," old woman, and shepherdess. In Massinger and Fletcher's *Very Woman* (1634) Paulo uses three different disguises within the limits of one scene (IV, 2).

a mad peasant (IV, 1, 6), when he leads Gloucester to the cliff. Then by simply changing his voice after the blind Gloucester supposes he has fallen, Edgar produces the effect of another disguise. In act V, scene 3 his identity is concealed by appearing in complete armor.

This completes the group of plays selected for the study of the rogue in multi-disguise. In harmony with the general theory that plays are rigidly conditioned by the physical demands and opportunities of the stage for which they are written, we have suggested in this chapter that the curious multi-disguise plays which the Admiral's Men performed within a period of six years or less may have been written in order to exploit the unusual abilities of one of their actors. Incidentally we have seen that, the vogue of multi-disguise plays once having been established, these plays exerted a traceable influence on certain other plays which followed.

Multi-disguise is seen occasionally on the modern French stage; see, for example, *Tricoche et Cacolet* by Meilhac and Halévy, acted 1871. In this play Tricoche disguises himself in seven characters and Cacolet disguises himself in nine characters.

CHAPTER VII

THE SPY IN DISGUISE

I . . . . am resolu'd therefore, to spare
spy-money hereafter, and make mine own discoueries.
                                                    — *Bartholomew Fair*

I

In war a very useful and thrilling disguise is that which enables a person to enter the enemy's camp and procure information not otherwise obtainable. During peace suspicion may sometimes make it necessary to spy on one who is professedly in faithful relations. In any case the situation is fascinating, for success depends entirely on the histrionic ability of the spy. The theatrical potentiality of the spy situation obviously recommends it to the dramatist. It is further recommended by its unique value in plot construction. We have already alluded to the distinctive structure of plays like *Measure for Measure* (Chapter II, page 7). In such a play the spy is somewhat like the man who sits behind the scenes and pulls the strings of a marionette show. But he differs from the marionette man by actually appearing on the open scene as a part of the show. The spy starts the action because of his disguise, he watches the action or participates in it protected by disguise, and he terminates the action by finally revealing his disguise.

The history of this figure in drama does not seem to go back earlier than Ruzzante's *Moschetta* (1551), already described in Chapter III.[1] Subsequent instances in Italian

[1] See page 49. See Child (III, 109), for various allusions to spy stories dating back to the twelfth century. Boccaccio and other non-

Renaissance drama are rather scattered and it is evident
that the spy situation had not become a traditional motive
in any dramatic literature from which English playwrights
drew their inspiration. But in England three allied situations — the spying husband, the spying father, and the
spying duke — soon became stock material, and the playwrights who used those motives did not hesitate to borrow
freely, each from his predecessor or contemporary.

The close kinship of the English spy plays is rather remarkable. We find in the father-spy and the duke-spy
plays, not only the frequent repetition of a certain dramatic
figure, but also interesting detailed parallelisms of plot. A
tracing out of these resemblances will emphasize the theory
— or perhaps it should be called truism — that a favorable
reception of any given disguise situation encouraged imitation, more or less close, in other plays coming shortly
after.

The husband spying in disguise, not uncommon in medieval
French and Italian tales, appears first in English drama in
Peele's *Edward I*, about 1590. Edward, upon learning that
Queen Eleanor has ordered two confessors from France,
suggests that he and his brother Edmund disguise themselves
as friars and trick the queen out of her secrets. Edmund
foresees the consequences and tries in vain to dissuade the
king. At the confession the queen states that she had
granted her favors to Edmund the night before the royal
marriage, whereupon "the king beholdeth his brother woe-
fully." She also says that her daughter Joan was begotten
by a friar. Then, at peace with her conscience, she dies,
never suspecting the identity of her confessors. The king
turns on Edmund, who declares that the queen "grew luna-
tic, Discovering errors never dreamed upon," but Edward

dramatic writers will be referred to in this chapter for analogies to the
English plays discussed.

curses him into exile. Joan dies from the shock of hearing that she is a "friar's base-born brat."[2]

The whole scene is a very effective representation of the triangular meeting of wife, husband, and paramour, where the wife unconsciously pulls down the tragic fate over all three. A number of early French and Italian tales which contain analogues to the husband confessor motive are mentioned by Dunlop (II, 113) and by Child (III, 258). All of these early tales present an ingenious turn by letting the wife declare that she had discovered her husband's disguise, and consequently framed her expression in equivocal language, meaning husband when she seemed to mean paramour. Peele elaborates the situation by presenting two friars — one the husband, the other, the paramour. This is an advantage for theatrical effectiveness.

From the stage manager's point of view this scene furnished a strong climax to the general stage business of *Edward I;* yet the situation is merely a dramatic episode, for it neither initiates nor resolves any main complication. Considered as an episode, however, it is skilfully done, with good action and tragic consequence.

Lyly used the husband spy momentarily in the *Woman in the Moon* (before 1595). But the scene (IV, 1) is mere horse-play. Stesias learns that his wife is wanton with three

---

[2] The same motive of the two friars appears in the seven ballads published by Child in vols. III and IV under the general title "156. Queen Eleanor's Confession." Child does not date these ballads very definitely. Thieme and Kroneberg in their respective dissertations on *Edward I* believe, but do not prove, that the material of the ballads antedates the play.

Later analogues in English drama are found in Davenport's *City Night Cap* (1624), where Lodovico, disguised as a friar, confesses his wife, who is wanton; and in Massinger's *Emperor of the East* (1631), where the husband in friar costume finds his wife faithful.

See also a husband confessor in the *Decameron, VII, 5.*

of his fellow shepherds; so he dresses in her apparel and goes to the rendezvous, where Melos, Learchus, aud Iphicles separately fall into the trap and are soundly cudgelled for their intentions.[3] The dialog in this scene covers only a page and a half; but perhaps, dialog is negligible in a cudgelling affair.

When the spy disguise is used basically, instead of incidentally as in Peele and Lyly, we find it almost conventional for the chief intrigant to declare, at the opening of the action, that he is going to travel away from home. However, after farewells have been said, the audience is informed that the person really intends to stay and spy in disguise. He then becomes, as we have suggested, the marionette man of the play. Straparola has a novel (*I, 5*) built somewhat on this principle. The plot concerns Dimitrio who, having been informed that his wife is unfaithful to him, pretends to go on board ship, but really goes to the house of a friend. He now disguises himself as a beggar and goes into his own house where he witnesses his wife's infidelity with a priest. He goes out, undisguises, and pretends to have just returned. This device, the pretended departure but actual remaining in disguise, was first used in English drama about 1600. It appears in the *Blind Beggar of Bednal Green* (before 1600), in the *Malcontent* (1601), and in the Cambridge Latin comedy *Zelotypus* (about 1600–03 [4]); it appears also in *Measure for Measure*, *Westward Ho*, the *Widow's Tears*, and the *Revenger's Tragedy*[5] between 1603 and 1606.

---

[3] A spy motive is found in *Jack Drum's Entertainment*, V (1600), where Brabant, Jr., learns of a meeting between his sweetheart and his friend Planet. He possesses himself of Planet's clothes and impersonates him only to learn in a brief scene that his lady is true.

An Italian play similar to the *Woman in the Moon* has been referred to in Chapter V, page 106.

[4] Churchill and Keller, 313.

[5] The *Revenger's Tragedy*, although not a spy play, resembles the type in the fact that the disguised intrigant engineers the fundamental

In *Zelotypus* Cassander, suspicious of his wife, announces his departure for Brindisi. In reality he remains at home and becomes the servant and pander of Ascanius and Valerius, two young men who are wooing his wife. Then, through a series of scattered incidents, he discovers that his wife is faithful. From this Latin play or its unknown source Marston may have borrowed the situation in the *Malcontent* (V, 2) where the disguised "Malevole" acts as pander to his own wife only to find her faithful.

The pretended departure but actual remaining in disguise was elaborated in *Westward Ho*, by Webster and Dekker, registered in 1605, but probably acted in 1604.[6] Justiniano, who believes he is a cuckold, tells his wife that he is going away. He really remains and disguises as a schoolmaster. In this professional capacity he pretends service to a couple of citizens' wives, but he really becomes their pander. In act IV, scene 2, comes a scene so frankly theatrical that it amounts to claptrap. Justiniano, masked and disguised like his own wife, pretends to keep an assignation with Earl. When Justiniano unmasks, Earl thinks he has to do with some old hag. Justiniano insists that he is Mistress Justiniano, but fails to get incriminating evidence against his wife. Finally he reveals himself and declares that he has killed his wife because of her unchastity. A curtain is drawn and the wife's body is discovered to prove the statement. But by this time Justiniano has been convinced of his wife's fidelity. She springs up from her feigned death, the husband commends her part in the test, and there is a happy reunion. The motiving and action in this scene will not bear close scrutiny, but the stage business was

action. One of Lope de Vega's plays, *El Ausente en el Lugar* (1617), uses the motive and indicates by its title the supposed absence but actual remaining.

[6] Hunt, 101.

doubtless vital to the gaping groundlings, who preferred the sensational to the subtle.

In the three plays just described, the wives, spied upon by their pandering husbands, were found faithful. But there are perhaps worse things than unfaithfulness, as may be seen by the skilful turn in the plot of Middleton's *Michaelmas Term* (1604).

Quomodo, who has cozened gulls through his disguises of his clever servants, decides (IV, 1) to test his wife by means of false report of death and spying in disguise.[7]   He spreads the news of his death, and then attends his own funeral disguised as a beadle (IV, 4).   The conduct of his wife proving quite satisfactory, he decides to reveal himself in a jest.   In signing a receipt for all claims due him in that house the "beadle" writes his real name, Quomodo, not realizing until too late that he has signed away all his right (V, 1).   Now comes his punishment.   The retributory wife insists on the letter of the document, and marries Easy, the former victim of her husband's gulling.   And Quomodo finds no redress in court.

It has been suggested that Middleton received his inspiration for this situation from *Volpone* (Christ, *Quellen*, 108), but no evidence has been offered to show that *Volpone* preceded *Michaelmas Term*.   Fleay, on the other hand, presents fair evidence that *Michaelmas Term* was acted in 1604, and *Volpone* in 1605 (Fleay, *Biog. Chron.*, II, 91; I, 372). But there is no need of seeking a source in *Volpone*.   The spy scene in question might have been suggested by a number of earlier spy plays.   As for the device of a disguised person reporting his own death, that too, was already old when *Michaelmas Term* was played.   The dramatic prototype of such false report is found in the *Electra* of Sophocles, where

---

[7] The situation reminds us somewhat of Steele's *Funeral, or Grief à la Mode*. However, in Steele's play the husband is not in disguise.

Orestes, unrecognized by his sister, reports his own death and presents her with an urn alleged to contain his ashes. In English drama similar false reports of death had been made by disguised persons in the *Blind Beggar of Alexandria* (1596), in *Antonio and Mellida* (1599), in the *Malcontent* (1601), in the *Two Maids of Moreclacke* (1603), and in *London Prodigal* (1603–05).[8] Thus we see that neither Middleton nor Jonson had to go far afield for this spy situation.

The trial of a suspected wife is worked out elaborately in Chapman's *Widow's Tears* (1605). This play is an interesting illustration of dramatic economy, as we have remarked in Chapter II.[9] Chapman cleverly reshaped an old story by combining with it the disguised spy. It will be noted that the alteration produced sensational stage business and made the action theatrical. Chapman's remodelling of his material in the coffin and tomb scene is an evidence that he considered disguise a valuable motive. The raw material for this scene is found in the *Satyricon* of Petronius Arbiter. An Ephesian matron lingers in a tomb weeping over the coffin of her dead husband. (In Petronius the husband really is dead.) A soldier makes love to the widow, whose maid eloquently pleads the soldier's cause. The widow, finally yielding, establishes a liaison with him, using the tomb as a meeting place. Meanwhile, a crucified body has disappeared. The soldier is in danger of prosecution, but the widow rescues him by nailing the corpse of her husband to the vacant cross. So runs the tale in Petronius.

[8] In the Middle English poem *King Horn* there is a similar false report of death. Horn returns to his betrothed in the disguise of a palmer, telling her that Horn is dead but had sent her the ring. When the grief-stricken lady threatens to stab herself the "palmer" rubs the black off his face and reveals himself. There is a similar situation in the *Decameron*, X, 9.

[9] See page 15.

Chapman borrowed all this gruesome material substantially and yet made an entirely new story by employing disguise in order to make the bewept but soon forgotten husband identical with the soldier lover. The dramatic economy and theatrical gain in this alteration is obvious. The wife thinks she is dealing with a lover; the audience knows she is being tested by her own husband; and the hero must exercise his skill in acting in order to maintain this dual rôle.[10] Chapman's plot is briefly as follows: Lysander, suspicious of his wife, Cynthia, tells her he is going away for a month. His brother Tharsalio, according to previous arrangement, reports Lysander dead, and his coffin is placed in the tomb. Here Cynthia sheds copious tears, a fact which is reported to the husband who is in hiding twenty miles away. Lysander now disguises as a soldier and comes to the tomb to woo the languishing Cynthia. She resists bravely for some time, but finally rewards the passionate "soldier" with kisses. While the "soldier" was busy making love, a crucified body was stolen from the tomb. Cynthia suggests putting the body of her late husband in place of it. The "soldier" now "confesses" that he had murdered Lysander. But Cynthia, out of a loving heart, forgives him this achievement! Lysander-"soldier" rages at his wife's shocking fickleness. Meanwhile the brother Tharsalio finds out that Lysander and the "soldier" are identical. Tharsalio, because he had not been confided this part of the plot, peevishly tells Cynthia who the "soldier" is. Lysander-"soldier" declares that he will brain Cynthia if she really attempts to unhearse her "dead husband's body." The unhearsing is about to be accomplished with a crowbar, when Cynthia declares that she had penetrated the "soldier" dis-

[10] The plot of Sir William Berkeley's *Lost Lady* (pr. 1639) might be considered an inverted parallel of the *Widow's Tears*. See Schelling, II, 367.

guise, that she had recognized her husband from the beginning, and had decided to give him what he was looking for. She departs in a huff, but the end of the play brings a reconciliation.

Chapman in writing this play altered the old plot by adding two motives which, as we have just seen, were popular in England during the few years preceding this play. The two additions we mean are the pretended departure but actual remaining in disguise, and the disguised person's report of his own death. An older motive, also discussed above, is the wife's fib that she was aware of her husband's disguise and had played on his jealousy.

Another example of the disguised spy added to a borrowed situation is seen in Markham and Machin's *Dumb Knight* (1607). One of the scenes (IV, 1) of this play is dependent for its theatrical value on the disguise of the King of Cyprus, who spies on his wife during revels at court. Cyprus has been told by Epire that the queen is unfaithful with Philocles. Consequently during the king's spying on the dances and on a card game his jealousy is whetted by a misinterpretation of all actions of the dance and the terms used in the game. He finally orders the arrest of Philocles. But in a later scene Epire is forced to confess that he has borne false witness against the queen. Good opportunities for acting are given by the asides between Cyprus and Epire, which the audience, being aware of Epire's plot, can appreciate fully. The misinterpreted card game is borrowed from act III, scene 2 of *A Woman Killed with Kindness*. In Heywood's play, however, the husband is not in disguise and is a participant in the game. The authors of the *Dumb Knight*, like so many contemporary playwrights, had enriched an old scene by adding disguise to it.

The re-shaping of an old plot by adding disguise happened again and again. Cervantes's *Curioso Impertinente*, a story told in *Don Quixote* (Part I, Chaps. 33, 34, 35), furnished the plot for Beaumont and Fletcher's *Coxcomb*, probably written about 1609 (Thorndike, *Infl.*, 68). The spying on the wife is not very sincere or serious, but serves to emphasize Antonio's character as a coxcomb. The disguise is introduced by Beaumont and Fletcher largely for theatrical effect, as may be seen by a summary of the plot. The Irish brogue and horse-play of act II, scene 3, and the sensational discovery, as well as the ludicrous attitude of the judge in the last scene, were certain guarantees of applause. Antonio, desirous of proving his wife's fidelity, urges his friend Mercury to tempt her. Antonio assists Mercury by disguising himself as an Irish footman. The wife penetrates Antonio's disguise but keeps the secret, and orders him soundly beaten by the servants (II, 3). Later, disguised as a postman, he urges her to be the best possible friend of Mercury. She again recognizes Antonio but says nothing. Finally she yields to Mercury. In the last scene Mercury and Antonio's wife are being tried on the charge of having murdered Antonio, when the "postman" reveals himself as Antonio. The judge remarks that "It was not honestly done of him to discover himself before the parties accused were executed!"

It is very fitting that, after so much spying on one side of the family, the wife should turn around and spy on her husband. The spying wife[11] had appeared in 1603, in the *London Prodigal* (acts IV and V). A more basic use is in Robert Daborne's *Poor Man's Comfort* (1613). Lucius, a nobleman, flees to Arcadia and there, calling himself Lisander, marries Urania, a shepherdess. But when he receives news of his restored favor at court, he deserts his wife. Urania in disguise goes to town, and, taking service

---

[11] See the *Alcestis* of Euripides for a spying wife, who, however, is not in disguise.

with Mistress Gulman, a bawd, meets her husband Lucius, who is a caller on the courtesan Flavia (II, 3). This gives an effective little scene, in places reminiscent of Shakespeare.[12] Flavia asks "Castadora" (Urania) to sing.

> "*Luc.* Have you a good voice Castadora?
>
> *Vra.* (*Disguised*) A sad voice Sir.
>
> *Flav.* Ile ha' you sing a merry song, I am a maid and I cannot mend it.
>
> *Vra.* I have no variety, I can sing but one song.
>
> *Luc.* Let's have that, What's the subject?
>
> *Vra.* Tis of a haplesse shepheardesse forsaken by her false lover.
>
> *Luc.* Tis too sad, I do not like it.
>
> *Vra.* I would you did not, I might sing merrily then.
>
> *Surd.* (*Servant of Lucius*) This wench has been with a Conjuror I hold my life. She knows all my Lords Knavery."

When the king hears of the desertion he gives Lucius four days in which to find Urania. Meanwhile the unfaithful husband is in love with the strumpet Flavia, but "Castadora" (Urania) declares (IV) that she will cure her husband of this by showing that Flavia is "base and mercenary." In act V, 1, after Urania sees that Lucius is repentant, she reveals herself. The three scenes in which husband, courtesan, and wife-in-disguise appear together are full of appealing action. This triangle of characters reminds us of the situation in Peele's *Edward I*, where queen, paramour, and husband-spy meet.

The last use of the husband-spy before 1616 was in *Faithful Friends*, attributed to Beaumont and Fletcher, and probably written about 1614. Tullius, a Roman general, receives word that his wife is being solicited by the king. Tullius

[12] See *Two Gentlemen* (IV, 2) where Julia-page puns on musical terms while her lover serenades her rival. Another reminiscence of that scene is Lucius's remark that Urania is dead (V, 1), just as Urania enters. Compare also the *London Prodigal*. See below, page 151.

returns and while attending a masque disguised as a fury he hears the king invite the wife to lodge at court during the night (IV, 3). In some disguise Tullius enters his wife's lodging and hides behind the arras, where he becomes the witness of the king's treachery and his wife's faithfulness (IV, 4). When Tullius suddenly reveals himself the king declares that he had no evil intentions, but was merely protecting and testing the young wife.[13]

In summing up these husband-spy plays we must admit that none are models of dramatic construction. However, the ingrafting of the disguise resulted in considerable theatrical value. The tragic climax in *Edward I*, the cudgelling in the *Woman in the Moon*, the surprising revelations in *Zelotypus*, the farcical impersonations in *Westward Ho*, the funeral in *Michaelmas Term*, the coffin scene in *Widow's Tears*, the card game in the *Dumb Knight*, the drubbing scene and the final discovery in the *Coxcomb*, the involved dialog in the *Poor Man's Comfort*, the amorous soliciting in *Faithful Friends* — all these depend on the fact of disguise for their theatrical effectiveness. It was this theatricality which favored the conventionalizing of the disguised spy situations. Their popularity is attested to, not only by the plays just mentioned, but also by the numerous fatherspies and political spies who were stealthily treading the rushes during this decade and a half.

---

[13] The husband spying in disguise was not uncommon in plays after 1616. For example, in William Rowley's *Match at Midnight* (1623) the "Widow's" husband spreads the report of his death and returns in disguise, serves his wife incognito, and finds her faithful. In Ford's *'Tis Pity She's a Whore* (1627) the husband spreads the report of his death, returns disguised as a physician, and tries to avenge himself on her lover. In Shirley's *Hyde Park* (1632) the husband, supposed dead, returns in disguise and spies on his wife.

II

The situation of the father spying in disguise, which sprang into popularity about the middle of the decade 1600–1610,[14] seems to have been first used in England in the *London Prodigal*, about 1603.[15] The most commonly imitated feature of this plot is the device of a half-indulgent father, with a turn for roguery himself, spying on a spendthrift son, while serving in disguise as his menial.

Perhaps it is well to relate the main events of the *London Prodigal*, especially since the plot was paralleled rather closely in *II Honest Whore*, which we shall presently compare with 'the *London Prodigal*. Flowerdale, Sr., who is supposedly away in Venice, returns in the disguise of a sailor calling himself "Kester," and reports his own death to his son Matthew, to whom he also presents his own will, a facetious document which does not provide for the son. "Kester" now becomes the faithful servant of Matthew and generously offers to assist him financially with twenty pounds. At a tavern Matthew grandiloquently courts Luce, while "Kester" pays the bill. The match with Luce is opposed by her father, but he is won over by discovering that Matthew has made a will in favor of Luce. This will, by the way, is false, and the drawing of it was instigated by "Kester." Matthew confides to "Kester" that he does not love Luce, but

[14] Some incidental spying by a father in disguise appears earlier in a loosely constructed play, the *Rare Triumphs of Love and Fortune* (1582), but the father is not deliberately a spy. There is a slight but pretty and paradoxical situation in the *Downfall of Robert, Earl of Huntington* (1598), where Fitzwater spies on his daughter Marian and Robin Hood by pretending that he is a blind old man. He says:

"I'll close mine eyes as if I wanted sight,
That I may see the end of their delight."

[15] Fleay, *Shakespeare*, 300. The *London Prodigal* was printed in 1603.

will marry her for her money. The disguised father is now dis-
gusted with his son and orders the Uncle to arrest him at the
first opportunity. On the wedding day Matthew is arrested.
"Kester" testifies that the will is false, and the bridegroom
is denounced by all except Luce, his wife, who asserts her
faith in him. But Matthew advises her to turn prostitute,
and proceeds to curse his father before "Kester." "Kester"
disguises Luce as a "Dutch Frow" and makes it possible for
her to spy on her husband Matthew. One day the prodigal,
who has borrowed money on the assertion that his wife is sick,
meets the "Dutch Frow" and tells her that his wife is dead.
The "Dutch Frow" gives him money. Matthew, on pretence of love for this supposed new acquaintance, tries to induce her to steal plate for him. Presently he is about to
be arrested on the charge of killing his wife. The "Dutch
Frow" stands by him and, when threatened with arrest, undisguises, revealing her identity as Luce. This devotion so
impresses Matthew that he turns over a new leaf. "Kester"
reveals himself as the father, and fortune smiles.

In this play we see how the prodigal son story, already
long popular on the stage, was improved theatrically by the
addition of the disguise motive. The art lay in the combination of old material. By 1603 a spy in disguise was no
longer a novelty. Flowerdale's report of his own death is, as
we have seen above, an old device. Matthew's statement to
his disguised wife that she is dead reminds us of Proteus's
remark in the *Two Gentlemen*, when he declares to Silvia that
his old sweetheart Julia is dead, a remark overheard by the
disguised Julia (IV, 2; IV, 4). The spying wife, making
her English debut here, is a natural variation of the spying
husband.[16]

The *London Prodigal* is a strikingly close parallel of *II
Honest Whore*, which was presented in 1630, but probably

[16] See above, page 148.

acted as early as 1604.[17] Since this resemblance has apparently not hitherto been noticed, let us describe it in detail. The motives common to both plays are: 1. A father attends his child disguised as "serving man." 2. Flowerdale poses as a sailor, while Friscobaldo says that he "has sailed about the world." 3. The "serving man" talks about the father to the child. 4. The "serving man" assists financially to the extent of 20 pounds. 5. The "serving man" roguishly leads the child into worse complications. 6. The "serving man" secretly assists the child. 7. The father, by means of his disguise, learns the real character of the child. 8. In the dénouement the "serving man" reveals his identity as the father. The similarity of the two plots is further emphasized if we compare the husbands in the plays. We note first their identity of name, Matthew and Matheo. These two men are of the same stripe. Each one is a dissolute prodigal; each begs his wife to commercialize her sex; and each is arrested only to be devotedly defended by his wife.

It is perhaps somewhat superfluous to argue that these resemblances taken together constitute a close parallel, and it seems to me a necessary inference that Dekker (or Middleton) [18] had the disguise plot of the *London Prodigal* in mind when contriving the plot of the *II Honest Whore*. This inference assumes that Fleay is correct in his chronology of the two plays. Perhaps there is presumptive evidence in support of Fleay in the obvious fact that the *II Honest Whore* has better technic than the *London Prodigal*, the presumption being that the more effective of the two parallel plots is the copy. The *II Honest Whore* employs the disguise to the greater theatrical advantage; there is much more veiled allusion in the dialog between father and child; and the

---

[17] Fleay, *Biog. Chron.*, I, 132.

[18] Neither Miss Hunt (*Dekker*) nor Bullen (*Works of Middleton*) attempts to fix credit for the authorship of the *II Honest Whore*.

disguised father submits his child to a severer test.   Friscobaldo, too, is a more active intrigant that Flowerdale.   A
very effective turn (not borrowed from the *London Prodigal*)
is where Friscobaldo appears in his own shape (IV, 1),
roundly berates Matheo and his daughter, and accuses the
"serving man" of being an accomplice with Matheo in a
robbery.   Friscobaldo then goes out and re-enters as "serving man."   Matheo curses Friscobaldo behind his back (as
he thinks) and together with the "serving man" plots to rob
him.   This device of shifting out of the disguise and back
again was used contemporaneously in *Measure for Measure*,
and earlier in the *Malcontent*.[19]

Since Middleton may have been part author of the *II
Honest Whore* it is interesting to note his incidental use of
the father-spy disguise in *Michaelmas Term*, which also
appeared in 1604 (Fleay, *Biog. Chron.*, II, 91).   The motive
occurs in the sub-plot and is sketched somewhat abruptly
and crudely.   The Country Wench's Father decides to serve
his daughter, who has run away to London.   He knows
the evils of this city and protects his child unrecognized,
finally succeeding in forcing a marriage between her and her
lover.

The sincere flattery of imitation is manifest in Edward
Sharpham's *Fleire*, entered in 1606.   It not only adopts the
spying father, but it draws inspiration from two of Marston's
spy plays which had preceded it.[20]   The father is a cynical,
sneering character resembling Malevole in the *Malcontent*.
He further resembles Malevole in being a deposed duke in
disguise.   Note also that his real name is Antifront, while
Malevole's real name is Altofront.   In Sharpham's play the
disguised duke is called the "Fleire," that is, a fleerer, or
sneerer.   This reminds us of the way Marston made the

---

[19] See further discussion of shifting, below, page 166.
[20] For dates and synopses see below, page 162 ff.

name "Fawn" from the verb "to fawn," for his disguised
Duke Hercules. There is further resemblance in the fact
that both the "Fleire" and the "Fawn" are disguised dukes
and spying fathers.[21] A disguised father's manipulation of
events so as to force the marriage of his daughter and a favored lover reminds us of Middleton's *Michaelmas Term*. In
that play, as in the *Fleire*, the couple is brought before a
judge. A brief summary of the *Fleire* may be of service to us.
Duke Antifront disguises as "The Fleire" and takes service
with his two daughters, who have turned prostitutes. In
the course of a tangled love plot "The Fleire" learns that
his daughters are planning to poison two men whom they
had wanted to marry, but had wooed in vain. "The Fleire"
now disguises as an apothecary and sells a sleeping potion
instead of poison to his daughters' agents, Havelittle and
Piso. "The Fleire" then disguises as a judge,[22] and at the
trial of Havelittle and Piso brings out his daughters' complic-
ity in the supposed murder. "The Fleire" was anxious to
have his daughters marry Havelittle and Piso. It so happens that Piso's father was the usurper of Antifront's ("The
Fleire's") throne. Piso, Sr., dies and Piso, Jr., orders Antifront restored. "The Fleire" now reveals himself as Antifront and the couples are married.

Day's *Law Tricks*, printed in 1608, seems reminiscent of
the *London Prodigal* in one particular, and of the absent duke
plays in general. Ferneze, Duke of Genoa, makes his ne'er-
do-well son Polymetes deputy ruler, while he plans to go to
Pisa to direct the search for his daughter Emilia, who has
been kidnapped by the Turks. Meanwhile Emilia comes

[21] See Nibbe, *The Fleire*, 10–25. Dr. Nibbe evidently had not con-
sulted Sampson, *The Plays of Sharpham*, in *Studies — in Honor of J. M.
Hart*. Cf. Nibbe, 13; Sampson, 443.

[22] Observe that these three changes of costume are somewhat in
the manner of the multi-disguise plays. See Chapter VI.

home, and, calling herself "Tristella," is wooed by her brother, who has not seen her since infancy.[23]   In the course of time the duke enters in disguise (IV) and reports his own death to the son (now an old device).   Polymetes at the first word of the sad news joyfully proclaims himself duke and plans a prodigal life (somewhat like the *London Prodigal*).   The disguised duke expresses his amazement in an aside to the audience, and says to his son, "Were your father Alive to note these hopeful parts in you, How would it move him and surprise his heart?"   Polymetes merely dismisses him with a tip for his "good news."   Before the end of the scene the arrival of the duke is announced.   Duke Ferneze returns to his own, and pretends to be gulled by his son, who poses as honest and dutiful.

Day uses the spying father again in *Humour Out of Breath*, printed in 1608.   In this play the duke Octavio advises his sons to go a-wooing, which they do with alacrity.   The duke disguises and spies on his sons in time to catch them plighting troth to the daughters of an enemy.   He undisguises and forbids the bans.   However, before the end of the play, he yields, and the lovers are paired off happily.

The six plays we have just discussed show that the father spying in disguise was a very popular motive during the brief period from 1603 to 1608.   It reappears about three years later in the *Captain*, (1611–12 Thorndike, *Infl.*, 89) by Beaumont and Fletcher.   The father of a wanton young widow disguises, first as an old soldier, and afterwards in "brave apparel."   In the latter he is seen though not recognized by his daughter, and becomes the object of her lust. He captures his daughter after her lewd soliciting at a banquet, and ultimately by a shrewd plot inveigles the cowardly gull Piso into marrying her.   A daughter's tempting her dis-

---

[23] A similar mistaken wooing is effected through disguise in the *Four Prentices*, which appeared several years earlier.

guised father (a bit of tragic irony skilfully wrought by disguise) seems to be original in this play; but the dénouement in which the father undisguises after having by strategy forced a lover to marry his daughter seems reminiscent of *Michaelmas Term* or of the *Fleire*.

Beaumont and Fletcher used the spy also in the *Scornful Lady* (1611, Thorndike, *Infl.*, 87). This is not a father-spy play, but we treat it here because of its literary relations with the plays under discussion. Some of the motives hark back to the *London Prodigal*. In the *Scornful Lady* a man supposedly absent returns disguised as an old sailor, reports his own death, receives thanks for such good news, and presents his own will. These four points are the same as in the *London Prodigal* [24] except that one hero deals with his son, and the other deals with his brother. From this point forward another story is worked out. The hero, Elder Loveless, was supposedly exiled because of the scornful lady who would not listen to his love suit. In his rough sailor disguise Elder Loveless comes to tell her (III) that Elder Loveless died a victim of her cruelty. She betrays her real sentiment by weeping, but immediately says she will marry a rival. Elder Loveless now throws off his disguise. But the lady declares she knew his identity all the time. The lady's attitude when the disguise is revealed is somewhat like the situation in the *Widow's Tears*. Thus we see how Beaumont and Fletcher time and again recognized the theatrical values of disguise situations, and did not hesitate to borrow from their predecessors or fellow dramatists.

Shakespeare, who borrowed almost all of his disguise situations, introduced the spying father in the *Winter's Tale*. The royal father's spying on his son and the theatrical

[24] The relation between these two plays was suggested by Koeppel, *Quellen*, 53.

unmasking (IV, 4) are not in Greene's novel, but such a
situation was, as we have seen, a well-established tradition
in the plays immediately preceding the *Winter's Tale*. The
effect of Shakespeare's veiled and subtle dialog quoted
below must have reminded the audience of many similar
situations, where the son unknowingly revealed his heart
secrets to a disguised father. Polixenes has just suggested
to his son Florizel that he should take counsel with his
father concerning his proposed marriage to Perdita, when
the following ironical dialog takes place:

> "*Flo.*   I yield all this;
>   But for some other reasons, my grave sir,
>   Which 'tis not fit you know, I not acquaint
>   My father of this business.
> *Pol.*   Let him know 't.
> *Flo.*   He shall not.
> *Pol.*   Prithee, let him.
> *Flo.*   No, he must not.
> *Shep.*   Let him, my son: he shall not need to grieve
>   At knowing of thy choice.
> *Flo.*   Come, come, he must not.
>   Mark our contract.
> *Pol.*   Mark your divorce, young sir."
>
> > (*Discovering himself.*)

The addition of disguise to an old plot is, as we have often
remarked, a tribute to the practical value of disguise as a
dramatic device. Shakespeare paid this tribute not only in
the *Winter's Tale* but also in *King Lear*, which had been
played a few years earlier. The familiar figure of Kent in
disguise, serving and protecting his helpless king, has obvious
dramatic kinship with the motive of a father in disguise,
serving and protecting his child. It is significant that the
Kent disguise is not to be found in Shakespeare's immediate
sources. Perillus in the old *Chronicle History of King Leir*

becomes the faithful companion of the king.   But Perillus is not in disguise, and, although at first unrecognized, he is afterwards continually addressed by name.   Possibly Shakespeare got a hint from an anonymous comedy *Timon* (1600), where the hero is attended by a faithful servant in disguise. But, whether Shakespeare owes anything to *Timon* or not, it is clear that the Kent disguise bears a strong family resemblance to the spying father who serves and protects his child.   Shakespeare, like the other master playwrights, did not hesitate to adopt good situations that were popular favorites, but, unlike many of them, he usually bettered what he borrowed.   He tinges this situation with pathos by making the banished Kent remain in disguise to serve his king unrecognized to the end.[25]   It is a maximum dramatic effect with a minimum of complication.

Thus we have seen that the *London Prodigal* is of considerable importance as a disguise play, since it inspired to a greater or less degree the disguise situations in *II Honest Whore*, *Michaelmas Term*, the *Fleire*, *Law Tricks*, *Humour Out of Breath*, the *Captain*, the *Scornful Lady*, the *Winter's Tale*, and *King Lear*.   It also may have been remembered by Jonson in the *Staple of News* (1625), where a disguised father, after having reported his own death, spies on his spendthrift son.[26]   But it is not our purpose at present to trace out any disguise tradition beyond our arbitrary stopping place of 1616.   We have analyzed enough plays to show how the spy in disguise became conventional dramatic

---

[25] Lamb, however, in *Table-Talk, by the late Elia*, interpreted the scene poetically as of "the old dying king partially catching at the truth, and immediately lapsing into obliviousness."   For Lamb's appreciative estimate of the character of Kent see *On the Genius and Character of Hogarth.*

[26] Compare also Shirley's *Royal Master* (1638), where a disguised father spies on his son.

material. The dramaturgic function of this disguise (to conceal the intrigant of the plot) has been obvious, especially in such plays as the *London Prodigal*. This functional use of disguise is still more interesting in the plays containing spying dukes, or political spies in general, a type of disguise which we shall discuss in the following paragraphs.

III

One of the most perfectly constructed of all the spy plays is Shakespeare's *Measure for Measure*. When we study *Measure for Measure* in the light of its predecessors we learn that Shakespeare, as usual, had a sharp eye for a favorite situation of the moment, but we learn also that he had a sure hand in weaving a telling plot. The stage effectiveness of the action of the disguised Duke Vincentio is achieved through rare dramatic economy.

First let us glance at the ancestors of Shakespeare's duke, or at least at the pioneers who prepared the way for this spy. The playwright got the criminal and unjust judge, as well as a hint for the disguise, from Whetstone's *Promus and Cassandra*, which was printed in 1578 but never acted. In this play Andrugio, because of his misconduct with Polina, is condemned to death by Lord Promus, who rules in the absence of the king. Andrugio's sister, Cassandra, vainly sacrifices her virtue to Promus upon his promise to save the brother's life. Promus breaks the promise, but Andrugio, though supposedly executed, is saved by a jailer's trick and escapes to the woods. In the course of events the king returns, the deviltry of Promus is exposed, and he is sentenced to death. Rumor of this reaches Andrugio in the forest, and he returns to the court "disguised in some long blacke Cloake." After two or three days of observation he appears in his own character in time to save Promus from execution.[27] The absent king has almost no dramatic value in this play. He is not a disguised intrigant like Shakespeare's Duke Vincentio. Yet the absence of the king and the disguise of Andrugio doubtless united to inspire the disguised duke of *Measure for Measure*.

Perhaps it is fair to assume that Shakespeare owed something in general to all cases where royalty disguised for the purpose of political spying.[28] The device of a king in disguise roaming through his realm is familiar in all literatures, and this literary motive is doubtless based on many historical facts. The earliest use in English drama,[29] so far as we can discover, is in *Fair Em* (1590), where a king disguises himself and goes off on a wooing expedition. The anonymous comedy *A Knack to Know a Knave* (1592), presents a king and two courtiers who disguise themselves and with the assistance of "Honesty" inveigle "Coneycatcher" into false swearing, thus spying out one of the knaves in the land. This play perhaps dimly foreshadows Jonson's *Bartholomew Fair*. In *George a Greene, the Pinner of Wakefield* (mentioned by Henslowe in 1593), the spy motive is used incidentally (V, 1) but with much comic irony and theatrical effect. King Edward and King James disguise them-

---

[27] In Cinthio, *Heccatommithi, VIII, 5*, which was Whetstone's source, this disguise could not have been used, for Andrugio's prototype was actually killed.

The somewhat melodramatic ending of Whetstone's play is paralleled in *A Knack to Know an Honest Man* (1595), where Sempronio, supposedly slain by Lelio, goes off in disguise, but returns and reveals himself just in time to save Lelio from execution.

[28] Note that in Shakespeare's *Henry V* (1599) the King goes unrecognized among his soldiers, not because he is disguised, but because he is without royal insignia, like a "common man."

[29] In the English metrical romance of *Sir Orpheo* the hero, disguised as a minstrel, spies briefly on his steward who has been in charge of the household during the hero's absence.

selves as yeomen in order to observe the exploits of George a Greene. At Bradford the kings are forced to vail their staves or fight the shoemakers. George a Greene and Robin Hood, also disguised, come along and, calling the kings "base minded peasants," fight a valiant bout with the shoemakers. Presently all identities are revealed, and the kings praise the heroes and pardon the rudeness of the shoemakers, confirming their pardon by dubbing their trade forever after "the gentle craft."[30] Armin's *Valiant Welshman* (1595) presents incidentally the hero disguised as a common soldier spying on his enemy. In *I Sir John Oldcastle* (1598) Henry V disguises himself and starts for Westminster. While waiting for a boat he is robbed by Sir John, a parson, who does not recognize him. Later in a dice game with Sir John, the king regains his gold and reveals himself. In Samuel Rowley's *When You See Me You Know Me* (1603, Bayne, 371) Henry VIII disguises himself and goes out at night to spy on the London watches, constables, and criminals. The king gets into a fight with the notorious Black Will, and is jailed. Black Will adds insult to injury by taunting the king with comments on his poor fencing. After the king has heard various tales of abuse from prisoners, his identity is revealed. Black Will now changes front, but is doomed to stay in prison until his services may be used in some battle.

All these plays helped to make political spying in disguise familiar to playgoers. Let us now turn to more tangible and definite literary influences on Shakespeare. He is clearly indebted to Marston's *Malcontent* for the general effect and some details in *Measure for Measure*. The *Malcontent* was

---

[30] The writer of the *Pinner* has taken over the disguises from the prose romance by the same title as the play. Compare Heywood's *I Edward IV* (1594), where the king in disguise learns from Hobs, the tanner, that he is respected by his subjects, and gets Hob's opinions on affairs of government.

produced in 1601.[31] It was printed in 1604, the year when
Measure for Measure was acted at Whitehall (Ward, II, 153).
In connection with these two plays we must consider Marston's *Parasitaster, or the Fawn*, which was printed in 1606,
but had been acted in 1604 according to Fleay (*Biog. Chron.*,
II, 79). The *Fawn* has been spoken of as being a rival of,
or partly influenced by, Shakespeare's *Measure for Measure*.[32]
We cannot, of course, presume to settle the question of
general relations here. But with respect to the disguise
plot it is significant that the motives which the *Fawn* and
Measure for Measure have in common may be found earlier
in the *Malcontent;* and that much of the other dramatic
material in *Measure for Measure* was first used by Marston.
The evidence which we are about to present tends to show
that Shakespeare was influenced by Marston, instead of
Marston by Shakespeare, as Fleay and Koeppel would
have it. As we glance at the plots of these plays let us
keep in mind the relative theatrical effectiveness of the disguise situations. The synopses of the plots follow:

The Malcontent [33]

"Malevole," living at the court of Pietro, tells the audience in a soliloquy that he is Altofronte, the real Duke of
Genoa, whose throne has been usurped by Pietro. "Malevole" tortures his enemy Pietro by accusing him of having

[31] See Stoll, 55–60; also see Fleay, *Biog. Chron.*, II, 78.

[32] Fleay, *Biog. Chron.*, II, 79: "The whole plot reminds us of *Measure for Measure*, which this play was meant to rival."

Koeppel, *Quellen*, 28: "Es ist wohl möglich, dass Marston diesen an
und für sich gänzlich überflüssigen, verkleideten Herzog und den Ge-
danken der abschliessenden Gerichtsitzung dem Shakespeare-drama
"Measure for Measure" entlehnt hat."

[33] Koeppel, *Quellen*, (1895) had not found a source for the *Malcontent*. I observe that one situation is like the husband-confessor motive
in *Edward I*, namely act IV, scene 2, where Pietro tests his wife by
confessing her while he is disguised as a hermit. Compare also "Male-

been cuckolded by Mendoza. He further injures Pietro by assisting in a love intrigue involving the latter's wife. The sly Mendoza, who has been made heir of Pietro, now begs "Malevole" to help him by murdering Pietro. Further, Mendoza tells "Malevole" that he wants "to marry Maria, the banished Duke Altofront's wife" (III, 1). "Malevole" discloses the murder plot to Pietro, and disguises him in a hermit's gown. Later they report to Mendoza, when Pietro eloquently describes his own death, and "Malevole" "confesses" to have killed Pietro! Mendoza now declares himself Duke; instructs the "hermit" (Pietro) to poison "Malevole" and "Malevole" to poison the "hermit"; and finally sends "Malevole" as pander to Maria ("Malevole's" wife). Meanwhile, the Duke of Florence, having been informed of the corruption in Genoa, declares that the Duchess (his daughter) must die; that Duke Pietro must be banished, and Duke Altofront ("Malevole") be re-accepted. Pietro promises to restore the dukedom to Altofront, when "Malevole" undisguises and proves to be Altofront. Altofront as "Malevole" again tests the faithfulness of his own wife by wooing her for Mendoza. Later Mendoza attempts to poison "Malevole," who feigns death. A masque is given in which "Malevole," Pietro, and others are presented as Genoan Dukes. "Malevole" unmasks and unceremoniously dismisses Mendoza. He pardons Pietro on condition that he take vows of repentance.

Measure for Measure

Duke Vincentio, making Angelo his deputy ruler, pretends to go away, but actually remains at court disguised as a friar. Claudio, who has been arrested for getting Julietta with child, begs his sister Isabella to intercede with Angelo.

vole's" trial of his wife in act V, scene 2. A disguised husband as pander to his wife occurs in *Zelotypus*. See above, page 143.

She does so with the result that Angelo falls in love with her, and offers to free the brother at the price of Isabella's virtue. She refuses, but Claudio begs his sister to yield. A certain "Friar" proposes a stratagem by means of which Isabella is to make an assignation with Angelo and then substitute Mariana, Angelo's betrothed, for herself. This plan is carried out and Angelo enjoys Isabella, as he thinks. But he breaks faith by ordering his provost to send him Claudio's head. Now the "Friar" perverts this sentence by presenting an order from the Duke (himself), to substitute the head of some one else. The "Friar" now amuses himself by telling Isabella that her brother has been executed. Incidentally he engages in conversation with Lucio, who declares that he "can tell pretty tales of the Duke." The Duke, resuming his own character, now pretends to have just returned to court and ironically expresses his trust in Angelo. Isabella makes her charges against Angelo. The Duke pretends to scout them, but asks Isabella for some witness who was in her confidence. She refers to the "Friar." Incidentally Lucio tells the Duke that the "Friar" "slandered His Grace," — a gratuitous fib. The Duke disguises as "Friar" again. Lucio now accuses the "Friar" of having slandered the duke. The "Friar" declares Lucio did the slandering, which was true. Angelo is about to arrest the "Friar" at Lucio's behest, when he undisguises and proves to be Duke Vincentio. The duke compels Angelo to marry Mariana, and then sentences him to death. Finally he pardons him in response to the prayers of Mariana and Isabella. Claudio is ordered to marry Julietta. The Duke asks Isabella to marry him.

The Fawn

Hercules, Duke of Ferrara, wants his son Tiberio to marry Dulcimel, daughter of Gonzago. When Tiberio refuses to

do this, Hercules decides to marry Dulcimel himself, and
sends Tiberio as a wooer by proxy. Hercules then disguises
as "Faunus" and goes to Gonzago's court, where under
cover of disguise he observes matters develop so that Tiberio
finally does fall in love with Dulcimel. Hercules uses his
disguise also in order to spy on roguery in Gonzago's realm.
At the end of the play in the Masque of Cupid, "Faunus"
sentences a number of "humourous" gulls to the ship of
fools. Among them is Gonzago, who tried to cross love,
but really became the unconscious go-between for Dulcimel
and Tiberio. The bride and groom enter, and Hercules
("Faunus") "enters in his own shape" to welcome them to
Ferrara.

Let us now compare these three plays with respect to their
interdependence, their dramaturgy, and their theatrical
effectiveness. The basic motive which these plays have in
common is that a duke in disguise spies on crime or roguery.
In the *Malcontent* and *Measure for Measure* he pretends to
go away but remains as a spy at his own court. The motive
of a ruler temporarily abdicating to a bad deputy had been
used in the tragedy *Cambises* (1570) as well as in Shakespeare's immediate source *Promus and Cassandra* (1578), but
neither of these plays has a ruler actually remaining in disguise to spy at his own court. Shakespeare, therefore, may
have borrowed the duke supposedly absent but really
present in disguise, from Marston's *Malcontent*. With
regard to the initial disguise situation it is perfectly
clear that if the *Fawn* was inspired by *Measure for
Measure*, *Measure for Measure* was first inspired by the
Malcontent. Hence it seems likely that Marston in the
Fawn borrowed from himself directly rather than from
Shakespeare.

Shakespeare's duke shifts out of his disguise and back
again. This was an effective device used by Marston in

the *Malcontent*.[34]   And as far as the final scene is concerned
we find a number of resemblances between *Measure for
Measure* and the *Malcontent*.   Shakespeare's deputy and
Marston's usurper are both forgiven by the dukes, and
wished happiness together with their wives.   Each duke
deals unmercifully with one villainous character.   Each
duke compliments a friend and an officer.   And each duke
is still sentimental enough to take a woman to his heart.
So far, then, Shakespeare seems indebted to Marston.

Koeppel suggested, as we have seen above, that Marston
owed his Masque of Cupid in the *Fawn* to the last scene
in *Measure for Measure*.   Let us see if there is anything in
the resemblances of the two scenes which would determine
chronology.

The last scene in the *Fawn* is a mock judgment.   Cupid
sits as a judge, surrounded by Drunkenness, Folly, and six
other abstractions.   "Faunus" has drawn up a number of
acts and statutes in elaborate legal jargon, and pleads his
complaints before Judge Cupid, who sentences the "humourous" courtiers to the ship of fools.   One is sentenced because
of a "plurality of mistresses"; a second is acquitted of the
charge of "counterfeiting Cupid's royal coin"; a third is
pardoned for slandering his wife; a fourth is sentenced for
being a "mummer"; and a fifth is sentenced for trying to
"make frustrate" the sweet pleasure of love.

How much does all this resemble *Measure for Measure?*   In
a brief section of only two hundred lines the duke compels
Angelo to marry Mariana.   He then condemns him to death,
but later pardons him; Claudius is commanded to marry
the woman he wronged, and Lucio is sentenced to marry a
"punk," after which he is to be whipped and hanged.
Escalus is thanked for his goodness.   The Provost is first

[34] The device of shifting goes back at least as far as Roman comedy.
See Chapter III, page 37.

discharged and afterwards promoted. And Isabella is chosen to become the duke's wife.

From this comparison there surely can be no inference that anything in the Masque of Cupid either borrows or burlesques any incident in the final scene of *Measure for Measure*. And consequently this internal evidence (or lack of it) does not convince us that Marston's scene was inspired by Shakespeare's. We can only repeat what we have already remarked, namely, that Shakespeare seems, on the whole, rather to be indebted to Marston.

As a pure piece of technic *Measure for Measure* is clearly superior to its predecessors and rivals. Marston's dukes spy on their courts with cynical and even vile comment and action; but they do not utilize their disguise to any great extent to shape events in the plays. In the *Malcontent* the restoration of the duchy is brought about by the arch villainy of Mendoza, and not by any cleverness of "Malevole." In the *Fawn* Dulcimel's hinting accusations and her father's folly unite to bring about her marriage to Tiberio. This marriage is what "Faunus" desired, but he does not employ his disguise to accomplish the result. But in *Measure for Measure* the duke is more than a spy. He is himself the manager of the whole plot. He initiates, directs, and resolves the entire action. And his disguise serves him in his double purpose of spying on scoundrels, and of bringing tragic complications to a happy resolution.

The theatrical possibilities of the disguised spy were realized more fully by Shakespeare than by Marston. In turning his duke into a counterfeit friar Shakespeare was utilizing a disguise costume that had long been popular in English drama.[35] Besides it was eminently fitting that a friar have

[35] By 1604, the friar, or the hermit, disguise had been used in *Magnificence, Satire of the Three Estates, Dr. Faustus, Mucedorus, Ed-*

free access to prisoners, and advise maidens in distress. The duke realized the necessity of mimetic dissimulation and bade Friar Thomas instruct him how he might "formally in person bear Like a true Friar." Costume, as well as action, were distinctive in the case of Duke Vincentio. Just how distinctive the costume was in the case of a malcontent or a fawner it is hard to tell.

In handling disguise Marston does not always show a keen sense of values in stage business. For example, at the end of act IV of the *Malcontent* "Malevole" "undisguiseth himself" in the presence of the usurper. This stage effect is repeated at the end of the play, where "Malevole" unmasks and spreads terror among the villains. A sudden revelation at the end of a play is as ancient as Æschylus. But Marston discounts its effectiveness in this play by giving it twice — the first time in act IV. In the *Fawn* the undisguising is off the stage. Contrast this with Shakespeare's method. In act V, scene 1 of *Measure for Measure* the duke enters the city in his own habit, giving no suspicion that he had been the "Friar." With comic irony he listens to the complaints of his subjects, and expresses complete confidence in Angelo. He even hears complaints about the "Friar," who is presumably near at hand. The duke retires and presently the "Friar" enters. In an altercation which ensues Lucio calls the "Friar" a "bald pated lying rascall" and, pulling off the friar's hood, discovers the duke.[36]

ward I, *Look About You*, *Merry Devil of Edmonton*, *Malcontent*, *Fair Maid of Bristow*, and *I Honest Whore*.

The friar disguise was ridiculed in *May Day* as having been worn "threadbare on every stage." *May Day* possibly preceded *Measure for Measure*. See Chapter IV, page 87.

[36] A brief but interesting spying situation occurs in *II Henry IV* (II, 4), where Prince Hal and Poins, disguised as drawers, hear themselves denounced to Doll Tearsheet by Falstaff. Compare also the

Veiled allusions in the disguise dialog are plentiful in all three of the plays under discussion.[37]   A quotation from *Measure for Measure* may suffice to illustrate.

"*Lucio.*   . . . . By my troth, Isabel, I lov'd thy brother; if the old fantastical duke of dark corners had been at home, he had lived.

Duke.   (*as Friar*) Sir, the duke is marvellous little beholding to your reports; but the best is, he lives not in them.

Lucio.   Friar, thou knowest not the duke so well as I do: he's a better woodman than thou takest him for.

Duke.   Well, you'll answer this one day.   Fare ye well.

Lucio.   Nay, tarry; I'll go along with thee: I can tell thee pretty tales of the duke.

Duke.   You have told me too many of him already, sir, if they be true."

In conclusion we may say that *Measure for Measure*, though imitative in plot, was, because of its compactness, the integral relation between its disguise and the dramatic complications, the subtlety of the disguise dialog, and the theatricality of its action a better play than its predecessors or contemporaries of the same type.

In connection with *Measure for Measure* and Marston's two plays let us recall the plot of Middleton's *Phœnix*,[38] which bears some resemblance to all three.   The *Phœnix* was printed in 1607, but the date of composition was probably several years earlier.   The dates cannot be settled at

incidental spying which results from the disguise of Barabas in the *Jew of Malta* (IV, 6).

[37] Veiled allusions in *Measure for Measure* are found in III, 1; III, 2; IV, 2; IV, 3; V, 1.

[38] It has been thought that the *Phœnix* is founded on the *Force of Love*, a Spanish novel.   But K. Christ (*Quellen*, 105) says: "Es ist mir nicht gelungen, eine novelle dieses Titels in der spanischen Literatur zu finden."

present, but the presumption is that the *Malcontent* preceded the *Phœnix*.   The plot is somewhat loose, but presents
in general Prince Phœnix's discovery of corruption while
he travels in disguise in his father's duchy.   This theme we
shall see later in Jonson's *Bartholomew Fair*.

Jealous courtiers prevail on the Duke of Ferrara [39] to send
his son Phœnix away to travel.   Phœnix, pretending to go,
really remains at home in disguise.   First, Phœnix exposes
Tangle, who is a past master in the art of perverting justice
by shrewd law tricks.   Next he catches and punishes a mercenary sea captain who has sold his wife.   Then he discovers
the crookedness of Justice Falso, who maintains a pack
of thieves as servants.   Next he becomes the confidant of
Proditor, who plots with his new friend the downfall of
Prince Phœnix!   He accidentally rings a doorbell and is
pulled into a farcical dark scene with the Jeweller's wife,
who converses with him at length, mistaking him all the time
for her paramour, the Knight.

Finally, Phœnix is hired to assassinate Duke Ferrara and
Prince Phœnix.   He and the arch plotter, Proditor, are
present for this purpose in the court scene.   A servant
announces that Prince Phœnix has returned and is about
to enter.   The servant presents a document from the Prince
which contains specific charges against the traitor (Proditor),
the gamblers (Lussurioso and Infesto), and the nefarious
Justice Falso.   Charges are brought orally against the
Jeweller's wife.   Suddenly Phœnix undisguises and pardons
all except Proditor, who is banished.

It should be noticed that the general structure in this
dénouement is like the *Malcontent* and *Measure for Measure*.
The announced return of the hero, his presence in disguise,

---

[39] Slight resemblances between the *Phœnix* and the *Fawn* are that
the duke in each play is the Duke of Ferrara, and that the spying heroes
occasionally break into verse soliloquies over their discoveries.

his judgment and pardon of all except one man — these
motives are alike in the three plays. It is interesting to
see how in a brief period, say from 1601 to 1604, the disguised
spy was used as the basic element in four plays so important
as the *Malcontent*, the *Fawn*, *Measure for Measure*, and the
Phœnix.

Another play of Middleton's in which the detection of
roguery is facilitated by disguise is *Your Five Gallants* (1607).
The plot is said to be original (Christ, *Quellen*, 106), which
may be true of particular situations, but is not true of the
main theme of a disguised spy seeking out rogues. Furthermore, the plot, which is dominated by the spy, is resolved
through a masque in which specific accusations are brought
against the offenders. A masque dénouement contrived by
a disguised spy had been employed in Marston's *Malcontent*,
and a similar masque with definite revelation of roguery was
given at the end of the *Fawn*. This comparison of the
Phœnix and *Your Five Gallants* with Marston's two plays
makes it apparent that for the construction of spy plays
Middleton had been studying the success of Marston. In
employing these masque revelations[40] with a variety of
spectacular costumes and properties together with sensational and brisk stage business, both playwrights showed a
fondness for the "grand finale" which is still familiar in
certain theaters.

When a motive has become so thoroughly familiar and
conventionalized as the disguised spy it is not surprising to

[40] A cruder form of masque dénouement had been used by Marston
in *Antonio's Revenge*, where Antonio and companions are able to kill
Piero while pretending to be masquers at his wedding. A much earlier
masque scene with a similar purpose, though not a dénouement, occurs
in act IV of the *Tragedy of Richard II*, where King Richard and companions, disguised like Diana's knights in a masque, capture Wood-
stock, Duke of Gloucester. See also the masque dénouement in the
Revenger's Tragedy (printed 1607).

find even the proverbially independent Jonson adopting it as
the main element of a comedy plot.[41] His *Bartholomew
Fair* (1614) has not hitherto been spoken of as dependent
on earlier plays.   Ward (II, 370), for example, calls it "Absolutely original, so far as is known, in both conception and
construction."   Koeppel says: (Quellen, 14) "Weder für die
ganze Handlung, noch für einzelne Scenen dieses Stückes
lassen sich literarische Beeinflussungen nachweisen."

Now in the light of our account of the disguised spy it
seems pretty obvious that Jonson was not "absolutely
original," and that literary influences are not far to seek.
The chief ingredient in Jonson's play is, of course, the
Fair, with its "humour" characters.   But as far as plot
goes, an important, if not the main interest is Justice Overdo's determination to spy out "enormities," his humiliation
because of his disguise, and his final revelation and specific
accusation of the rogues.

In a broad sense Justice Overdo has predecessors in all the
spies we have discussed in this chapter; for they assumed
their disguise purposely to search out villainy.   But if we
limit the motive to the man of high authority who spies
on petty roguery in his own community, we find predecessors
in *A Knack to Know a Knave,* where a king in disguise looking
for knavery catches a perjurer; in *I Sir John Oldcastle,*
where the king traps a thieving parson; in Samuel Rowley's
When You See Me You Know Me, where the king spies on
corrupt watches and constables, and other unworthy citizens; in Middleton's *Phœnix,* where a prince discovers a
tricky lawyer who abuses his knowledge of the law, and a
corrupt judge who maintains a pack of thieves; and in the

---

[41] In *Volpone* (1606) Volpone, after having given out the report
that he is dead, haunts the house disguised as a *commandadore* and
taunts the sycophants. But the disguise is assumed for the sake of
gloating over, rather than spying upon, them.

same author's *Your Five Gallants*, where a gentleman in disguise discovers cheating, theft, and bawdry. Thus we see that in the general purpose and method of the disguised spying, Jonson was by no means original.

We have already indicated Middleton's probable indebtedness to Marston for the general plan of his dénouements in the two plays just mentioned. Now let us in turn note the similarity between the dénouements of *Your Five Gallants* and of *Bartholomew Fair*. Fitzgrave, after rounding up the rogues, discovers himself and says:

> "'Twas I framed your device, do you see? 'twas I!
> The whole assembly has took notice of it.
> That you are a gallant cheater,
> So much the pawning of my cloak contains; (*to Goldstone*)
> You a base thief, think of Combe Park (*to Pursenet*) and tell me
> That you're a hiréd smockster (*to Tailby*); here's her letter,
> In which we are certified that you're a bawd. (*to Primero*)"

Justice Overdo, after revealing his identity, proceeds very much in the same fashion in act V, scene 6.

> " . . . . stand forth you weedes of enormity, and spread. (*To Busy*) First, *Rabbi Busy*, thou *superlunaticall* hypocrite, (*To Lantern*) next, thou other extremity, thou prophane professor of *Puppetry*, little better than *Poetry*: (*To the horse courser, and Cutpurse*) then thou strong Debaucher, and Seducer of youth; witnesse this easie and honest young man; (Then *Cap. Whit,*) now thou Esquire of Dames, *Madams*, and twelue-penny *Ladies*: (*and Mistresse Littlewit*) now my greene *Madame* her selfe, of the price. Let mee vnmasque your Ladiship."

This comparison shows that Jonson was presenting an old spying situation, namely, the sudden revelation of disguise with an alignment and specific accusation of the rogues who had been spied upon.[42] It shows that he was not "ab-

---

[42] The alignment of rogues without the use of disguise is a feature of some of Jonson's earlier plays, as *Cynthia's Revels* and *Every Man Out of His Humour*. As usual the addition of disguise improved the dramatic effectiveness.

solutely original," but was to a certain extent dependent on Middleton and others for a good dramatic device.

There is no intent of calling Johnson an imitator because of these parallels. His creative genius was sufficient to make an old thing new. He made the spy a "humour" character, a man who is so zealous in his nosing into "enormities" that he actually sympathizes with and wants to protect a promising young pickpocket. The justice is mistaken for a rogue and put into the stocks, a theatrical bit of comic irony. He hears his own name constantly harped on by the mad Trouble-all. He finds that he can have his choice of two "greene" madames for a shilling, and he speaks more truth than he suspects when he says "This will proue my chiefest enormity," for one of them turns out to be his wife! All of these situations have dramatic values which compensate fully for any lack of dramatic novelty, and reveal Jonson as a skilful playwright.

With this we shall close the study of spy plays. In the notes we have frequently alluded to plays which come after 1616, but our purpose in this chapter has been to show by an examination of thirty or more plays how the spy disguise became a dramatic tradition in England during the early years of the seventeenth century. Our division of these plays into three groups has been for purposes of convenience, but it must be remembered that, from the technical point of view, all disguised spies are alike, whether they are spying upon wife, child, or subject. Dramatically each served, as it were, to advertise the other until spying in disguise became a well established tradition.

The study of the spy motive, as of all disguise, has a tendency to fix our attention on the physical, momentary, theatrical values of certain dramatic situations. There were repetitions, variations, and conventionalizing. The little writers borrowed from the big, and the big from each other.

And we have seen in this chapter that the playwrights, all the way from the forgotten ones up to Jonson and Shakespeare, drew on their predecessors, not necessarily because of poverty-stricken imagination, but because of shrewd recognition of theatrical success.

CHAPTER VIII

THE LOVER IN DISGUISE

O, sir, know that vnder simple weeds
The gods have maskt.
— Greene's *Orlando Furioso*

I

THE use of disguise in love affairs is a practice approved
by Jupiter himself. The device is especially convenient in
the drama of intrigue; secret love needs disguise. A lady
may be strongly guarded by parent or husband, but the
lover overcomes such obstacles by sheer ingenuity. If he
cannot reach his lady's chamber in his own shape, he may
do so in the assumed identity of her maid, her physician, her
spiritual adviser, or even in the character of the husband
himself. But the presence of a disguised lover in a play
does not always imply an amour. In situations of romantic
love the wooer often appears in disguise. In some English
plays such disguises may be relics of vulgar intrigues which
have been idealized. In certain other plays disguise is used
because it gives a peculiarly romantic turn; as, for example,
when a lady is wooed and won by a man in lowly station
only to learn that he is a prince in disguise. In some plays,
Love's Labor's Lost, for example, the disguises are not technically of great value to the plot; but they add a certain
theatrical glamor. They are conceived in the spirit of the
masque dominant in the courtly life of the period.

The chief tributaries of the current of disguised lovers in
Renaissance drama are Roman comedy and Italian *novelle*.
One would expect to find the motive also in French *fabliaux*,

177

but the influence from that source, if any, is slight.   An
example of *novella* influence may be seen in Parabosco's
Viluppo (1547), where the servant Viluppo gets clothes
from his associate Negromante and, thus disguised, has an
amour with Negromante's wife.   This situation, which
Parabosco used again in *l'Hermafrodit*, is borrowed from the
fiftieth novel of Bandello.[1]   Boccaccio's disguised lovers[2]
have no important bearing on English drama.   Salernitano
in the twelfth novel of his *Novellino* (1476) introduced a
lover disguised as a woman, a device which afterwards had
a long career in the drama.

   We shall consider in this chapter: first, the *Supposes* and
the shrew plays;   second, the impersonating lover in the
Amphitruo school of comedy;   third, the lover disguised as
girl; fourth, the disguised lover tricked; and fifth, the romantic situation of the noble lover in lowly disguise.

   The earliest use of a disguised lover in English drama is
in Gascoigne's *Supposes* (1566), a play which was drawn
upon for the underplot in the *Taming of A Shrew* and Shakespeare's *Taming of The Shrew*.   Gascoigne's play is an adaptation of Ariosto's *Suppositi*, and Ariosto was himself partly
indebted to earlier drama.   His play contains one motive
which goes back at least as far as the *Frogs* of Aristophanes,
and two which have good analogies in Plautus's *Amphitruo*
and Terence's *Eunuchus*.   The lover posing as servant, the
master and servant exchanging rôles, and the comic conflict
when an impostor in disguise attempts to outface the man
he is impersonating—these are old traditions in drama.   It
is curious how often the disguised lover and the doubles
situation are combined.   The association of these two motives necessitates an inclusive discussion in the first part of
this chapter.

[1] See Creizenach, II, 334.
[2] See the *Decameron, III, 7*, and *IV, 2*.

First, let us relate the plot of the *Supposes*. Erostrato, a nobleman, carries on an amour with Polynesta for two years, being disguised during the time as the servant of her father. Meanwhile, the nobleman's servant Dulipo has been masquerading as the nobleman. A complication arises when a rich doctor of laws seems about to secure the parental consent to marry Polynesta. In order to offset this, the servant Dulipo, posing as the nobleman, is instructed to act in the capacity of a rival suitor. But he must have a father to offer a dower; hence they induce a stranger to pose as the nobleman's father. We now have three wooers — the hero posing as a servant, his servant posing as the hero (together with a bogus father), and the rich doctor of laws. Presently Polynesta's father learns of her affair and jails the nobleman-servant. Philogano, the real father of the nobleman, arrives but is denounced as an impostor by the servant and by the false Philogano. Dulipo, the servant disguised as nobleman, is recognized by Philogano, but Dulipo insists that he really is the nobleman, and that Philogano is an impostor. Finally the doctor of laws identifies Dulipo as his own son. Polynesta's father learns that his daughter's partner is a nobleman and an acceptable husband. The real Philogano proves his identity and all ends happily.

The *Supposes*, although a popular play, is weak in stage values because most of the plot is narrated. The hero and heroine never appear on the stage together until the last scene, and in that scene he speaks two words, and she, none! The servant, disguised as master, poses as the wooer of his master's lady, but he never has a scene with her nor with her father. The value of the plot is in the incidents narrated, rather than in the situations represented. There is no scope for sentiment, character delineation, or charming dialog. Let us see how the Italian love plot was developed through *A Shrew* into *The Shrew*.

The underplot of the *Taming of A Shrew* (1588) is in many respects less dramatic than the *Supposes*. For example, there are no rival lovers to whet our interest. The play is not so convincing either. Aurelius, a nobleman in love with Philema, disguises himself as the son of a rich merchant; but there seems to be no reason for his assuming such a disguise. There seems to be no reason why the servant should pose as the master. These elements are disintegrated relics of the earlier plot. Despite such dramaturgic defects the play has many merits. It illustrates the tendency of some Elizabethans to chasten realistic situations. The vulgar intrigue is turned into a romantic situation of pure sentimental love. The wooers and their ladies are given poetic dialog in two scenes (II, 1, and III, 6). A new motive is the music teacher and his lute lesson.[3] The servant Valeria assumes this disguise and attempts to teach Kate, in order that her younger sisters may have freedom to meet their wooers. The lute and the music teacher disguise was borrowed and employed to better purpose in *The Shrew*. We must not forget, in criticising *A Shrew*, that the author deserves much credit for combining the three plots — the Sly plot, the disguise plot, and the shrew plot — thus furnishing the source of Shakespeare's play.[4]

When we examine the *Taming of The Shrew* we find that it improves on *A Shrew* by raising the love situations into a still higher sphere of charming sentiment. Yet *The Shrew* is by no means an airy poem. It has theatrical effectiveness obtained through careful dramatic economy. The main situations of the underplot are Bianca and her four wooers,

[3] Compare Molière's *Malade Imaginaire*, where the lover Cleante poses as a music master. See also Lope de Vega's *Maestro de Danzar*, Calderon's *Maestro de Danzar*, and Wycherly's *Gentleman Dancing-Master*.

[4] Boas, *A Shrew*, xxv.

and the amusing play between the counterfeit and the real father of one of the wooers. It will be remembered that the wooers are: Lucentio, disguised as schoolmaster; his servant Tranio disguised as Lucentio; Hortensio, disguised as a music teacher, and Gremio, who makes the mistake of employing Lucentio-schoolmaster as his proxy. After much comedy Lucentio explains to the heroine's father that he has just wedded his daughter "While counterfeit supposes bleer'd thine eine."

Let us see how Shakespeare has used the lover disguises of his source. In *A Shrew* the disguise of the lover is unmotivated, and the servant as master of the lute has only the value of buffoonery. When we turn to *The Shrew* we find that the lover Lucentio avails himself of the tutor's gown to cloak his wooing of Bianca, and disguises his words of love under the shape of a Latin lesson.[5] But we find also that the buffoonery of the music teacher is preserved. This disguise is given to Hortensio, another of Bianca's suitors, and it serves, not only to introduce the horse-play of the lute, and the situation of a disguised rival, but to give comic irony. Hortensio comes to woo, but unwittingly gets himself into humiliating difficulties which he had not foreseen. Lucentio's Latin lesson and Hortensio's music lesson furnish ample opportunity for facial expression, gesture, and stage business. Thus in *The Shrew* both disguise motives count with the fullest theatrical value.

The most significant thing, however, about the lover situations in the *Supposes*, *A Shrew*, and *The Shrew* is, not the difference in dramaturgic values, but the fact that an Italian intrigue was shaped by English writers into a romantic wooing, thus gaining in charm, and incidentally gaining in dramatic value.

[5] A lover disguised as private tutor appears in Lope de Vega's *Domine Lucas*.

II

In the plays just considered there is a situation more effective theatrically than that of the disguised wooing. It is the scene where the real father is called an impostor by a man impersonating him — a typical doubles situation. In a series of plays the disguised lover is one of the doubles. He actually impersonates either the husband or a favored lover. Usually in these plays the heroine is deceived in identity; and the arrival of the real subject of the impersonation produces the comedy of doubles. Plautus's *Amphitruo* is probably the prototype of such plots.

The earliest plot of English composition in which the impersonation of a lover leads to a doubles dénouement is probably *Sir Clyomon and Sir Clamydes*.[6] The knightly lover Clamydes is betrayed by his servant into the power of Bryan Sans Foys, an enchanter. The enchanter charms Clamydes into a ten days' sleep, and takes his silver shield, his clothing, and the serpent's head, the trophy which Clamydes was to bring his lady Juliana. Thus disguised Bryan goes to the court, and is joyfully received by Juliana, who thinks he is Clamydes and prepares for their nuptials. Soon the real Clamydes appears at court and the princess spurns him as a counterfeit. But when Clamydes challenges the pretender to mortal combat the latter confesses the fraud without a moment's delay. In another early play, *I Ieronimo*, the impersonating lover comes to a tragic end. Alcario, who "affects" Bellimperia, is advised to get access to her by impersonating her accepted lover Andrea. Alcario plays his part well and meets the lady, but is temporarily sent away by her. He has proceeded only a step or two when he is killed by an assassin who mistook him for the

---

[6] See Chapter IV.

real Andrea.   The latter arrives on the scene in time to hear
Bellimperia mourning over his supposed death.[7]

The influence of *Amphitruo* on the two plays just discussed is traceable though slight.   But a much more direct
and obvious influence is to be seen in the four plays which
we shall next consider.   The second act of Heywood's
Silver Age (1595), which is really the main plot of the play,
is a fairly close version of *Amphitruo*.   The substance of
Heywood's rendering is as follows: Amphitrio, Alcmena's
husband, who is away at war, is hourly expected to return.
Ganymede, disguised as Amphitrio's servant Socia, heralds
Amphitrio's arrival, and Alcmena prepares a banquet.   But
the supposed husband whom she banquets and beds is really
Jupiter in disguise.   During the night the real Socia comes
to announce the real Amphitrio, but Ganymede-Socia, who
is on the watch, outfaces the poor servant, beating him and
maintaining that he (Ganymede) is the only and original
Socia, and proves it by giving an account of everything that
has happened to the real Socia.   At early dawn Jupiter-
Amphitrio bids Alcmena farewell with the excuse that he
must hurry back to war.   Meanwhile, Socia, sorely perplexed and doubtful of his own identity, astonishes Amphitrio by saying that the other servant is he, that the other
servant proved that he was Socia, and that he has been beaten
by himself (Socia).   A situation of cross-purposes arises when
Amphitrio reaches the house.   He thinks that Alcmena is
mad when she insists that he was with her two hours earlier;
and she does not understand why he should have returned so

[7] A parallel occurs in Freeman's *Imperiale* (1639), where Francisco,
disguised like Imperiale, pursuing an intrigue, is slain by an assassin
who meant to kill Imperiale.   See also Addison's *Cato* (IV, 1), where
the disguised lover is mistaken for some one else and killed.

An impersonation which results in a mistaken (though fortunate)
marriage appears in Lyly's *Mother Bombie* (1590), where Candius and
Livia exchange clothes with a couple who are about to be married.

suddenly and be in such bad humor. She tells him the
account of his battles (which omniscient Jupiter had already told her), and finally convinces him that he has already been with her, by producing the very gold cup which
he had intended to give her, and thought that he still had
under lock and key. Amphitrio, though puzzled, decides
that his wife is a strumpet, and goes off vowing revenge.
The next minute Jupiter-Amphitrio enters, and Alcmena is
astonished that her husband should be so soon appeased.
Ganymede-Socia bars the gates against Amphitrio and
taunts him from the wall. Amphitrio a few minutes later
upbraids the real Socia for these taunts. Finally the two
Amphitrios and the two Socias appear together. Jupiter-
Amphitrio declares that he is the genuine one, with the
result that the two captains, the shipmaster, a servant, and
even Alcmena declare in his favor, because of his mildness
and nobility. In the end Jupiter appears in his glory under
a rainbow, and assures Amphitrio that "faire Alcmena . . .
neuer bosom'd Mortall saue thee."

Another Amphitruo play is the *Birth of Hercules* (1610).
It introduces an additional servant, and elaborates some of
the comic situations; but, on the whole, the play corresponds
closely with Plautus.[8] We might have had still another
play on this theme if Ben Jonson had not been overcritical
of theatrical realism. According to Drummond, as we saw
in Chapter II,[9] Jonson had "ane intention to have made a
play like Plautus's *Amphitrio*, but left it of, for that he could
never find two so like others that he could persuade the
spectators they were one."[10]

Considering the *Amphitruo* plot as a story of intrigue we
must admit that no lover could ever assume a more successful disguise than that of Jupiter. It was an impersonation

---

[8] Wallace, 171.   [9] See page 29.
[10] On the acting of doubles see Chapter II, pages 28-9.

of mind as well as of body. But the main theatrical value
in this comedy is the situation where the real husband is
unable to prove his identity before the impostor, and the
servant has to admit that somebody else is himself. The
curious fact that the doubles scene should be so persistent
an accompaniment of the disguised lover in English plays
is due to the initial impulse given by Plautus. We have
already observed these motives in the *Supposes*, in the two
Shrew plays, in *Sir Clyomon*, in *I Ieronimo*, in the *Silver Age*,
and in the *Birth of Hercules*.

Marston's use of Plautian situations inherited through
Sforza d'Oddi's *Morti Vivi* [11] is so interesting that perhaps
we may be pardoned a detailed examination of his play
What You Will (1601). Marston's great contribution to
the plot is the dramatic effect of supposed disguise.[12] His
plot is as follows: Albano is reported drowned; and his wife,
Celia, decides to marry Laverdure, a French knight. This
match is opposed by Albano's brothers and by Jacomo, a
disappointed suitor. They plan to disguise Francisco, a
perfumer, and to train him in impersonating Albano, their
scheme being to report that Albano had really saved himself by swimming. Laverdure gets wind of this plot; and
when Albano, who really is alive, enters the scene, Laverdure jeers him with "perfumer," "musk cat," etc., and
threatens him if he dare disturb the match. Albano, stut-
tering with rage, is stupefied when Jacomo and the brothers
pass by and congratulate him on his perfect impersonation!
Albano decides that he must have drowned and that his
"soul is skipped into a perfumer." Laverdure now decides
that it might be a pleasant trick to "clothe another rascal

[11] Becker, 42.

[12] Supposed disguise appears in several Italian plays. See *Gl' In-
gannati*, and Cecchi's *Incantesimi*, and *Pellegrine*. It appears in the
English plays *Philotus* (1600), *Eastward Ho* (1604), and *Honest Man's
Fortune* (1613). See also Chapter II, page 14, and Chapter IV, page 97.

like Albano" as a foil to the disguised perfumer. We must keep in mind that this plan is not executed. Presently Albano and his counterfeit appear together. Celia, believing that Laverdure has carried out his counterplot to disguise a fiddler like Albano, addresses both men as frauds, calling one a fiddler, and the other a perfumer. The brothers accept the fiddler myth, but now pretend that Francisco is the real Albano. A battle of words ensues, and since Albano has a natural stutter and Francisco must imitate him, this is a lively scene.[13] At the end Albano proves his identity by means of a birth-mark.

Thus we see how Marston by a very skilful introduction of supposed disguise multiplies and intensifies the comic complications of the original plot. Laverdure's hint that it would be fun to disguise another man is acted upon as though the suggested disguise had already been effected. This makes it impossible to reveal the identities by simultaneous appearance of the doubles; because the real Albano, whom the conspirators first mistook for their histrionic assistant, is now mistaken by them for a supposed second impersonator. Laverdure cannot convince any one that he has not disguised some fiddler like Albano; and Albano's efforts to identify himself by mere words only deepens the comic irony. But the birth-mark remains. Marston conceived his play quite in the spirit of the Italian plot makers, who multiplied their intricate confusions until it was almost impossible for the spectators to disentangle the various threads.[14]

[13] Imitation of a stutterer by a disguised person occurs also in *Look About You*, somewhat earlier than Marston's play. See also Steele's *Conscious Lovers* (III, 1) where the servant Tom has to stutter when disguised as Target.

[14] Plautian doubles occur in *Albumazar* (1614) by Tomkins, a play adapted from della Porta's *L'Astrologo*. But this play has almost completely lost sight of the disguised lover motive.

In some English plays the character of the Plautian impersonating lover was altered, and he became, not the paramour, but the honorable wooer. An example of this is the *Fair Maid of the Exchange* (1602), partly by Heywood.[15] Frank loves Phyllis, but she favors the Cripple, who is unselfish enough to disguise Frank in his own habit. Thus attired and acting like the Cripple, Frank plights troth to the unsuspecting girl. He gets the father's consent in his own character, after which he reappears as the Cripple. The revelation of his identity is forced by the unmotivated intrusion of the real Cripple craving audience with the heroine. In the end Phillis decides to accept Frank.[16] A similar but less dramatic situation occurs in the *Two Noble Kinsmen*, where the gaoler's daughter is in love with Palamon and talks distractedly of him. Palamon pays no attention to her, but her ardent suitor, by disguising himself as Palamon, woos her successfully.

The conclusion we come to, after studying the *Amphitruo* influence in English, is that there was a general pull away from the Jupiter-Alcmena intrigue toward more ideal, that is, less realistic situations. However, this pull was resisted by the tenacity of a good stage complication. From the stage manager the demand was persistent, not so much for the lover, as for the theatrical effect of the doubles situations which involve the real and counterfeit husband, and the real and counterfeit servant.[17]

[15] See Aronstein.

[16] An inverse parallel to this occurs in *Much Ado About Nothing* (I and II), where Don Pedro disguises himself and woos a lady, not for himself, but for Claudio, whom he impersonates. This disguise is not in Shakespeare's sources as given by Furness.

[17] The popularity and influence of *Amphitruo* is further attested to by three interesting plays which fall outside our scope. They are Rotrou's *Deux Sosies*, Molière's *Amphitryon*, and Dryden's *Amphi-*

We have seen how Shakespeare in *The Shrew* idealized the
original of his disguised lover; and how Marston in *What
You Will* elaborated the theatrical value of a Plautian
situation. We shall now see how English drama borrowed
the Italian intrigue of the lover disguised like a woman,
without veiling any of its salaciousness. If this motive had
any dramatic change at all in England it was the development into farce. Morally such a change was perhaps a
healthy phenomenon. With relation to the progress of the
plot this disguise is usually incidental or episodic, introduced
perhaps chiefly for comic relief.

The lover's disguise as a girl was, as we have remarked
above, a motive in Salernitano's *Novellino* (1476), *novel 12.*
How much earlier the story had appeared in literature we
cannot say.[18] Salernitano tells of a youth who dresses in
the garb of a widow in order to get access to an innkeeper's
wife. The unsuspecting innkeeper puts the pretended
widow to bed with his wife. Similar stratagems are often
found in Italian drama. In Chapter III we have described
da Bibbiena's *Calandria* (1513), where one of the Plautian
twins disguises himself as a girl while carrying on an intrigue.
We have also described della Porta's *Fantesca* (pr. 1592),
where the lover, disguised as a maid servant, dwells with

tryon. For other adaptations and analogues I refer to Reinhardstöttner.

Landau suggests (71) that *Amphitruo* influenced the *Decameron,
III, 2.* In this tale a groom impersonates his master and enjoys his
mistress, who is deceived. The dialog is reminiscent of Plautus.

[18] The story of a lover disguised as a woman occurs in a Hebrew and
in a Spanish version of the *Seven Sages.* See Landau, 42, and Tabelle
B., No. 36.

In Calderon's *Monstruo de los Jardines* (pr. 1672) Achilles disguises
himself as a girl in order to prosecute a love affair with Deidamia.

his lady at the home of her father. In Secchi's *Camariera* (1583), the lover disguises himself as a chambermaid, and in Gelli's *Errore* (1555) a similar disguise is used. The lover disguised as girl appears in another of della Porta's plays, *La Cintia* (pr. 1606), which was translated into Latin at Cambridge under the title of *Labyrinthus*.[19]

A lover's safe access under the protection of petticoats was often as frankly represented in England as in Italy. The exploits of Achilles perhaps never got into English drama; but Jupiter in Heywood's *Golden Age* (1595) fulfils his desires with Calisto by disguising as a nymph. In *Englishmen for My Money* (1598) a lover, disguised as a neighbor girl, comes to the home of his beloved, and asks for lodging. The unsuspecting family, like the innkeeper in Salernitano's novel, send the supposed girl to the bed-chamber of the beloved. A similar ironical mistake favors a disguised lover in *Philotus* (1600).[20] The preliminaries to the lover disguise are that the doting Philotus wishes to marry Emelia, who escapes from her father's house by dressing as a man. It so happens that about the same time Emelia's twin brother returns to the village. He is mistaken for the disguised Emelia by her father and by old Philotus. When the brother sees the mistake he plays up to the joke and pretends to be a girl disguised as a man. After girls' clothes have been procured for the captive, old Philotus, still thinking he has caught Emelia, takes "her" home with him and, for safe-keeping until the wedding, puts "her" under the care of his own daughter, who shares her bedchamber with this prospective bride of her father. A situation somewhat like this develops in Day's *Isle of Gulls* (1605).[21] Lisander, disguised as an amazon, gets

---

[19] See Chapter IV, page 81, and Chapter V, page 110.
[20] See Chapter V, page 112, for other aspects of the plot of *Philotus*.
[21] See discussion of this play in Chapter V.

access to the Arcadian court of Duke Basilius.   Through a
series of ironical complications Lisander-Amazon is admitted
to Violetta by her father, the duke himself.

Beaumont and Fletcher in the *Scornful Lady* (1609) and
Fletcher in *Monsieur Thomas* (after 1610) did not gloss over
the affairs of disguised lovers.   In *Monsieur Thomas* the
hero, by dressing in his sister's clothes, gets safe access to
the home of his sweetheart.   The maid, with a sidelong look
at the audience, pretends to mistake the lover for his sister,
and lets him in to the lady's chamber.   In the *Scornful
Lady* a disguise is used to help two men in their designs.
One man, who has vainly wooed the scornful lady, decides
to make her jealous.   He appears one day with a creature
whom he introduces as his fiancée.   This supposed young
lady is another man in disguise.   But the ruse works.   The
scornful lady decides to accept the hero immediately, much
to his joy.   Now the supposed fiancée pretends to be very
dejected, swoons, and is comforted by the lady's sister, who
takes "her" to bed with her and is not angry when the
sex is discovered.

What might have been a situation similar to that in
Salernitano's novel is slightly altered in Jonson's *The
Devil Is an Ass* (1616).   Wittipol, who is in love with Mrs.
Fitzdottrel, disguises himself as a Spanish lady and makes
such an impression on Squire Fitzdottrel that the latter
places his wife in the "Spanish Lady's" care.   His judgment
is further reflected upon by the fact that he makes over his
estate to the "Spanish Lady."   The loss of the estate is
the serious consequence of the disguise; for, through some
strange law of comic justice, Wittipol and Mrs. Fitzdottrel
develop only the intimacy of friendship.

The course of love is still further turned aside in Field's
Amends for Ladies (1611).   The aggressive lover, Bold, disguises himself as a waiting woman and becomes chummy

with Lady Bright.   They indulge in loose talk until bedtime,
when Lady Bright invites her new friend to sleep with her.
Another scene intervenes; but the next we hear of the
affair the insulted lady has become aware of Bold's identity
and drives him naked into the street.

Of all the disguise stratagems of lovers the one of gaining
access to a lady protected by a female habit is, as we have
seen from the plays just described, the most nearly crystal-
lized into a dramatic tradition.   In the dozen or more plays
here discussed the playwrights borrowed from their predecessors or contemporaries, not only the general idea of
female disguise, but also many of the details of the
scene.

The costume of the lover as a girl was, of course, in no
sense traditional.   Any dress would do, whether of lady or
servant girl, wife or widow.   But, if we turn to disguised
lovers in general, we find that one disguise costume, the
lover as doctor, had become conventional in Italian drama
and was frequently used in English drama.   It occurs in
Macchiavelli's *Mandragola*, in Bentivoglia's *Geloso*, and in
Grazzini's *Gelosia*, to mention a few Italian examples.   The
lover disguised as a doctor was one of the conventions of
the *commedia dell' arte*.[22]   The various influences from Italian
doubtless suggested the doctor disguise in the English plays
noted below.   In *Grim the Collier of Croyden* (1600) Bel-
phagor disguises himself as a doctor in order to hide a love
intrigue.   In Middleton's *Mad World, My Masters* (1606)
Penitent Brothel, before turning penitent, avails himself of
a doctor's disguise in order to carry on an amour with Mrs.
Hairbrain.   Later in the play he has an awakening of conscience and the affair is not continued.   In Field's *Amends
for Ladies* (1611) a wedding is about to begin when the bride
suddenly feigns illness.   Her lover, dressed like a doctor,

[22] See Chapter III, page 52.

comes to treat her in her chamber, and marries her without a moment's delay, having brought a parson along.[23]

To return from this digression on a conventional costume, let us take leave of the lovers dressed like girls by remarking that in England this motive, like most cases of men dressed as women, was treated as farce.

IV

A playwright could produce farce from any given situation involving a disguised lover by merely playing a laughable trick on the confident intriguing gallant. We have just described the fate of Bold who, at the moment of hoped for joy, was driven *sans culottes* into the street. We are familiar with the ill luck which befell Hortensio, who stepped into a room to teach a music lesson and returned with his head projecting through a broken lute. No one forgets the results of Falstaff's amorous adventures with the merry wives. Almost equally vivid is the picture of Volpone, disguised as a mountebank, being beaten away by the irate husband of his inamorata.[24]

The difficulties that a disguised lover might get into are manifold. In the Cambridge play *Hymenœus* (1580) by A. Fraunce the lover enters his lady's chamber in a masque costume, but inadvertently drinks a sleeping potion. His lady believes him dead and puts him into a neighbor's chest, which is presently carried off by thieves. The lover, upon

[23] In plays after 1616 the lover disguised as a doctor appears in Dekker's *Wonder of a Kingdom* (1623), and in Marmion's *Fine Companion* (1633). See also Molière's *L'Amour Médecin*, and Sheridan's *Scheming Lieutenant*.

[24] The mountebank scene is borrowed from *commedia dell' arte*. See Smith, 187. Other cases of disguised lovers being caught and beaten are found in Giancarli's *Cingana*, Piccolomini's *Alessandro* (the original for Chapman's *May Day*), Mercati's *Lanzi*, and Cenati's *Silvia Errante*.

reviving, is arrested and is completely at a loss to explain his adventure. Finally the truth is discovered, and the lover is pardoned on the ground that the sleeping potion had prevented his doing any harm.[25]   In Chapman's *May Day* (adapted from the Italian *Alessandro*) one of the plots is the gulling of Lorenzo, who desires an affair with Franciscina, Quintiliano's wife.   He thinks of using a friar disguise, but a comrade declares that "that disguise is worne thread bare vpon euery stage, and so much villainy committed vnder that habit; that 'tis growne as suspicious as the vilest."[26]   Lorenzo is finally persuaded to impersonate Snail, the chimney sweep.   He is waylaid and plagued by some companions who know of the disguise but pretend that they think he is Snail.   When he has reached his lady, she, by arrangement with an accomplice, pretends that her husband is knocking at the door, and hides poor Lorenzo-Snail in the coal house.   Finally the husband really does return, finds the unlucky lover in the coal house, and tortures him with threats.   When Lorenzo is released he goes off muttering: "A plague of all disguises!"

In some plots the lover is tricked into marrying a woman he did not want.   Such is the case in the three examples which follow.   In Monday's *Fidele and Fortunio* (an adaptation of Pasqualigi's *Fedele*) the pedant, disguised as a beggar, gets access to the maid Attilia.   Later he induces the braggart Captain Crackstone to assume this beggar disguise in order to meet a certain lady in Attilia's clothes — so the pedant tells him.   But this lady proves to be Attilia, and the captain, caught in the clutches of the law, is forced to

---

[25] The *Hymenaeus* plot, with the exception of the disguise of the lover, is imitated from the *Decameron IV, 10*.

[26] Compare the following comment in II, 2, of *Swetnam, Arraigned by Women* (1618–19): ". . . this habit; 'tis the best To cover, or to gain a free accesse, That can be possible in any project."

marry the servant girl. In the *Wise Woman of Hogsdon* the double wedding, in which all parties are disguised, is so engineered that Young Chartley marries the very girl he intended to abandon. A similar exchange of intended brides occurs in *Cupid's Whirligig* by Sharpham. Lord Nonsuch is in love with Sir Timothy's wife. After having wooed her in vain, while disguised as a serving man and as a poor soldier, he succeeds in inducing Sir Timothy to divorce his wife. He recommends a certain Nan as the second wife of Sir Timothy. A masked marriage is to follow. When it comes tokens are exchanged through the foresight of a servant, with the result that Sir Timothy marries his divorced wife, and Lord Nonsuch gets Nan.

Such cases of the trickster tricked are legitimate bits of dramatic action. They combine theatrical circumstance, sometimes amounting to broad farce, with a sense of moral justice. If any one is to have a lute crushed over his head, or be cast into a river along with soiled linen, or be locked up in a trunk or a coal bin, the intriguing lover is the most deserving of the punishment — at least, thus the undisguised lovers in the audience may reason. The gallant himself may reflect otherwise upon the fates that permit the feet of love to become entangled in the toils of circumstance.

V

In strong contrast with the farcical elements of the plays above described is the idealized situation of a royal personage, disguised in lowly costume, and wooing a lady of high station, who, when prepared to sacrifice her social standing, is rewarded by learning that her suitor is a prince or king in disguise.[27] In England one of the earliest examples of such

[27] For continental analogues to this situation see Mariano's *Pieta d'Amore* (1518), and Lope de Vega's *Ilustre Fregona*, which is an adaptation of Cervantes's novel of the same name.

romantic wooing is found in *Mucedorus*, a play which was doubtless old before its publication in 1598.[28] Mucedorus, Prince of Valencia, disguised as a shepherd, has the happy adventure of rescuing Princess Amadine from a bear, while her fiancé takes to his heels. Later the fiancé returns and attempts to have the "shepherd" assassinated. He fails to kill the rival, but banishes him. The princess decides to accompany her hero, telling him that she honors him, "sovereign of my heart." He replies: "A shepherd and a sovereign nothing like." But she maintains: "Yet like enough, where there is no dislike." Later in the play the princess is saved from a wild man by her lover, now disguised as a hermit. In the end the princess is made doubly happy by learning that her lover is the Prince of Valencia.

The *Chronicle History of King Leir* (1594) contains a general resemblance to the above situation. The King of France, disguised as a palmer, addresses Cordella, saying that he is wooing for the King of France. Cordella advises him: "Cease for thy King, seek for thyself to woo." Finally, when she has proved her devotion by declaring: "I'll hold thy palmer's staff within my hand, And think it is the sceptre of a queen," the king reveals his identity.

Fair Em (before 1590), a rather loosely constructed play, has a romantic wooing of slight dramaturgic value. Em, supposedly the Miller's daughter, is wooed by three gentlemen in alleged disguises. Their change of costumes does not result in mistaken identity. Another episode in the play is the presence of William the Conqueror in disguise at the Danish court, where he had come to woo Blanch, the Danish princess. William really falls in love with another girl, with whom he arranges to elope. She, by a stratagem of substi-

[28] H. W. Hill has shown (31) that much of the plot of *Mucedorus*, including the prince's disguise as shepherd, is parallel to the episodes in Sidney's *Arcadia*.

tution, sends Blanch in her place. But this, of course, is not a complication resulting from William's disguise.

The noble lover in lowly disguise appears in Greene's *Friar Bacon and Friar Bungay*. This play has been compared with *Fair Em* in words that suggest a plot parallel between the two plays (Collins, *Greene*, II, 4). The similarities, however, are very general and not marked. Prince Edward falls in love with Margaret, a dairy maid, and sends Earl Lacy to woo her for him. Lacy, who disguises himself in country apparel, woos Margaret for himself. She falls in love with the "country swain" because he differs from the rest in being witty and of "courtesie gentle, smelling of the court." Presently his disguise is revealed and ultimately the lovers are married. This disguise episode was not in the romance from which Greene drew his material. The playwright, therefore, must have added it because he sensed a certain charm or theatrical value in the situation of the courtly gentleman pretending to be a country lad.

To this group of plays belongs also Dekker's *Shoemaker's Holiday* (1597–99). It contains a simple disguise spread thinly but charmingly throughout an entire play. The Earl of Lincoln, in order to cross the love of his nephew Lacy, sends him out of the country. But the young man contrives to send a substitute and remains in London, disguised as a Dutch shoemaker. He appears in his new rôle at the beginning of act II, but does not see his sweetheart Rose until the end of act III. The outcome of the affair is that the lovers elope and are married. Dramatically the disguise is of slight value except for the elocutionary opportunities in the part of Lacy-shoemaker, who speaks a delightful brand of Dutch. Besides there is a certain irony in the noble blooded Lacy's working as a shoemaker.[29]

[29] Situations of less honorable love-making occur in Heywood's *I Edward IV* (1594), where the king in disguise woos Jane Shore; and

These five plays, *Mucedorus*, *King Leir*, *Fair Em*, *Friar Bacon*, and the *Shoemaker's Holiday*, all contain aristocratic lovers who by their disguises pretend to belong to lower ranks of society. But aside from this the resemblances are slight. There is no conventionalizing of the action, no copying of plot patterns. Nor are these situations distinguished by the best craftsmanship; but they contain a sentimental appeal in the character of the heroine who is quite willing to sacrifice rank for love, and finds behind a disguise the best of both.

We have noticed all through this chapter that in general the plays containing disguised lovers do not possess so much cohesive continuity, as, for example, the female page plays. The explanation of this lies in the nature of the disguise. The lover had unlimited scope in choosing costumes; and the characters to be impersonated varied all the way from the lady's maid to her husband. Thus, while the purpose was single, the methods were many. We have remarked that the disguised lover plots in Italian *novelle* and drama failed to emphasize the spiritual relations. Therefore an English playwright, unless he desired to represent realistic intrigue, had to reduce a disguised lover plot to farce, or idealize it into sentimental wooing. From the plays examined we know that one course was taken as often as the other. Either, we maintain, was a dramatic improvement on the Italian tradition of disguise intrigue.

in Dekker's *Match Me in London* (1611–23), where the king in disguise woos Tormiella.

CHAPTER IX

CONCLUSION

LOOKING back over the plots we have examined and recalling the dramatic values we have perceived, we experience a growing consciousness that the disguise motive is richer in dramatic possibilities than any other mere physical contrivance. With respect to material, aside from technic, we are more and more impressed with the multiplicity of situations. A simple device used in the dawn of drama grew into solid usage, meanwhile ramifying constantly until it yielded a vast bulk of dramatic stuff. This extensive scope of disguise was due to its extreme flexibility. The motive could serve any type of drama and could be wrought in the spirit of any particular play. Its utility ranged from the farcical exploits of the boy bride in *Casina* to the romantic adventures of Rosalind; from the intrigues of *Eunuchus* or *Amphitruo* to the melodramatic spying of the *Malcontent;* from the domestic distresses of the *Honest Whore* to the tender heartache of the maid in *Philaster;* from the chameleon rogueries of Skink to the constant and pathetic service of Kent. Disguise was used by playwrights of diverse aims and methods — Lyly with his courtly fables, Middleton with his vivid impressions of London realities, Jonson with his "humours," and Shakespeare with his searching delineation of character.

The flexibility of disguise is evident, not only in the plays of various nature, but in the dissimilarities of similar situations. Thus the female page may serve her lover, or his mistress, her own rival; she may assume her part in order

to help a husband, or to slay a ravisher; she may unconsciously lead some lady into a mistaken wooing, or herself
be the victim of ironical demands. A boy may disguise himself as a nymph or an old witch, as an amazon or a bride.
The ingenious deviltries of a rogue end only when the theatrically impossible begins. The spy may secretly observe
his subjects or his enemy, his brother or his friend, his child
or his wife, or the wife may spy on her husband. The lover
may pursue his designs with various success in the disguises
of servingman, eunuch, tutor, dancing master, gardener,
doctor, priest, chambermaid, or sister; he may impersonate
some favored lover or the husband himself.

Flexibility characterized the general method as well as
the content of a disguise action. Whether the motive was
basic, incidental, or episodic, it was manipulated in various
manners. We have contrasted the expository forewarning
with the surprise plot. We have felt the dramatic value of
suspected disguise, and the refreshing diversion in supposed
or pretended disguise. We have seen single disguises develop
into exuberant multiplications, or become involved in retro-
disguise. Therefore, the first thing we remark about disguise is its flexibility and consequent scope.

In spite of all this flexibility the disguise motive had
peculiar tenacity, too, a persistent tendency toward historical continuity. The preceding chapters in this book have
indicated the main channels of influence. The traditional
and conventional types that became well recognized by the
dramatist need no further definition here. In exploring the
literary currents of disguise we are impressed by length as
well as by depth. From the disguises in *What You Will* or
the *Taming of The Shrew* we trace our way back to Plautus
and Terence. Upstream from *Epicœne* is *Casina*. The
multi-disguises in *Look About You* derive one element, the

exchange of costumes, from Aristophanes, and the other element, rapid shifting, from Plautus. The female page of Shakespeare was a century old in Italian drama and had her youth in the days before the medieval romances. The spy was already a venerable figure when Shakespeare wrote *Measure for Measure*. Retro-disguise was not new in England. The unforeseen discovery of disguise was apparently an English contribution to dramaturgy, but such a surprise was after all a substitute for the obsolete Greek device of an unforeseen discovery of rank or family relationship, or the sudden solution by the *deus ex machina*. All our study of literary relations emphasizes the dramatic reliability of the disguise situations that were old yet ever novel. In the broadest sense, disguise is as old as the art of acting, for acting is itself disguise. Our second comment on dramatic disguise is that it is curiously tenacious, that the various situations chronologically arranged possess a remarkable cohesiveness, and constitute a firmly linked chain that binds the technicians of Athens with those of London.

Why was the disguise motive basic and so extensive in Elizabethan drama? There are many answers: first, because of the literary inheritance from Italian drama, and from Italian *novelle*, directly, or through English non-dramatic literature; second, because of the similar influence from ballads and other literature of British origin; third, because of stage conditions, such as the custom of boys playing female parts, or the presence in a company of a skilful mimic and impersonator. Furthermore, disguise was popular in England, and was constantly added to plots which did not originally contain it, for the same reason that it was popular in Italian or Spanish drama, namely, because of its great dramatic utility. This dramatic utility, as we have shown in Chapter II, applies both to the weaving of the plot, and to its representation on the stage. We recall that disguise was useful to the writer because it initiated, developed, and terminated plots easily, because it made the action compact, and because it permitted veiled allusion in the dialog; that it was useful in the theater because it permitted pantomime, bodily mimicry, and stage business in the manipulation of costume and the accessories of make-up, and because it permitted elocutionary dissimulation, most subtle of all in the veiled allusions. The dramatic utility of disguise situations, when once recognized by the playwrights, would alone have insured repetition and conventionalizing on the Elizabethan stage. Yet three hundred years later in our theater the criterion of stage verisimilitude deprives us of the delightful improbabilities of romantic disguise plots.

What influence disguise plays exerted on the technic of English drama is an interesting speculation. Doubtless many playwrights learned the lessons of compact technic, and of mechanical unity, the logical connection between the beginning and the end of an action, from their experimentation with disguise plots. The best lesson in technic was learned from the surprise plays. The influence of plays like *Epicœne* and *Philaster* tended to do away with unnecessary exposition of plot. It is true, as we saw in Chapters IV and V, that complete surprise is an extreme method involving many defects, but it is also true that copious explanation of an action about to take place is another extreme. The better dramaturgy lies between. It gives suspense without shock, and permitted the suspicions of penetrating spectators to develop into dramatic realization. From about 1608 onward there was, on the whole, less and less expository narration and forewarning, especially in disguise plays.

Perhaps there was a harmful influence, also, exerted by the success of disguise plots. It is easy for a poor playwright

to upset the moral motivation of a play by the intervention
of mere physical (and sometimes accidental) circumstance.
Such failure to subordinate the mechanical devices of dramaturgy to the higher purposes of dramatic action are manifest
in any plot where screaming farce interrupts the progress of
comedy, or where the initial improbabilities of a situation
can hardly be accepted. However, such dramatic defects
can be only relatively defined. It depends on taste. Most
of us would agree that Chapman's *Blind Beggar of Alexandria*
is quite improbable and is farcical beyond laughter; but
that play is an extreme case, and probably the only one upon
which we could agree. By glancing back at the best plots
discussed in the preceding chapters we can soon decide that
there is nothing incompatible in a moral motive for action
and the use of disguise. One is an impelling cause, the other
is an enabling means.

Before taking leave of our subject it may be pleasant to
observe again the difference between the disguise plays of
England and those of Italy. Speaking broadly and ignoring
exceptions we may say that the playwrights of England substituted the freshness of idyllic, romantic, or sentimental
situation for the stuffy air of realistic intrigue; they placed
dramatic emphasis on situation and not on a succession of
incidents; they preferred the portraiture of an engaging character to the intricate tangles of plot. Shakespeare is typical; he does not illustrate all the uses of disguise plots, but
he illustrates the best.

APPENDIX A

[A list of the critical or historical works which have been referred to in the text or foot-notes of this book.]

ANDERS, H. R. D. *Shakespeare's Books.* Berlin, 1904.

ARONSTEIN, P. *Die Verfassenschaft des Dramas The Faire Maid of the Exchange.* In *Eng. Stud.,* xlv.

ARNOLD, M. L. *The Soliloquies of Shakespeare.* New York, 1911.

BAXMAN, E. *Middletons Lustspiel "The Widow" und Boccaccios "Il Decamerone,"* III, 3, und II, 2. Halle, 1904.

BAYNE, R. *Lesser Elizabethan Dramatists.* Chapter xiii, in vol. v of the *Cambridge History of English Literature.*

BECKER, P. *Das Verhältnis von John Marston's "What you Will" zu Plautus' "Amphitruo" und Sforza d'Oddi's "I Morti Vivi."* Halle, 1904.

BOAS, F. S. (Ed.) *The Taming of A Shrew.* London, 1908.

—— (Ed.) *The Works of Thomas Kyd.* Oxford, 1901.

BOND, R. W. *Early Plays from the Italian.* Oxford, 1911.

BROCKHAUS, H. *Analyse des 6. Buches von Somadeva's Märchensammlung.* In *Berichte ü. d. Verh. d. Kgl. Sächs. Gesellsch. d. Wissensch. z. Leipzig,* xii, 1860.

BULLEN, A. H. (Ed.) *The Works of Thomas Middleton.* 8 vols. London, 1885–86.

—— (Ed.) *The Works of George Peele.* 2 vols. Boston, 1888.

CAPPS, E. (Ed.) *Four Plays of Menander.* Boston, n. d.

CEDERSCHIÖLD, G. *Fornsögur Suðrlanda.* Lund, 1884.

CHILD, E. J. (Ed.) *The English and Scottish Popular Ballads.* 5 vols. Boston, 1882–1898.

CHRIST, K. *Quellenstudien zu den Dramen Thomas Middletons.* Borna-Leipzig. 1905.

CHURCHILL, G. B. UND KELLER, W. *Die lateinischen Universitäts-Dramen in der Zeit der Königen Elizabeth.* In *Jarhbuch,* xxxiv.

COLLINS, J. C. (Ed.) *The Plays and Poems of Robert Greene.* 2 vols. Oxford, 1905.

CREIZENACH, W. *Geschichte des neueren Dramas.* vols. i–iv, Halle, 1893–1909.

DODSLEY, R. *A Select Collection of Old English Plays* . . . enlarged by W. C. Hazlitt. 15 vols. London, 1874–76.

DRUMMOND, W. *Notes of Ben Jonson's Conversations with William Drummond of Hawthornden.* Repr. Shak. Soc., 1842.

DUNLOP, J. C. *History of Prose Fiction.* 2 vols. London, 1911.

ECKHARDT, E. *Die lustige Person im älteren englischen Drama bis 1642.* Berlin, 1902.

FEUILLERAT, A. *John Lyly.* Cambridge, 1910.

FISCHER, H. *Nathaniel Fields Komödie "Amends for Ladies," eine literarhistorische Untersuchung und Quellenstudie.* Kiel, 1907.

FLEAY, F. G. *A Biographical Chronicle of the English Drama.* 2 vols. London, 1891.

—— *A Chronicle History of the Life and Works of William Shakespeare.* New York, 1886.

FORSYTHE, R. S. *Some Parallels to Passages in the First Part of Jeronimo.* In *Mod. Lang. Notes,* xxvii.

FOURNIER, E. *Le Théatre Français avant La Renaissance.* Paris, 1872.

FREEBURG, V. O. *A Sanskrit Parallel to an Elizabethan Plot.* In *Mod. Lang. Notes,* xxvii.

FURNESS, H. H. (Ed.) *Much Ado About Nothing.* Philadelphia, 1899.

GAYLEY, C. M. (General Editor) *Representative English Comedies,* with Introductory Essays and Notes. 3 vols. New York, 1903–1914.

GIFFORD, W. (Ed.) *The Works of Ben Jonson.* 9 vols. London, 1816.

GOSSON, S. *The Schoole of Abuse.* Ed. by E. Arber. Westminster, 1895.

GOTHEIN, M. *Die Frau im englischen Drama vor Shakespeare.* In *Jahrbuch,* xl.

GREG, W. W. (Ed.) *Henslowe's Diary.* 3 vols. London, 1904–19.

GUSKAR, H. *Fletchers Monsieur Thomas und seine Quellen.* In *Anglia*, (n. f.) xvi, xvii.

HAIGH, A. E. *The Attic Theatre.* Oxford, 1889.

HART, H. C. (Ed.) *The Merry Wives of Windsor.* London, 1904.

HENNIGS, W. *Studien zu Lope de Vega Carpio.* Göttingen, 1891.

HENRY, A. (Ed.) *Epicœne.* New York, 1906.

HENSLOWE, P. See Greg.

HERBST, C. *Cupid's Revenge by Beaumont and Fletcher und Andromana, or the Merchants' Wife in ihrer Beziehung zu einander und zu ihrer Quelle.* Königsberg, 1906.

HICKIE, W. J. (Tr.) *The Comedies of Aristophanes.* 2 vols. London, 1869–87.

HILL, H. W. *Sidney's Arcadia and the Elizabethan Drama.* In *Univ. of Nevada Studies*, 1908.

HUNT, M. L. *Thomas Dekker.* New York, 1911.

JACKSON, A. V. W. *Disguising on the Stage as a Dramatic Device in Sanskrit Plays.* In *Proc. Am. Philol. Assoc.*, xxix.

JACOBI, G. A. *Die Frauengestalten der Beaumont-Fletcherischen Dramen.* Halle, 1909.

KELLER, W. (Ed.) *The Wars of Cyrus.* In *Jahrbuch*, xxxvii.

KLEIN, J. L. *Geschichte des Dramas.* 13 vols. Leipzig, 1865–76.

KÖLBING, E. *Riddarasögur.* Strassburg, 1872.

KOEPPEL, E. *Quellen-Studien zu den Dramen Ben Jonson's, John Marston's und Beaumont und Fletcher's.* Erlangen und Leipzig, 1895.

KRONEBERG, E. *George Peele's "Edward the First." Ein literarhistorische Untersuchung.* Jena, 1903.

LACROIX, P. (Ed.) *Recueil de Farces, Soties, et Moralités.* Paris, 1859.

LAMB, C. AND M. *The Complete Works of.* Ed. E. V. Lucas, 7 vols. London, 1903.

LANDAU, M. *Die Quellen des Dekameron.* Stuttgart, 1884.

LEE, A. C. *The Decameron; Its Sources and Analogues.* London, 1901.

LEE, SIR SIDNEY. *The French Renaissance in England.* Oxford, 1910.

LUCE, M. (Ed.) *Apolonius and Silla*. New York and London, 1912.

MABILLE, E. (Ed.) *Choix de Farces, Soties, et Moralités*. 2 vols. Nice, 1872–73.

MACGILLIVRAY, J. *Life and Works of Pierre Larivey*. Leipzig, 1889.

MATTHEWS, B. *Molière*. New York, 1910.

—— *A Study of the Drama*. New York, 1910.

MELVILLE, SIR JAMES. *Memoirs*. Glasgow, 1751.

MEYER, P. *Notice sur le Roman de Tristan de Nanteuil*. In *Jahrbuch f. Rom. u. Engl. Lit.*, ix.

MÉZIÈRES, A. *Shakespeare. Ses Œuvres et Ses Critiques*. Paris, 1865.

NIBBE, H. (Ed.) *The Fleire*. In *Materialen zur Kunde*. 1912.

NORTHUP, G. T. (Ed.) *La Selva Confusa*. In *Revue Hispanique*, xxi.

PAINTER, W. *The Palace of Pleasure*. 3 vols. London, 1890.

PARROT, T. M. (Ed.) *The Plays and Poems of George Chapman*. 3 vols. London, 1910–1914 (vols. 1 and 2).

PEPYS, S. *The Diary of*. 9 vols. London, 1893–99.

PERCY, T. *Reliques of Ancient English Poetry*. London, 1765.

PRICE, W. T. *The Technique of the Drama*. New York, 1892.

REINHARDSTÖTTNER, K. VON. *Plautus*. Leipzig, 1886.

RENNERT, H. A. *Life of Lope de Vega*. Philadelphia, 1904.

RICHTER, K. *Beaumont und Fletcher's "The Honest Man's Fortune" und seine Quellen*. Halle, 1905.

ROSENBERG, S. L. M. See Calderon, *La Española de Florencia*.

SAMPSON, M. W. *The Plays of Edward Sharpham*. In *Studies in Language and Literature in Honor of J. M. Hart*. New York, 1910.

SCALA, FLAMINIO. *Il teatro delle favole, etc.* Venice, 1611.
(The author has made use of Miss Winifred Smith's translations (in manuscript) from this collection of *commedie dell' arte*.)

SCHACK, A. T. VON. *Historia de La Literatura y del Arte Dramatico en España*. trad. . . . E. de Mier. 5 vols. Madrid, 1885–87.

SCHELLING, F. E. *Elizabethan Drama, 1558–1642.* 2 vols. London, 1908.

SCHULZ, E. *Das Verkleidungsmotiv bei Shakespeare mit Untersuchung der Quellen.* Halle, 1904.

SCHUYLER, M. *A Bibliography of the Sanskrit Drama.* New York, 1906.

SMITH, W. *The Commedia dell' Arte.* New York, 1912.

STIEFEL, A. L. *Zur Quellenfrage von John Fletcher's "Monsieur Thomas."* In *Eng. Stud.*, xxxvi.

STOLL, E. E. *John Webster; Periods of his Work as Determined by his Relations to the Drama of his Day.* Cambridge (U. S. A.), 1905.

THORNDIKE, A. H. *The Influence of Beaumont and Fletcher on Shakespeare.* Worcester, 1901.

SYMONDS, J. A. *The Renaissance in Italy.* 2 vols. New York, 1882.

TENNANT, G. B. (Ed.) *The New Inn.* New York, 1908.

TEUFFEL AND SCHWABE. *History of Roman Literature.* London, 1891.

THIEME, W. *Peele's Edward I und seine Quellen.* Halle, 1903.

TOLMAN, A. H. *Shakespeare's Part in the "Taming of the Shrew."* In *Pub. Mod. Lang. Assoc.*, v.

WALLACE, M. W. (Ed.) *The Birth of Hercules.* Chicago, 1903.

WARD, A. W. *A History of English Dramatic Literature.* 3 vols. London, 1899.

WHITE, R. G. *Studies in Shakespeare.* Boston, 1896.

WILSON, H. H. *Select Specimens of the Theatre of the Hindus. Translated from the Original Sanskrit.* 2 vols. London, 1871.

WINTER, W. *Shakespeare on the Stage.* Second Series. New York, 1915.

WURZBACH, W. VON. *Lope de Vega und seine Komödien.* Leipzig, 1899.

ZÜGE, K. *Das Verkleidungsmotiv in den englisch-schottischen Volksballaden.* Halle, 1908.

APPENDIX B

[The following is a list of the plays, novels, romances, ballads, etc., which have been discussed in this book. The items here classified according to author will be found listed according to title in the index. A few of the plays here named do not contain the disguise motive.

For the full titles represented by the names Dodsley, Klein, Scala, etc., the reader should refer to Appendix A.]

ANONYMOUS PLAYS:

—— *Albion Knight.* Fragment in *Shak. Soc.*, 1844.

—— *Ballad of Gude Wallace.* See Child.

—— *Beggar's Daughter of Bednal Green, The.* See Percy.

—— *Birth of Hercules, The.* Ed. M. W. Wallace. Chicago, 1903.

—— *Capitani Simili, Li Due.* See Scala.

—— *Capitano, Il.* See Scala.

—— *Common Conditions.* Repr. *Quell. u. Forsch.*, lxxx.

—— *Comte d'Artois, Le Liure du tres Chevalereux, et de sa Femme.* Ed. J. Barrois. Paris, 1837.

—— *Creduta Morta, La.* See Scala.

—— *Cromwell, Thomas Lord.* Ed. C. F. T. Brooke. *Shakespeare Apocrypha*, 1908.

—— *Disguises, The.* (Not extant. See Chapter VI, page 122.)

—— *Doctor Disperato, Il.* See Scala.

—— *Fair Em.* Ed. C. F. T. Brooke. *Shakespeare Apocrypha*, 1908.

—— *Fair Maid of Bristow, The.* Ed. A. H. Quinn. Philadelphia, 1902.

—— *Faithful Friends.* In the *Works of Beaumont and Fletcher*, vol. ii.

—— *Famous History of George a Greene, The.* Described and printed in part in Collins's *Greene.*

—— *Felix and Philomena.* (Not extant. See Chapter IV, page 68.)

—— *Fidi Amici, Li Tré.* See Scala.

—— *Fidi Notari, Li Due.* See Scala.

ANONYMOUS PLAYS:

—— *Finta Pazza, La.* See Scala.

—— *Fortuna di Flavio, La.* See summary by Miss Smith in *Mod. Phil.*, viii.

—— *Grim the Collier of Croyden.* Dodsley, viii.

—— *Ieronimo, The First Part of.* Boas, *Kyd.*

—— *Ingannati, Gl'.* Tr. by T. L. Peacock, *Works.* 1875, vol. 3.

—— *Jack Juggler.* Dodsley, ii.

—— *Jew The.* (Not extant. Mentioned by Gosson.)

—— *King Horn.* E. E. T. S. Old Series, xiv.

—— *King Leir, The Chronicle History of.* Ed. Sir Sidney Lee. London, 1909.

—— *Knack to Know an Honest Man, A.* Printed by *Malone Society,* 1910.

—— *Knack to Know a Knave, A.* Dodsley, vi.

—— *Lœlia.* Ed. G. C. Moore Smith. Cambridge, 1910.

—— *London Prodigal, The.* Ed. C. F. T. Brooke. *Shakespeare Apocrypha,* 1908.

—— *Look About You.* Dodsley, vii.

—— *Lusty Juventus.* In Hawkins's *Origin of the English Drama,* i.

—— *Magus saga.* In Cederschiöld, *Fornsögur.*

—— *Marito, Il.* See Scala.

—— *Marriage of Wit and Wisdom, The.* Shak. Soc., 1846.

—— *Mirmans saga.* In Kölbing, *Riddarasögur.*

—— *Mucedorus.* Ed. Warnke and Proescholdt. Halle, 1878.

—— *New Custom.* Dodsley, iii.

—— *Pellegrino Fido Amante, Il.* See Scala.

—— *Philotus.* Repr. *Bannatyne Club,* 1835.

—— *Pidinzuolo.* Described by Creizenach.

—— *Queen Eleanor's Confession.* Child, iii and iv.

—— *Rare Triumphs of Love and Fortune, The.* Dodsley, vi.

—— *Richard II, The Tragedy of King.* *Jahrbuch,* xxxv.

—— *Roi Flore et de la Belle Jehane, Du.* In Moland and Héricault's *Nouvelles Françoises.* Paris, 1856.

—— *Sir Clyomon and Sir Clamydes.* In Bullen's *Peele.*

—— *Sir Orpheo.* Ritson's *Ancient English Metrical Romances.* London, 1802, ii.

ANONYMOUS PLAYS:

—— *Specchio, La.* See Scala.

—— *Sposa, La.* See Scala.

—— *Swetnam, the Woman Hater, Arraigned by Women.* Ed. A. B. Grosart. Manchester, 1880.

—— *Taming of A Shrew, The.* Ed. F. S. Boas. London, 1908.

—— *Thracian Wonder, The.* In Hazlitt's *Webster.*

—— *Timon.* Ed. A. Dyce. *Shak. Soc.*, 1842.

—— *Tom Tyler and his Wife.* Ed. F. E. Schelling, *Mod. Lang. Publ.*, xv, 1900.

—— *Tragici Successi, Li.* Tr. by Miss Winifred Smith in *Mod. Phil.*, xii.

—— *Travagliata Isabella, La.* See Scala.

—— *Tristan de Nanteuil (or Guy de Nanteuil).* Ed. P. Meyer. Paris, 1861.

—— *Vecchio Geloso, Il.* See Scala.

—— *Wars of Cyrus, The.* Repr. *Jahrbuch*, xxxvii, 1901.

—— *Zelotypus.* Described by Churchill and Keller.

ADDISON, J. *The Poetical Works of.* New York, 1860.

—— *Cato.*

ÆSCHYLUS.

—— *Choephori.* *Tr.* by T. G. Tucker. Cambridge, 1901.

ARETINO, PIETRO. *Quattro Comedie*, n. p., 1588.

—— *Marescalco, Il.*

—— *Talanta, La.*

ARIOSTO, L.

—— *Suppositi, I.* Venice, 1602.

ARISTOPHANES. *The Comedies of.* Tr. by J. Hickie. London, 1869–87.

—— *Acharnians, The.*

—— *Ecclesiazusæ.*

—— *Frogs, The.*

—— *Thesmophoriazusæ.*

ARMIN, R.

—— *Two Maids of More-Clacke, The History of the.* Ed. A. B. Grosart. Manchester, 1880.

ARMIN, R.
—— *Valiant Welshman, The.* Ed. V. Kreb.   Erlangen and Leipzig, 1902.
BANDELLO, M.   *The Novels.*   Tr. by J. P. Collier, 6 vols.   London, 1890.
—— *Book I, Novel 18.*
—— *Book I, Novel 50.*
—— *Book II, Novel 27.*
—— *Book II, Novel 36.*
BARREY, L.
—— *Ram Alley.*   Dodsley, x.
BEAUMONT AND FLETCHER.   *The Works of.*   Cambridge, 1905–12.
—— *Beggar's Bush.*
—— *Captain, The.*
—— *Coxcomb, The.*
—— *Cupid's Revenge.*
—— *Love's Cure.*
—— *Maid's Tragedy, The.*   Ed. A. H. Thorndike.   Boston, 1906.
—— *Philaster.*   Ed. A. H. Thorndike.   Boston, 1906.
—— *Scornful Lady, The.*
BENTIVOGLIO, ERCOLE.
—— *Geloso, Il.*   Described by Klein.
BERKELEY, SIR WILLIAM.
—— *Lost Lady, The.*   Dodsley, xii.
BERRARDO, GIROLOMO.
—— *Cassina.*   Described by Reinhardstöttner.
BHAVABHUTI.
—— *Mālatī and Mādhava.*   Tr. by Wilson.   See Appendix A.
BIBIENA, B. DOVIZI DA.
—— *Calandr(i)a, La.*   In *Biblioteca Classica Italiana.   Teatro Classico.*   Trieste, 1858.
BOCCACCIO.   *The Decameron.*   Tr. by L. Flameng.   Philadelphia, 1881.
—— *Day II, Novel 2.*
—— *Day II, Novel 3.*
—— *Day II, Novel 9.*
—— *Day III, Novel 2.*

Boccaccio.

—— *Day III, Novel 7.*

—— *Day III, Novel 9.*

—— *Day IV, Novel 2.*

—— *Day IV, Novel 10.*

—— *Day VII, Novel 5.*

—— *Day VIII, Novel 4.*

—— *Day X, Novel 9.*

Brome, R. *The Plays of.* 3 vols. London, 1873.

—— *City Wit, The.*

—— *Damoiselle, The.*

—— *English Moor, The.*

—— *Mad Couple Well Matched, The.*

—— *Northern Lass, The.*

Calderon de La Barca, D. Pedro. *Las Comedias de.* Ed. J. J. Keil, 4 vols. Leipzig, 1827–30.

—— *Amor, Honor y Poder.*

—— *Cenobia, La Gran.*

—— *Devotion of the Cross, The.* Tr. by D. Florence MacCarthy. Dublin, 1870.

—— *Española de Florencia, La.* Ed. S. L. Rosenberg. Philadelphia, 1911.

—— *Joseph de las Mugeres, El.*

—— *Maestro de Danzar, El.*

—— *Monstruo de los Jardines, El.*

—— *Selva Confusa, La.* See Northup, Appendix A.

—— *Vida es Sueño, La.* Ed. W. W. Comfort. New York, 1904.

Calmo, Andrea.

—— *Travaglia, Il.* Described by Creizenach.

Carliell, L.

—— *Deserving Favorite, The.* Ed. C. H. Gray. Chicago, 1905.

Cecchi, Giovanni Maria.

—— *Incantesemi, Gl'.* In Frighetti, *Teatro Comico Fiorentino,* 1750, vol. i.

—— *Pellegrine, Le.* In *Commedie Inedite.* Ed. G. Tortoli. Florence, 1855.

—— *Rivali, I.* Described by Klein.

CENATI, BERNARDINO.
—— Silvia Errante, La. Described by Stiefel in *Jahrbuch*, xxxv.
CERVANTES, MIGUEL de.
—— Curioso Impertinente, El. In *Don Quixote*, Part 1, chaps.
        33, 34, 35.
—— Dos Donzellas, Las. In *Exemplary Novels*, Tr. by N. Maccol.
        Glasgow, 1902.
—— Ilustre Fregona, La. In *Exemplary Novels*, Tr. by N. Maccol.
        Glasgow, 1902.
—— Laberinto de Amor, El. In *Teatro Completo*. 3 vols. Madrid,
        1896–97.
CHAPMAN, G. *The Plays and Poems by.* Ed. T. M. Parrot. 3
        vols. London, 1910–14 (vols. 1 and 2).
—— Blind Beggar of Alexandria, The.
—— May Day.
—— Widow's Tears, The.
CHETTLE, H.
—— Blind Beggar of Bednal Green, The. (With Day) See Day.
—— Robert, Earl of Huntington, The Downfall of. (With Munday)
        See Munday.
CINTHIO, GIRALDI.
—— Arrenopia. Described by Klein.
—— Heccatommithi, Day III, Novel 1. In *Heccatommithi*, 2 vols.,
        Venice, 1580.
—— Heccatommithi, Day VIII, Novel 5. In *Heccatommithi*, 2
        vols., Venice, 1580.
CONGREVE, W. In *Mermaid Series*, London, n. d.
—— Double Dealer, The.
—— Mourning Bride, The.
DABORNE, R.
—— Poor-Man's Comfort, The. London, 1655. *Anglia*, xxi.
DAVENPORT, R.
—— City Nightcap, The. Dodsley, xiii.
DAY, J. *Works.* Ed. A. H. Bullen. London, 1881.
—— Blind Beggar of Bednal Green, The. (With Chettle) Ed. W.
        Bang. Louvain, 1902.
—— Humour Out of Breath.

DAY, J.
—— *Isle of Gulls, The.*
—— *Law Tricks.*
—— *Maid's Metamorphosis, The.* In Bullen, *Old Plays*, i.
DEKKER, T. *Dramatic Works*, 4 vols. London, 1873.
—— *I Honest Whore, The.* (With Middleton)
—— *II Honest Whore, The.* (With Middleton)
—— *Match me in London.*
—— *Old Fortunatus.*
—— *Patient Grissil.* (With Chettle and Haughton) In *Shak. Soc.*,
     1841.
—— *Shoemaker's Holiday, The.*
—— *Westward Ho.* (With Webster)
—— *Whore of Babylon, The.*
—— *Witch of Edmonton, The.* (With Rowley and Ford)
—— *Wonder of a Kingdom, The.*
DOLCI, LODOVICO.
—— *Ragazzo, Il.* Described by Klein.
DRAYTON, M.
—— *Merry Devil of Edmonton, The.* Dodsley, x.
—— *Oldcastle, First Part of Sir John.* (With collaborators) See
     Munday.
DRYDEN, J. *Works.* Ed. Sir Walter Scott. Rev. by G. Saints-
     bury. Edinburgh, 1882–93.
—— *Amphitryon.*
—— *Rival Ladies, The.*
EURIPIDES. Tr. by A. S. Way. London, 1912.
—— *Alcestis.*
—— *Bacchæ.*
—— *Rhesus.*
FIELD, N.
—— *Amends for Ladies.* In *Nero and Other Plays.* London,
     1888.
—— *Woman is a Weathercock.* In *Nero*, etc.
FIORENTINO, GIOVANNI. *Il Pecorone.*
—— *Day III, Novel 1.*
—— *Day IV, Novel 1.* In Locella, *Novelle Antichi.* Leipzig, 1879.

FLETCHER, J.   See also Beaumont and Fletcher.
—— *Honest Man's Fortune, The.*   (With collaborators)
—— *Love's Pilgrimage.*
—— *Loyal Subject, The.*
—— *Monsieur Thomas.*
—— *Night Walker, The.*
—— *Pilgrim, The.*
—— *Two Noble Kinsmen, The.*   (With Shakespeare)
—— *Widow, The.*   (Attributed to "Jonson, Fletcher, and Middleton.")   In Bullen's *Middleton.*
FORD, J.   *Plays.*   In *The Dramatic Works of Massinger and Ford.*   London, 1869.
—— *Lover's Melancholy, The.*
—— *'Tis Pity She's a Whore.*
—— *Witch of Edmonton, The.*   (With Rowley and Dekker)
FRAUNCE, A.
—— *Hymenæus.*   Ed. G. C. Moore Smith.   Louvain, 1908.
FREEMAN, R.
—— *Imperiale.*   London, 1639.
GASCOIGNE, G.
—— *Supposes, The.*   Ed. J. W. Cunliffe.   Boston, 1906.
GAY, J.
—— *Three Hours after Marriage.*   (With Pope and Arbuthnot)   London, 1717.
GELLI, GIOVANNI BATTISTA.   *Delle opere di.*   Ed. F. Reina.   3 vols. Milan, 1804–07.
—— *Errore, L'.*
GIANCARLI.
—— *Cingana, La.*   Described by Creizenach; also by Stiefel, *Jahrbuch*, xxxv.
GIUSTI, VINCENZO.
—— *Fortunio.*   Described by Stiefel.   *Jahrbuch*, xxxv.
GLAPTHORNE, H.   *Plays and Poems.*   2 vols.   London, 1874.
—— *Hollander, The.*
GODARD, J.
—— *Desguisez, Les.*   Described by Sir Sidney Lee in *French Renaissance in England.*   Oxford, 1910.

Goffe, T.
—— *Careless Shepherdess, The.* London, 1656.
Grazzini, Antonio Francesco.
—— *Gelosia, La.* Described by Klein.
—— *Parentadi, I.* Described by Klein.
Greene, R. *The Plays and Poems of.* Ed. J. C. Collins. 2 vols.
    Oxford, 1905.
—— *Friar Bacon and Friar Bungay.*
—— *George a Greene, or the Pinner of Wakefield.*
—— *James IV.*
—— *Orlando Furioso.*
Guarini, Battista.
—— *Pastor Fido, Il.* Tr. by Sir Richard Fanshawe. London,
    1676 (?).
Halévy. See Meilhac and Halévy.
Harding, S.
—— *Sicily and Naples.*
Hathway, R.
—— *Oldcastle, First Part of Sir John.* (With collaborators.) See
    Munday.
Haughton, W.
—— *Englishmen for My Money, or a Woman Will Have her Will.*
    Dodsley, x.
Hausted, P.
—— *Rival Friends, The.* London, 1632.
Hawkesworth, W.
—— *Labyrinthus.* Described by Churchill and Keller.
Heywood, T. *The Dramatic Works of.* 6 vols. London, 1874.
—— *Brazen Age, The.*
—— *Challenge for Beauty, The.*
—— *I Edward IV.*
—— *Fair Maid of the Exchange, The.*
—— *I Fair Maid of the West, The.*
—— *Four Prentices of London, The.*
—— *Golden Age, The.*
—— *Silver Age, The.*
—— *Wise Woman of Hogsdon, The.*

HEYWOOD, T.
—— *Woman Killed with Kindness, A.*
HILL, A.
—— *Henry V.* London, 1723.
JONSON, B. *The Works of.* Boston, 1854.
—— *Alchemist, The.* Ed. C. H. Hathaway, Jr. New York, 1903.
—— *Bartholomew Fair.* Ed. C. S. Alden. New York, 1903.
—— *Case is Altered, The.*
—— *Devil is an Ass, The.* Ed. W. S. Johnson. New York, 1905.
—— *Epicœne.* Ed. Aurelia Henry. New York, 1906.
—— *Every Man in His Humour.* Ed. H. B. Wheatley. London, 1877.
—— *New Inn, The.* Ed. G. B. Tennant. New York, 1908.
—— *Sad Shepherd, The.*
—— *Staple of News, The.* Ed. De Winter. New York, 1905.
—— *Volpone.* Ed. H. B. Wilkins. Paris, 1906.
—— *Widow, The.* (Attributed to "Jonson, Middleton, and Fletcher.") In Bullen's *Middleton.*
KENNEDY, C. R.
—— *Servant in the House, The.* New York, 1908.
KYD, T. *The Works of.* Ed. F. S. Boas. Oxford, 1901.
—— *Soliman and Perseda.*
—— *Spanish Tragedy, The.*
LAMB, C. *The Works of.* Ed. E. V. Lucas. London, 1903–05.
—— *John Woodvil.*
LARIVEY, PIERRE. Plays described by Macgillivray.
—— *Fidelle, Le.*
—— *Laquais, Le.*
—— *Morfondu, Le.*
—— *Tromperies, Les.*
LAVIGNE, ANDRÉ DE.
—— *Farce du Munyer, La.* See Lacroix.
LOBEIRA, VASCO.
—— *Amadis of Gaul.* Tr. by R. Southey. 3 vols. London, 1872.
LODGE, T.
—— *Rosalynde.* Ed. W. W. Greg. London, 1907.

LYLY, J. *Works of.* Ed. R. W. Bond. Oxford, 1902.
—— *Gallathea.*
—— *Mother Bombie.*
—— *Woman in the Moon, The.*
LYNDSAY, SIR DAVID. *Poetical Works of.* 2 vols. Edinburgh, 1871.
—— *Satire of the Three Estates, A.*
MACHIAVELLI, NICCOLO. *Commedie Terzine.* (*Opere,* vol. 6) Cosmopoli, 1769.
—— *Mandragola.*
—— *Clizia.*
MACHIN, L. See Markham.
MARIANO
—— *Pieta d'Amore.* Described by Creizenach.
MARKHAM, G.
—— *Dumb Knight, The.* (With Machin) Dodsley, x.
MARLOWE, C. *Works of.* Ed. A. H. Bullen. 3 vols. Boston, 1885.
—— *Faustus, Doctor.*
—— *Jew of Malta, The.*
MARMION, S. *Dramatic Works of.* Edinburgh, 1875.
—— *Antiquary, The.*
—— *Fine Companion, A.*
MARSTON, J. *Works of.* Ed. A. H. Bullen. London, 1887.
—— *Antonio and Mellida.*
—— *Antonio's Revenge.*
—— *Dutch Courtesan, The.*
—— *Jack Drum's Entertainment.* In Simpson's *School of Shakespeare,* ii.
—— *Malcontent, The.*
—— *Parasitaster, or the Fawn.*
—— *What You Will.*
MASSINGER, P. *Works of.* Ed. W. Gifford. 4 vols. London, 1813.
—— *Bashful Lover, The.*
—— *Bondman, The.*
—— *City Madam, The.*
—— *Duke of Milan, The.*

MASSINGER, P.
—— *Emperor of the East, The.*
—— *Very Woman.*
MASUCCIO. (Salernitano) *The Novellino.* Tr. by W. G. Waters.
      2 vols. London, 1895.
—— *Novel 11.*
—— *Novel 12.*
—— *Novel 28.*
—— *Novel 33.*
—— *Novel 35.*
—— *Novel 39.*
—— *Novel 40.*
—— *Novel 43.*
MAY, T.
—— *Heir, The.* Dodsley, xi.
MAYNE, J.
—— *City Match, The.* Dodsley, xiii.
MEILHAC and HALÉVY. *Théatre de Meilhac et Halévy*, Paris, n. d.
—— *Tricoche et Cacolet.*
MENANDER. *Four Plays of.* Ed. E. Capps. Boston, n. d.
—— *Epitrepontes.*
—— *Hero, The.*
—— *Periceiromene.*
—— *Samia.*
MERCATI, FRANCESCO.
—— *Lanzi, I.* Described by Stiefel. *Jahrbuch*, xxxv.
MIDDLETON, T. *The Works of.* Ed. A. H. Bullen. 8 vols. London,
      1885–86.
—— *Anything for a Quiet Life.*
—— *Blurt, Master Constable.*
—— *Family of Love, The.*
—— *I and II Honest Whore.* See Dekker.
—— *Mad World, My Masters, A.*
—— *Michaelmas Term.*
—— *More Dissemblers besides Woman.*
—— *No Wit, No Help Like a Woman's.*
—— *Phœnix, The.*

MIDDLETON, T.

—— *Widow, The* (Attributed to "Jonson, Fletcher, and Middleton").

—— *Your Five Gallants.*

MOLIÈRE, JEAN BAPTISTE POQUELIN. *The Dramatic Works of.* Tr. by C. H. Wall. 3 vols. London, 1891–1901.

—— *Amour Médecin, L'.*

—— *Amphitryon.*

—— *Dépit Amoureux, Le.*

—— *Malade Imaginaire, Le.*

—— *Médecin Volant, Le.*

—— *M. de Pourceaugnac.*

"MOLINA, TIRSO, DE" (TELLEZ. G.) *Comedias de.* 2 vols. Madrid, 1906–07.

—— *Amor Medico, El.* Described by Schack.

—— *Averigüelo Vargas.* Described by Bourland.

—— *Don Gil de las Calzas Verdes.* Ed. by B. P. Bourland. New York, 1901.

—— *Huerta de Juan Fernandez, La.* Described by Schack.

—— *Mujer por Fuerza, La.*

—— *Quien Hablo, Pago.*

—— *Villana de la Sagra, La.* Described by Bourland.

—— *Villana de Vallecas, La.* Tr. by A. Royer. Paris, 1863.

MOLNAR, F.

—— *Devil, The.* Adapted by O. Herford. New York, 1908.

MONTEMAYOR, JORGE DE

—— *Diana, La.* In Hazlitt's *Shakespeare's Library,* vol. i.

MUNDAY, A.

—— *Fidele and Fortunio.* Repr. by *Malone Society,* 1910.

—— *John a Kent and John a Cumber.* In *Shak. Soc.,* 1851.

—— *Oldcastle, First Part of Sir John.* (With Drayton, Wilson, and Hathway.) Ed. C. F. T. Brooke, *Shakespeare Apocrypha,* 1908.

—— *Robert, Earl of Huntington, The Downfall of.* (With Chettle) Dodsley, viii.

NASH, T. *Works of.* Ed. A. B. Grosart. 6 vols. 1883–85.

—— *Unfortunate Traveller, The.*

D'ODDI, SFORZA.

—— *Morti Vivi, I.* Described by Becker. See Appendix A.

OTWAY, T.

—— *Caius Marius.*

OVID. *Metamorphoses.* Tr. by J. Dryden and Others. New York, 1837.

—— *Book IX.*

PAINTER, W. *The Palace of Pleasure.* Ed. J. Jacobs. 3 vols. London, 1890.

—— *Tome I, Novel 38.*

—— *Tome I, Novel 66.*

PARABOSCO, GIROLAMO.

—— *Fantesca, La.* Described by Creizenach.

—— *Hermafrodit, L'.* Described by Klein.

—— *Viluppo, Il.* Described by Klein.

PASQUALIGO, LUIGI

—— *Fedele, Il.* See Munday's adaptation, *Fidele and Fortunio.*

PEELE, G. *The Works of.* Ed. A. H. Bullen. 2 vols. London, 1888.

—— *Edward I.*

PETRONIUS ARBITER

—— *Satyricon, Le.* Tr. de L. Tailhade. Paris, 1902.

PICCOLOMINI, ALESSANDRO

—— *Alessandro.* See Chapman's adaptation, *May Day.*

—— *Ortensio.* Described by Klein.

PLAUTUS. *Comedies of.* Tr. by R. T. Hiley. 2 vols. London, 1852.

—— *Amphitruo.*

—— *Asinaria.*

—— *Bacchides.*

—— *Captivi.*

—— *Casina.*

—— *Cistellaria.*

—— *Epidicus.*

—— *Menæchmi.*

—— *Mercator.*

—— *Miles Gloriosus.*

PLAUTUS.
—— *Mostellaria.*
—— *Persa.*
—— *Pseudolus.*
—— *Rudens.*
—— *Stichus.*
—— *Trinummus.*
PORTA, G. B. DELLA. *Commedie.* 4 vols. Naples, 1726.
—— *Astrologo, L'.*
—— *Cintia, La.*
—— *Fantesca, La.*
PRESTON, T.
—— *Cambyses.* Dodsley, iv.
RAJAŚEKHARA
—— *Viddha- ś alá- bhanjika.* Tr. by L. H. Gray. In *Jour. Am.
Or. Soc.*, xxvii, 1906.
RICH, B. *His Farewell to Militarie Profession. Shak. Soc.*, 1846.
—— *Apolonius and Silla.* See Luce, Appendix A.
—— *Phylotus and Emelia.*
RICKETS, J.
—— *Byrsa Basilica.* Described by Churchill and Keller.
ROTROU.
—— *Deux Sosies, Les.* Described by Reinhardstöttner.
ROWLEY, S.
—— *When You See Me You Know Me.* Ed. K. Elze. Dessau and
London, 1874.
ROWLEY, W.
—— *Match at Midnight, A.* Dodsley, xiii.
—— *Witch of Edmonton, The.* (With Dekker and Ford.) See
Ford.
RUEDA, LOPE DE. *Obras de.* 2 vols. Madrid, 1895–96.
—— *Engaños, Los.*
—— *Medora.*
"RUZZANTE," (ANGELO BEOLCO).
—— *Anconitana, L'.* Described by Klein.
—— *Moschetta.* Described by Creizenach.
SALERNITANO. See Masuccio.

SECCHI (or SECCO), NICOLO.

—— *Camariera, La.*   Described by Klein.

—— *Inganni, Gl'.*   Described by Klein.

—— *Interesse, L'.*   Described by Klein.

SHAKESPEARE, W.   *The First Folio Edition.*   Ed. Charlotte Porter
     and Helen Clarke.   Boston.

—— *All's Well that Ends Well.*

—— *As You Like It.*

—— *Comedy of Errors, The.*

—— *Cymbeline.*

—— *II Henry IV.*

—— *Henry V.*

—— *King Lear.*

—— *Love's Labor's Lost.*

—— *Measure for Measure.*

—— *Merchant of Venice, The.*

—— *Merry Wives of Windsor, The.*

—— *Midsummer-Night's Dream, A.*

—— *Much Ado About Nothing.*

—— *Romeo and Juliet.*

—— *Taming of the Shrew, The.*

—— *Titus Andronicus.*

—— *Twelfth Night.*

—— *Two Gentlemen of Verona, The.*

—— *Two Noble Kinsmen, The.*   (With Fletcher)

—— *Winter's Tale, The.*

SHARPHAM, E.

—— *Cupid's Whirligig.*   London, 1607.

—— *Fleire, The.*   Ed. H. Nibbe.   *Materialen,* 1912.

SHERIDAN, R. B.   *The Dramatic Works of.*   Oxford, 1906.

—— *Critic, The.*

—— *Scheming Lieutenant, The.*

SHIRLEY, J. *Dramatic Works.*   Ed. W. Gifford and A. Dyce. 6 vols.
     London, 1833.

—— *Arcadia.*

—— *Doubtful Heir, The.*

—— *Grateful Servant, The.*

SHIRLEY, J.
—— *Hyde Park.*
—— *Imposture, The.*
—— *Love in a Maze, The Changes, or.*
—— *Love Tricks.*
—— *Maid's Revenge, The.*
—— *Royal Master, The.*
—— *Sisters, The.*
—— *Wedding, The.*
SIDNEY, SIR PHILIP
—— *Arcadia, The Countess of Pembroke's.* Ed. E. A. Baker. London, 1907.
SKELTON, J.
—— *Magnyfycence.* Ed. R. L. Ramsey. London, 1908. (*E. E. T. S.* Extra Series No. 98.)
SMITH, W.
—— *Hector of Germany.* Ed. L. W. Payne. Philadelphia, 1906.
SOMADEVA. See Brockhaus, Appendix A.
—— *Kirtisena, The Story of.*
SOPHOCLES. *Tragedies.* Tr. by Sir Richard C. Jebb. Cambridge, 1904.
—— *Electra.*
—— *Philoctetes.*
STRAPAROLA. *The Nights.* Tr. by W. G. Waters. 2 vols. London, 1894.
—— *Night I, Novel 5.*
—— *Night IV, Novel 1.*
SRI-HARSHA-DEVA
—— *Ratnavali.* Tr. by Wilson. See Appendix A.
STEELE, R. *Plays.* London, 1894.
—— *Conscious Lovers, The.*
—— *Funeral, or Grief à la Mode, The.*
—— *Tender Husband, The.*
TAILOR, R.
—— *Hog Hath Lost his Pearl.* Dodsley, xi.
TASSO, TORQUATO.
—— *Aminta.* Tr. by F. Whitmore. Springfield, 1900.

TERENCE. *The Comedies of.* Tr. by H. T. Riley. London, 1853.

—— *Adelphi.*

—— *Andria.*

—— *Eunuchus.*

—— *Heautontimorumenos.*

TOMKINS, T.

—— *Albumazar.* Dodsley, xi.

—— *Lingua.* Dodsley, ix.

TOURNEUR, C.

—— *Revenger's Tragedy, The.* Dodsley, x.

VEGA, LOPE DE. *Obras.* 13 vols. Madrid, 1890–1902.

—— *Alcalde Mayor, El.* Described by Hennigs.

—— *Ausente en el Lugar, El.* Described by Hennigs.

—— *Batuecas del Duque de Alba, Las.* Vol. xi.

—— *Bella Mal Maridada, La.* Described by Wurzbach.

—— *Burlas y Enredos de Benito, Las.* Described by Wurzbach.

—— *Domine Lucas, El.* Described by Wurzbach.

—— *Gallarda Toledana, La.* Described by Hennigs.

—— *Ginoves Liberal, El.* Described by Wurzbach.

—— *Hidalgo Bencerraje, El.* Vol. xi.

—— *Ilustre Fregona, La.* Described by Hennigs.

—— *Ingrato Arrepentido, El.* Described by Hennigs.

—— *Maestro de Danzar, El.* Described by Hennigs.

—— *Mas Pueden Celos que Amor.* Described by Hennigs.

—— *Mejor Alcalde el Rey, El.* Vol. viii.

—— *Peregrino en su Patria, El.*

—— *Quien Mas no Puede.* Described by Hennigs.

—— *Ramirez de Arellano, Los.* Vol. ix.

—— *Soldado Amante, El.* Described by Hennigs.

VIRUES, CRISTOBAL DE.

—— *Semiramis, La Gran.* Described by Klein.

VIŚAKHADATTA.

—— *Mudraraksasa.* Tr. by Wilson. See Appendix A.

WEBSTER, J. *The Dramatic Works of.* Ed. W. Hazlitt. London, 1857.

—— *Westward Ho.* (With Dekker)

WHETSTONE, G.
—— *I Promus and Cassandra:* In Hazlitt's *Shakespeare's Library.*
    London, 1875, vol. 6.
—— *II Promus and Cassandra.* See above.
—— *Heptameron, The. Day IV, Novel 1.*
WILSON, R.
—— *Cobbler's Prophecy, The.* Repr. *Jahrbuch,* xxxiii, 1897.
—— *Oldcastle, First Part of Sir John.* (With collaborators.) See
    Munday.
—— *Three Lords and Three Ladies of London.* Dodsley, vi.
WOTTON, SIR HENRY
—— *Courtlie Controuersie, A.* In Sarrazin's *Thomas Kyd und sein
    Kreis.* Berlin, 1892.
WYCHERLY, W. *Plays.* London, n. d.
—— *Country Wife, The.*
—— *Gentleman Dancing Master, The.*
—— *Plain Dealer, The.*

INDEX

VITA

Victor Oscar Freeburg was born in Stanton, Iowa, March 22, 1882. He holds the degrees of B.A. (1905) and M.A. (1908) from Yale University. He was University Scholar at Yale (1905–06).

He has taught English at the United States Naval Academy (1906–07), at the College of the City of New York (1908–13), and at Haverford College (1913–15).

Among his publications are: "A Sanskrit Parallel to an Elizabethan Plot," in Modern Language Notes, March, 1912; "Folknamnet Geatas i den Fornengelska Dikten Beowulf . . . af Henrik Schück" (A Review) in The Journal of English and Germanic Philology, April, 1912, and "Studier i Beowulfsagan . . . af Henrik Schück" (A Review) in The Journal of English and Germanic Philology, July, 1912.